Better Homes and Gardens®

HANDCRAFTED
GIFTS & TOYS

Cots   Pg 53

Cradle   31

Lace Collar.   34

Quilting machine Cover   77

Feline Cat   206

1984 by Meredith Corporation, Des Moines, Iowa.
All Rights Reserved. Printed in the United States of America.
First Edition. First Printing.
Library of Congress Catalog Card Number: 82-81729
ISBN: 0-696-01010-0

Better Homes and Gardens® Books
Editor: Gerald M. Knox
Art Director: Ernest Shelton
Managing Editor: David A. Kirchner

Crafts Editor: Nancy Lindemeyer
Crafts Books Editor: Joan Cravens
Associate Crafts Books Editors: Debra Felton, Laura Holtorf

Associate Art Directors: Linda Ford Vermie, Neoma Alt West,
    Randall Yontz
Copy and Production Editors: Marsha Jahns, Mary Helen Schiltz,
    David A. Walsh, Carl Voss
Assistant Art Directors: Harijs Priekulis, Tom Wegner
Senior Graphic Designers: Alisann Dixon, Lynda Haupert, Lyne Neymeyer
Graphic Designers: Mike Burns, Mike Eagleton, Deb Miner, Stan Sams,
    D. Greg Thompson, Darla Whipple, Paul Zimmerman

Vice President, Editorial Director: Doris Eby
Group Editorial Services Director: Duane Gregg

General Manager: Fred Stines
Director of Publishing: Robert B. Nelson
Vice President, Retail Marketing: Jamie Martin
Vice President, Direct Marketing: Arthur Heydendael

Handcrafted Gifts and Toys
Crafts Editors: Joan Cravens, James A. Williams, Debra Felton
Contributing Crafts Editors: Margo Garrity, Ciba Vaughan
Copy and Production Editor: Marsha Jahns
Graphic Designer: Lynda Haupert

One of the greatest joys of crafting is presenting to loved ones and friends the gifts and toys that you have made especially for them. Large or small, token or treasure, a handcrafted gift is an expression of thoughtfulness, appreciation, and love that no purchased present can match.

Creating gifts and children's toys has its own abundant rewards, as you'll discover when you meet the crafters in the first chapter of this book. Fanciful playthings, personal trinkets, elegant and practical gifts for the home, and imaginative package wraps to make fill every page. Some are quick-and-easy mementos, and others are lovely heirloom-quality treasures. Here, too, are projects to craft using all sorts of materials and techniques and for every level of skill, whether you're an all-thumbs beginner or an experienced and expert craftsperson.

Whatever your personal taste—or the preferences of the lucky recipient of your handiwork—you're sure to find just the right gift to suit any occasion or any person on your gift list.

Contents

Country-Style Gifts & Toys

A handsome tablecloth in the traditional pineapple pattern, comfy pillows and afghans, wooden toys, old-time rag and corn husk dolls, hand-carved decoys, a grapevine wreath and twig baskets are among the down-home projects in this chapter that are sure to please city folks and country cousins alike.

To Have & To Hold

Make this day memorable with tatted flowers and crocheted gloves for the bride, or other elegant accessories for her attendants. And for a wedding gift, embroider a sampler for the bride and groom, a guest book for their reception, or a beribboned frame for their favorite picture.

Heirloom Treasures

Here are tomorrow's heirlooms for you to craft today: rose-patterned needlepoint boxes and cushions, a picture frame and an afghan traced with vines and blossoms, exquisite doilies to crochet from golden threads, treasure boxes and keepsake books—all these, plus the prettiest dolls imaginable and elegant toys to round out the collection.

Celebrate the Joy of Sharing

If you love crafts, you will be delighted to meet this group of enthusiastic crafters. For many reasons, they all cherish what they do and relish the joy their various crafts bring to them and to the lucky recipients of their handmade gifts and toys.

Investing—and sharing—their time, energy, skills, and affections in this way yields unique satisfactions, as Melissa

Weston Luppi (opposite) has discovered. "I love color, working with fabrics, and children, so I combined it all," says Melissa of her cheerful clothing creations for youngsters.

Originally, Melissa wanted to purchase brightly colored playclothes for her nephews, but she couldn't find them anywhere. "When you can't get what you want in the shops," she reasoned, "that's the time to make it yourself." And make it Melissa did—a wonderful assortment of children's wear, including sprightly colored jackets and vests (left and below) adorned with whimsical animals hand-painted by her artist-friend, Harriet Sharkey (opposite).

From selecting and cutting the fabrics, then pinning and stitching them together, to feeding ribbon ties through the handmade casing (right), Melissa enjoys being involved in each step of construction. This attention to detail is evident in her beautiful rainbow-bright bunting (below, right), for which she shares her design on page 157 of this book.

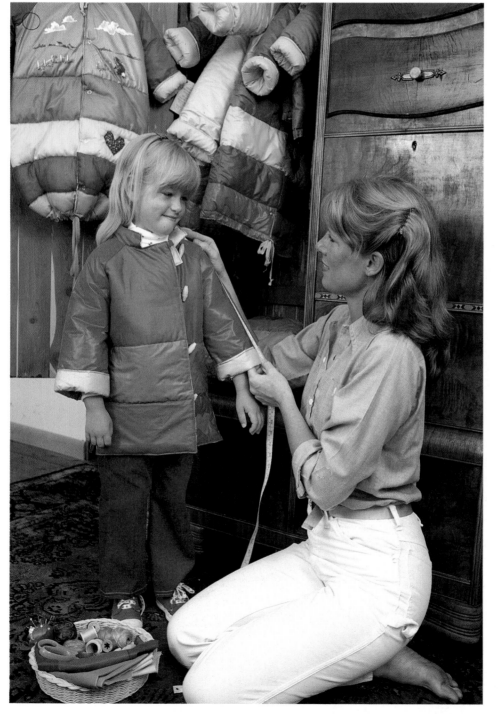

an eclectic family of dolls that reflect her personal tastes and talents. Although she's designed dozens of cloth dolls, Phyllis also creates characters out of sponges, wooden spoons, and almost any other material that comes to hand.

The prim Victorian trio (below and in progress, left) came into being when Phyllis chanced upon a stock of white clay pipes that "practically begged" to be made into dolls.

An adventurous and innovative designer, Phyllis eagerly shares her enthusiasm for doll-making through frequent classes, lectures, and demonstrations. Her tips for making your own clay-pipe dolls appear on page 143.

A lifelong fascination with dolls, particularly those based on historical models or fashioned from unusual materials, finally tempted California crafter Phyllis Dunstan (above) to design a few dolls of her own.

Blending traditional construction techniques with her unique sense of playfulness and a willingness to experiment, Phyllis gradually created

An unorthodox artist wielding needles and yarn in place of brushes and paint, New Jersey knitter Ben Sanders (left) shares his love of knitting with any and all comers. "Working with lively colors and patterns," Ben says, "helps to keep me young!"

While Ben knits away on new designs and patterns, his wife Dorothy (above) crochets leftover yarn scraps into colorful afghans and throws for a local hospital. Theirs might truly be called a close-knit relationship!

For Margot Carter Blair (right), working in fabric offers the opportunity to make a personal statement, and to share that statement with others. "Quilts and flags," she says, "are folk arts that come straight from the heart. They are a statement in cloth, as opposed to writing words."

An author and artist living in Virginia, Margot designed the quilt (far right) as an exercise in shape and color. The appliquéd calico flag (right) was created as a tribute to the nation's Bicentennial. (Flag how-to instructions appear on page 203.)

9

A reverence for the skills of the past led attorney Charles Lane (left) to take up the art of pewtering. His interest in this traditional craft began when he happened upon a pewtersmithing demonstration during a family trip to Colonial Williamsburg.

Hands-on instruction was difficult to come by, but eventually Charles found his way to John Q. Groot, a master pewtersmith working at Greenfield Village in Dearborn, Michigan. Groot, since retired, generously shared his

knowledge with the novice, and Charles now considers it his pleasure and privilege to pass on what he's learned.

Charles spends much of his time pewtering, and his enthusiasm for the craft is infectious. "To raise a blank chunk of metal into a lovely piece," he says, "is like

an artist painting a beautiful picture. Maybe it's even more satisfying, since you are producing something that's functional as well as pleasing to view."

Charles has perfected his pewtering skills through nearly twenty

years of patient practice—as evidenced by the exquisitely fashioned porringer, napkin ring, and berry spoon (above). But the pleasures of working with pewter are immediately apparent to even a novice smith. And because Charles is largely self-taught, he encourages others to try their hands at working with this wonderfully responsive material.

The beautiful little porringer (above, and in progress, left) is a gift you can give with pride, and it's a perfect project for beginners. For how-to instructions, turn to page 169.

From the time Susie Barber (below) was a young bride, she loved to roam the fragrant countryside, gathering the weeds that grow wild along Kentucky's fencerows. Weeds they may have been, but Susie found their blooms beautiful, and often fashioned them into arrangements for her home and to give as gifts to friends. Once dried, the blooms were even nicer, for now their charm was lasting.

Susie enthusiastically nurtured this love for "everlastings" in her life with Joe Barber, who managed his family's

farm near Springfield. At her insistence, he moved the fence behind the farmhouse out a few feet so she could have a small garden. Here she could grow statices and strawflowers to make pretty arrangements after the flowers were dried.

Gradually the simple dried bouquets she made as occasional offerings to family and friends led to more elaborate designs. Susie began to work dried flowers into small grapevine wreaths (left). Success with this idea led her to decorate antique baskets from flea markets and sell them to local shops. Soon Susie and Joe were constructing special racks to speed the drying of the flowers (above), and the family set to work turning a pleasant pastime into a paying business.

One order led to another, and over the years, Susie's little garden plot has expanded to eight acres, and her labor of love has grown into a substantial family business that now employs several dozen neighbors as well. Her successful dried-flower designs include decorated grapevine wreaths in several sizes, a host of sweetly scented potpourris, and herb-covered animals, as well as elegantly decorated women's straw hats (right).

Susie's creations now sell as far afield as New York and California, and provide an exciting opportunity for everyone involved to make his or her unique contribution to the enterprise. Joe has slowly altered his role from full-time farm manager to business partner, and the four Barber sons help, too, with cultivat-

ing, picking the flowers, and making potpourris and pomanders.

That the kids would be involved has been part of the Barbers' plan from the start. "There's no way," says Joe, "they could make a decent living from the farm; so once they left school they'd have to leave here, like most of the young people now. But we can give them the opportunity to participate in an ongoing business that'll make it possible for them to stay on the property."

By referring to the step-by-step photographs and using your imagination, you can create dried flower accessories of your own.

Quick-to-Make Gifts for Any Occasion

Unexpected occasions for gift giving crop up in even the most organized of schedules—a birthday remembered at the last minute, a friend's promotion, or a special achievement.

Whether the moment calls for a token of congratulations, celebration, sympathy, or affection, be prepared with a selection of handcrafted jars, boxes, and pretty catchalls. Tuck any small remembrance into one of these clever containers (left), and your gift becomes twofold—a pretty container as well as the gift inside.

♦ You might "etch" an elegant design on a dime-store canister with glass-frosting spray and fill with potpourri, candy, or bubble bath.

♦ Or, embellish unfinished wooden boxes with stenciled or woodburned designs and fill with a favorite candy or nuts, or with sewing notions or office supplies.

♦ If you're famous for your way around the kitchen, make some gift editions of your homemade goodies to put in mason jars topped with fancy cross-stitched lids.

♦ Crochet artists might turn bright scraps of yarn into appealing little granny-square boxes to fill with tiny tissue-wrapped treasures.

When it comes to last-minute gifting, remember: It may be the thought that counts, but it also helps to think ahead.

Instructions begin on page 22.

Quick-to-Make Gifts for Any Occasion

Silky fabrics, a flutter of lace, colorful ribbons and trims, and just a touch of embroidery are the basic ingredients for the dainty confections on these pages.

Using a few timesaving tools and techniques, you can create a batch of sweet sachets, lacy pillows, and a tiny pincushion or two in very little time. Stitch and stuff a few extras of each design to keep on hand for last-minute presents.

♦ The delectable little pincushion (right) not only resembles a piece of cake, but it's just that easy to make.

Use brocade fabric for the "cake," shiny satin for the "icing," and gathered ribbon trims for the pretty "frosting" rosette. And if pins and needles don't appeal, just stuff the fabric petits

fours creation with a bit of potpourri to make sweet-smelling sachets.

♦ Summer flowers bloom in rich profusion across the lace-bedecked pillows (opposite). The three petite pillows have

the look of fine hand embroidery, but crafty shortcuts help you turn them out in no time.

The seven-inch-square pillow with rose blossom and buds (opposite) is worked with cotton embroidery floss, using a special punch embroidery tool that allows you to complete the pattern in much less time than it would take to work in conventional embroidery stitches.

The mini-sachets, (opposite, top) begin with purchased floral appliqués. You only have to add a few stitches of hand embroidery—simple leaves and stems and an occasional French knot—to achieve the look of a richly textured embroidered surface. Add a delicate lace trim, stitch, and then stuff with dried blossoms for a fragrant treasure.

Quick-to-Make Gifts
for Any Occasion

Here's a quartet of gift ideas that make perfect presents for any home-oriented occasion.

♦ The natural-wood candlesticks (right) are a snap to make from scraps of lumber. They blend gracefully with any decor, from country to classic.

♦ For a gift idea that's custom-designed and unique, create the "tile" house-number plaque (below). Paint a floral design and the numbers on inexpensive Masonite hardboard using acrylic paints, then weather-proof the design with a coat or two of clear plastic finish.

♦ To make a stunning set of coasters (below, right) in next to no time, cut and glue floral note cards (new or old) to mat board. Cover with adhesive-backed plastic and back with felt.

♦ Grandparents and other family members are prime candidates for these colorful handcrafted gifts (above).

Capture individual handprints on scraps of muslin, then stitch the prints into place mats, potholders, tote bags, and aprons for special "signature" crafts.

♦ For a snappy set of storage jars (above), embellish jar tops with stickers, stencils, or stamped designs in an array of bright colors.

Quick-to-Make Gifts for Any Occasion

These striking gifts are relatively easy to make. The handsome home accessories sport simple lines and subtle coloring that are sure to appeal to many of the men on your gift list.

♦ For the gentleman whose taste runs to contemporary, create your own version of a magnificent modern masterpiece (right). It's easily accomplished with a simple pour-and-paint technique called "canning" that requires no artistic talent to achieve stunning results.

Re-create the angled, contemporary design shown here, or devise your own combination of stripes and gentle swirls of color to complement a particular decor.

♦ Help a busy young executive keep his important papers in order with a sophisticated

synthetic suede portfolio (below). The design features cutwork initials on the pocket flap.

With the wonderful variety of synthetic suedes and leathers currently available, you can make this handy work pad in almost any color combination you fancy. Use leftover scraps to cover small containers for stamps or clips, and to make other small desk accessories.

♦ Tasteful cross-stitch patterns and initialed designs turn purchased wooden trinket boxes

(above) into charmingly personal gifts.

Make several for the men on your list to hold playing cards, cuff links, or pocket change.

Many craft stores stock a wide selection of wooden boxes with recessed lids designed to accommodate a small piece of stitched and padded needlework.

Choose a box to suit one of the patterns shown here, or create your own stitchery or needlepoint patterns to fit boxes of different sizes and shapes.

Stenciled and Woodburned Boxes

shown on pages 14-15

Materials

Round Shaker-style wooden box; lightweight plastic or cardboard; craft knife or single-edge razor blade; acrylic paints in pink, brown, green, and light and dark blue; stencil brush; woodburning tool (available at craft and hobby shops); graph paper; masking tape; stain or varnish (optional).

Instructions

To make the stencil: Enlarge the design (above, right) onto graph paper. Vary the size by using a grid either smaller or larger than 1-inch squares.

Trace the design onto the plastic or cardboard. Then, using a craft knife or razor blade, cut out the design images, leaving the background intact. The cut-away portions of the design will form the painted or woodburned image.

To paint the design: Center the stencil on the lid of the wooden box and tape it in place. Referring to the photograph for colors, load your stencil brush lightly with paint. Dab the paint through the stencil with vertical movements. Let dry and remove the stencil.

To woodburn the design: Affix the stencil on the box lid, then trace the design onto the surface. Practice using the woodburning tool on scraps of wood, then incise the surface of the box lid along the traced lines.

Finish the box lids with stain or polyurethane; paint the sides, if desired.

Granny-Square Boxes

shown on page 14

Materials

Coats & Clark Speed-Cro-Sheen: No. 1 white, No. 48 hunter green, No. 90A bright gold, and No. 126 Spanish red (1 ball of each color makes several boxes); size C aluminum crochet hook; ¼ yard solid fabric (outer lining); ¼ yard polka dot or print lining fabric; ¼ yard quilt batting; ¼-inch-wide ribbon.
Abbreviations: See pages 218-219.

1 Square = 1 Inch

Instructions

The finished boxes measure 3¼ inches high and 4 inches square.

Granny-square motif: With white, ch 4, sl st to form ring.

Rnd 1: Ch 3 (counts as 1 dc), 2 dc in center of ring, ch 3, * 3 dc in center of ring, ch 3. Rep from * twice more, join with sl st to top of beg dc. Fasten off.

Rnd 2: Attach gold to any ch-3 sp, (ch 3, 2 dc, ch 3, 3 dc) in same corner sp, ch 1, * (3 dc, ch 3, 3 dc) in next ch-3 sp, ch 1. Rep from * twice more, join with sl st to top of beg dc. Fasten off.

Rnd 3: Attach red to any ch-3 corner sp, (ch 3, 2 dc, ch 3, 3 dc) in same corner sp, ch 1, * (3 dc, ch 1, 3 dc) in next ch-1 sp, ch 1, (3 dc, ch 3, 3 dc) in next ch-3 sp, ch 1. Rep from * twice more; join with sl st to top of beg dc. Fasten off.

Rnd 4: Attach green to any corner sp and work as for Rnd 3, adding 1 more 3-dc grp along each side.

Rnd 5: Attach red and rep Rnd 4, adding one 3-dc grp along each side.

Large box: Make 5 granny squares with 5 rnds each. From both solid lining and polka dot or print lining fabrics, cut six 4½-inch squares—2 for each side of box, plus top and bottom. Cut six 4-inch squares from batting.

To assemble the box, place a solid and a polka dot or print square together, right sides facing. Center batting on squares; pin in place.

Machine-stitch fabric pieces together, using ¼-inch seams and leaving an opening for turning. Turn; slip-stitch closed. Repeat for remaining 5 sides. Whipstitch box together, stitching top of box along 1 side for hinge.

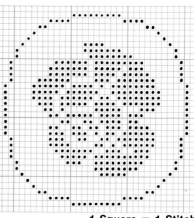

1 Square = 1 Stitch

Pin granny squares to sides and top; whipstitch squares together and tack to fabric. Add ribbon closures.

Small box: Work as for large box, making 5 granny squares with 4 rnds each. Cut fabric squares to 4x4 inches; cut batting to 3½x3½ inches.

Cross-Stitched Canning Jar Lids

shown on page 14

Materials

Squares of white hardanger; canning jars and ring lids; blue or red embroidery floss; embroidery needle and hoop; padded round forms for jar lids (available at craft stores).

Instructions

Cut a 6-inch square of hardanger. (The size depends upon the jar used.)

Stretch the cloth in an embroidery hoop. Use two strands of floss; work stitches over two threads of fabric. Following the rose design (above), stitch motif so it is centered in the square.

Stretch the completed rose over the padded form. Trim excess cloth and insert it in the jar lid.

"Fool-the-Eye" Etched Glass

shown on page 15

Materials

Glass jars; stencils; glass-frosting spray (available in craft stores); clear adhesive-backed plastic; craft knife.

Instructions

Using the glass-frosting spray, "etch" glass by covering it with a stencil, then spraying over it. To ensure an even coating of spray, practice first.

When planning your stencil design, remember that the area on the jar that is exposed will be "etched."

Trace the stencil design onto clear adhesive-backed paper. Cut it out with a craft knife, then adhere it to the jar.

Ventilate your work area well. Then, following the instructions on the spray can, apply a smooth, even coat of spray etching material. Let dry as directed on the can, then peel off the stencils.

Piece-of-Cake Pincushion

shown on page 16

Materials

White satin for base and icing; striped fabric for cake; quilt batting; cardboard; polyester fiberfill; glue; ribbon; scraps of green and pink satin.

Instructions

Cut a 3-inch square from cardboard and quilt batting; cut a 4-inch square from white satin. Glue batting to cardboard. Cover with satin fabric; turn under and glue raw edges of fabric.

Cut four 3½-inch squares of striped fabric for cake and stitch these pieces together into one long row, using ¼-inch seam allowances. Press the seams open, turn under raw edges, and whipstitch the striped fabric to the cardboard base. Stuff firmly with polyester fiberfill.

Cut two 3½-inch squares of quilt batting; cut a piece of white satin large enough to cover the batting. Fold under ½ inch on the edges of the satin; baste the satin to the batting. Pin the icing to the cake so the edges of the icing extend slightly beyond the cake; slip-stitch the pieces together.

Gather strips of ribbon and pink satin to form roses; make leaves from folded pieces of green satin. Stitch flowers and leaves in place atop icing.

Floral Sachets

shown on page 17

Materials

4½-inch squares of muslin and calico; purchased floral appliqué; ½ yard lace edging; embroidery floss; polyester fiberfill or potpourri.

Instructions

Referring to photograph for design ideas, tack appliqués to muslin. Embroider stems and leaves using stitches and colors of your choice.

Baste lace trim around edge of muslin square, then sew muslin and calico squares together, right sides facing. Leave one edge open for turning. Turn, press, and stuff with fiberfill or potpourri mixture.

Rose Punchwork Pillow

shown on page 17

Materials

⅜ yard of white, medium-weight, closely woven fabric; matching thread; polyester fiberfill; embroidery needle; iron-on transfer pencil; 8-inch embroidery hoop; screw-adjustable punch-embroidery three-needle tool set.

Also, 1 yard of 2-inch-wide gathered white eyelet lace trim; 1 yard of ½-inch-wide pink satin ribbon; 1 skein DMC floss in the following colors: medium pink (603), light pink (605), light green (907), medium green (904).

Instructions

Cut two 12-inch squares of fabric. Enlarge the designs (above, right) and transfer them (including cutting line) to the *back* side of fabric using iron-on pencil. Tape the fabric to a window and trace the stem lines to the front side with a pencil.

Using two strands of light green floss and embroidery needle, work outline stitch for stems on right side of fabric. Stretch fabric tautly in hoop.

Begin punching with No. 1 needle set at 8 mm. Use one strand of white floss to outline all sections of large rose with two rows of punching. Next, change to a strand of medium pink to fill in rose center and punch one row of stitches inside white outline of large rose (refer to photograph).

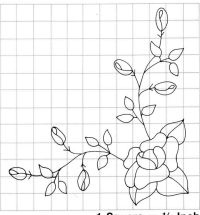

1 Square = ½ Inch

With a strand of light pink floss, fill in large rose and outline buds. Then, with medium pink, fill in buds. With light green, outline the large leaves. Next, with medium green, fill in large and small leaves.

Weave ribbon through lace beading. Hand-stitch to pillow top, placing it inside sewing line. Carefully miter the corners. Pin and baste eyelet trim on seam line of right side, gathering extra lace in corners. Stitch three sides of pillow; turn, stuff, and stitch closed. Tie small bows from satin ribbon and hand-stitch to pillow corners.

Wooden Candlesticks

shown on page 18

Materials

(To make one candlestick): Four 1x1⅝x2½-inch pieces of pine or other fine-grained wood; wood glue; clamps; drill with ⅞-inch-diameter bit; sandpaper; paint, stain, or polyurethane.

Instructions

Using a butt joint, glue two pieces of wood together into an L shape. Wipe off the excess glue and clamp the pieces together until dry. Repeat with the other two pieces.

Referring to the diagram on page 24, glue the pairs together. Clamp until dry. At the intersection of the pieces, drill a hole ⅞ inch in diameter and 1⅜ inches deep.

Sand smooth and finish with paint, stain, or polyurethane.

continued

23

House Numbers

shown on page 18

Materials

9¼x17½-inch piece of Masonite hardboard; router; wood sealer; No. 400 wet-and-dry sandpaper; acrylic paint in blue, white, bright red, maroon, bright yellow, dark forest green, and leaf green; Crystal Sheen; graphite paper; paint thinner; glass container; paintbrush; graph paper; ice-pop stick.

Instructions

With a router, make "tile" grooves in hardboard in a 4-inch grid. Seal the board with wood sealer. Let dry.

Sand with wet-and-dry sandpaper. Paint the surface with two coats of blue acrylic paint. While the paint is still wet, sand the board in a circular motion until the surface is smooth.

Enlarge patterns (far right) onto graph paper. Referring to the photograph for design ideas, trace patterns onto board using graphite paper.

To paint the design: Apply a base coat of white paint to the petals of the tulips. When they're dry, apply two coats of bright red. Use maroon paint to shade each flower; add highlights to the tips of the petals using bright yellow paint mixed with a bit of red.

Apply a base coat of forest green paint to the leaves and stems, then highlight them with leaf green.

To emphasize the "tile" look, paint the "grout" lines (the 4-inch grid) on the board white. Paint the numbers white; let dry.

If any tracing lines are still visible, remove them with a cloth dipped in paint thinner. Then check the board to make sure there is no lint or dust. The surface must be absolutely clean for the Crystal Sheen to cover successfully.

To apply the Crystal Sheen, warm both bottles in hot water. Pour exactly ½ of each bottle into a glass container. With an ice-pop stick, mix the solution well for a minute, scraping the sides and bottom of the container as you stir.

Quickly pour an equal amount onto each "tile" on the board. Spread the solution evenly over the entire surface of the board. With the side of the stick, pull through each grout line to leave an indentation. To remove any bubbles, blow gently on the tile board.

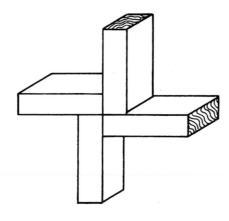

Wipe any excess solution from the bottom of the board. Then raise the board on a block and set it inside a box to prevent dust from settling on it. Allow the board to dry for 24 hours, and to cure for one week.

Check surface after three days for smoothness. If necessary, repeat procedure above. After the curing period, frame the board and hang.

Greeting Card Coasters

shown on page 18

Materials

Greeting cards; scraps of colored mat board; white glue; clear adhesive-backed plastic (available in discount or variety stores).

Instructions

For each coaster, cut the front of a card into a square, hexagon, or other pleasing shape. Then cut a piece of mat board the same shape, but slightly larger than the card.

Center the card shape on the mat board and glue in place. Cover the coaster with clear plastic (or laminate it, if desired).

Handprint Projects

shown on page 19

Materials

Cotton fabric; purchased pattern; fabric paint; aluminum or plastic tray; water-erasable pen; quilt batting.

Instructions

Trace cutting lines of pattern pieces onto fabric. Pour paint into tray; lay

1 Square = 1 Inch

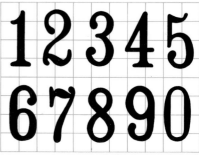

1 Square = 1 Inch

palm of hand in paint. Quickly press palm onto fabric. Repeat, coating palm with paint before each printing and arranging prints within marked lines.

Let dry, then outline handprints with water-erasable marker. Machine-quilt along outlines and assemble project according to pattern instructions.

"Canned" Wall Hanging

shown on page 20

Materials

Unbleached muslin or other solid-color cotton fabric; textile ink in assorted colors; small can or film canister with both ends removed; masking tape; scraps of paper; newspapers; artist's stretcher strips; large piece of cardboard; craft knife.

Instructions

"Canning" is done by pouring ink into a can that is open at both ends, then running the can over fabric. The ink will make a stripe as it is pushed across the fabric.

For your project, choose a simple design and add impact by varying the colors. As you practice, you may wish to work with more difficult shapes or overlapping images.

Lay the fabric out on a flat surface and tape the edges, pulling the fabric taut to stretch out all wrinkles.

Draw the desired pattern on cardboard. Cut out the shape with a craft knife. Lay the pattern on the fabric and position it for your first stripe.

With the help of another person, set the open-ended can on a sheet of scrap paper next to where you want to begin. Pour ink into the can and run the can over the fabric along the pattern edge of the cardboard, *firmly holding the can and applying even pressure.*

At the fabric edge, run the can onto scrap paper. To make an adjacent stripe, position the cardboard edge the can's diameter away from the first stripe and repeat the canning process.

If you wish to overlap stripes, wait until each stripe is thoroughly dry before adding the next stripe.

When completed, stretch fabric on artist's stretcher strips and hang.

Portfolio Cover

shown on page 20

Materials

¾ yard of rust-colored synthetic suede; scrap of ecru suede or other heavy fabric; rust-colored thread; mat board; fleece; quick-drying craft glue; purchased alphabet stencil for monogram; craft knife; water-erasable pen.

Instructions

From rust suede, cut an 8x10-inch piece, a 9½-inch square, and two 13x19½-inch rectangles. These pieces include ¼-inch seam allowances. Use a T square to ensure straight cuts.

From mat board, cut two 9x12-inch rectangles. Cut four 9x12-inch pieces of fleece and glue them to both sides of each piece of mat board.

To assemble, lay one rectangular suede piece on top of the other, wrong sides together and matching raw edges. To make a slanted-edge pocket, cut a 5¼x6x7⅞-inch triangle from one corner of the 8x10-inch piece of suede. With right side up, lay the pocket on

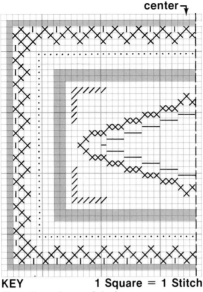

center ⌐

KEY   1 Square = 1 Stitch
- ⊡ **Yellow Cross-Stitch**
- ☒ **Burgundy Cross-Stitch**
- ⧄ **Burgundy Half-Cross**
- ⊟ **Coral Cross-Stitch**
- ⊞ **Tan Cross-Stitch**

the lower left-hand corner of the rectangles, matching the side and bottom raw edges. Pin in place.

To make a square pocket for a tablet of paper, position the 9½-inch square of suede in the lower right-hand corner of the large rectangles, matching edges. Clip or tape the layers together.

Machine-stitch through layers along three sides, leaving long edge of rectangle open so the inner and bottom edges of the pockets are still loose.

Insert a piece of padded mat board into the opening in the bottom and push it to the left. Using a zipper foot, topstitch ¼ inch from the center, along the right edge of the cardboard. Do not stitch the edge of the slanted pocket.

Slip the remaining mat board in and to the right. With a water-erasable pen, mark the left-hand edge of the mat board on the suede. Remove, and stitch along the marked line from the top to bottom, catching the square pocket in stitching. Insert the mat board in the right-hand side of cover; topstitch bottom closed. Trim near the stitching.

To make initials, slip heavy cardboard behind the slanted pocket. Position the stencils and trace onto the pocket. Using a craft knife, cut out the letters. Remove cardboard and cut a piece of ecru fabric to fit. Glue to inside of the pocket so the fabric shows through the cutout areas.

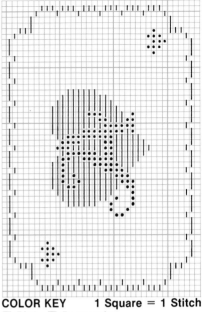

COLOR KEY   1 Square = 1 Stitch
   ⊞ Pink   ⊡ Burgundy

Cross-Stitched Boxes

shown on page 21

Materials

Wooden boxes with openings in lids; hardanger or other even-weave fabric; embroidery floss; embroidery hoop and needle; foam-core board; quilt batting.

Instructions

Measure the opening in the lid of the box. Cut fabric the size of the lid, plus 2 inches on each side. With two strands of floss in the colors indicated in the color keys beneath the charts (above), stitch patterns as follows:

For the ace-of-hearts card box: Begin in the center of fabric and the center of chart (above); work toward edges.

For the initialed box: Work the pattern (above, left), adjusting the borders to fit your box. (Flop the pattern along the center line to complete the pattern.) If desired, stitch initials within the center diamond. Stitch the shaded areas with solid gobelin stitches worked from the lower left to upper right.

To finish designs and insert in box lids: Cut foam-core board slightly larger than the lid opening. Pad board with one or more layers of quilt batting, then stretch the stitchery over the board and insert it in the lid.

Toys and Dolls to Stitch and Build

As anyone who's ever given a youngster a gift knows, simple toys are often the best loved. We've put together a quick-to-make collection of playthings that really proves the point.

Crafted of sturdy materials in cheerful colors, these kid-pleasing toys are designed to take a whole lot of loving.

♦ Pint-size animal lovers will go wild for these huggable bears and bobcats (right).

In next to no time you can stitch a whole pack of creatures from brightly colored bandannas. You'll need a pair of bandannas for each stuffed toy, plus a couple of buttons for the eyes, a scrap of felt for the nose, and a strand of floss to embroider the mouth.

To beautify your beasts, add a fabric bow, snappy suspenders, or an apron or vest fashioned from the remaining scraps of the bandanna fabric.

And don't forget that these winsome animals make appealing pets for teens as well as toddlers.

Instructions begin on page 32.

Toys and Dolls
to Stitch and Build

Toddlers who are learning to build will adore these vibrant wooden blocks (right). They're a snap to make from 4x4-inch fir posts or lumberyard scraps.

Just use an electric saw to cut geometrically precise shapes, such as the cubes shown here, plus rectangles and triangles, if you wish. Sand the blocks till they're smooth as glass, tint them with colored stain, and finish with varnish.

♦ The snuggly, slithery snake (below) makes an imaginative playtime pal for the nursery set. Fashioned of flexible dryer vent hose covered with pieced velour fabrics, the snake can be curled into lots of wiggly shapes for hours of fun.

♦ For a fanciful switch on the traditional hobby-horse theme, stitch up our hobby *giraffe* (right). With a shy expression and heart-shaped spots, he's a jaunty mount for junior equestrians.

♦ The adorable baby bear (below) is a delightful toy for a small child to cuddle. Barely 11 inches tall, he's stitched in washable velour and is softly stuffed.

Embroider his features using two strands of black cotton floss. Then dress him in shirt, shorts, and a kerchief made from fabric scraps for a wonderful, huggable toy.

Toys and Dolls
to Stitch and Build

Our freckle-faced poppet (left) is an up-to-date version of that old-fashioned favorite, the rag doll.

A generous 18 inches tall, with movable arms and legs, this young lady is the perfect companion for a little girl. And her calico and eyelet outfit snaps on and off, so she's an easy doll for small hands to dress.

Embroider the doll's cheerful features in simple stem and satin stitches, then add a scattering of tiny French knots for her freckles.

Plait her pigtails using a single skein of flaming red sport-weight wool—or make her a golden blonde or a brunette if you wish. (You're sure to win the heart of this doll's lucky new owner if you gift her with a perky look-alike!)

♦ When nap time rolls around, any little girl would like to have a sweet heart cradle (above) for her favorite doll—or a restless pet.

Ours is modeled after an antique and features a rocker bar so that the cradle can be gently rocked by hand or foot, just as generations of mothers (and fathers) have done in the past.

Make this 15x22-inch cradle easily, using ½-inch-thick birch plywood pieces joined with simple slat and peg construction. For side rails, drill holes into the head- and footboards and insert smoothly sanded dowels.

Finish the cradle with a light stain and several coats of oil, varnish, or wax. Or paint the cradle in pastel or primary colors and embellish with simple floral designs.

Bandanna Bears and Bobcats

shown on page 27

Materials

Bandannas in various colors; ½-inch-diameter buttons; black felt; black embroidery floss; polyester fiberfill; ribbon scraps; thread; butcher paper.

Instructions

Enlarge the patterns (right) onto butcher paper and cut them out.

For each bear or bobcat, place two identical bandannas, right sides facing, on a table. Place patterns on the bandannas to maximize the printed design (see photograph for ideas). Trace around the pattern piece onto the top bandanna.

Pin the bandannas together and machine-stitch along the drawn line, leaving an opening for turning. Trim the seams, clip the curves, and turn right side out. Stuff firmly with fiberfill and slip-stitch closed.

Piece bandanna scraps to make the bobcat tail. Sew as for the body, leaving an opening at the upper end for turning. Stuff the tail and stitch it to the back of the bobcat.

Sew on button eyes and a nose cut from black felt. With black floss and outline stitches, embroider the mouth lines. Add whiskers to the nose of the bobcat with black floss or thread.

Caution: To protect small children who may swallow buttons, sew felt circles on the stuffed toy for eyes or other button details.

For the bear clothing, cut pieces from bandanna scraps. The suspenders are ½-inch-wide grosgrain ribbons fastened with small buttons or felt circles. Bows are 2x20-inch bandanna strips.

For the bear vest, cut two vest fronts from bandanna scraps; hem and trim their edges with ribbon. Tack the fronts to the bear and add buttons or felt circles at front, center.

For the bear apron, cut one front from a bandanna scrap. Cut a 1½-inch-wide bandanna ruffle long enough

to go around the apron. Hem one edge of the ruffle. Gather and stitch the other edge to the apron front. Add a waistband to the straight edge of the apron and sew 1x20-inch ties on each side. Tie apron around the bear and tack to the body if desired.

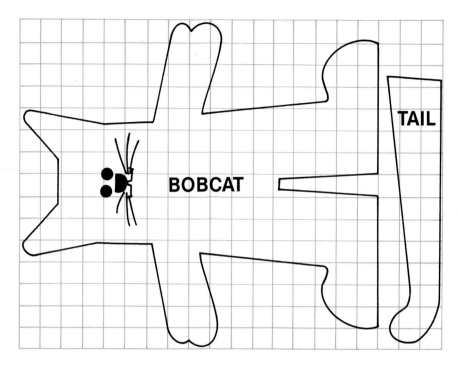

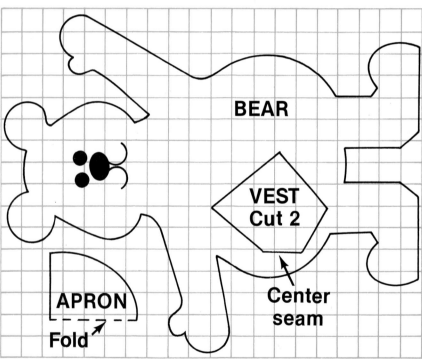

**Small Animal—1 Square = 3/4 Inch
Large Animal—1 Square = 1 Inch**

Fashion other garments from bandanna scraps by measuring the bodies and working with squares and rectangles for pattern pieces.

Wooden Blocks

shown on page 28

Materials

4x4-inch fir posts or lumberyard scraps; electric saw; sandpaper; fabric dye in assorted colors; polyurethane.

Instructions

With an electric saw, cut the fir posts into 4x4x4-inch blocks, or cut lumberyard scraps into any other desired shapes. Sand all surfaces until they are smooth, and sand the edges so they are slightly rounded.

Mix fabric dye according to package directions and dip the blocks one at a time into the desired dye solution. Let dry, then finish with several coats of polyurethane.

Striped Snake

shown on page 28

Materials

Six ½-yard pieces of acrylic fleece, velour, or other stretchy fabric in assorted colors; polyester fiberfill; 8 feet of flexible dryer vent hose; scraps of black and yellow felt; buttons for eyes.

Instructions

Cut fabric into strips 2 to 6 inches wide and 18 inches long. Sew all strips together, alternating colors, to make a long, striped piece of fabric 18 inches wide and 8 feet long. With right sides facing, stitch fabric into a tube that fits over the dryer vent hose (diameters vary). Turn the tube right side out.

Enlarge the patterns (above, right). (The patterns include ½-inch seam allowances.) Cut two each of the head, tail, and mouth pieces. With right sides facing, sew each mouth piece to the top and bottom head pieces along the curved edges. Then stitch mouth pieces together across the straight edge. Turn the head right side out and stuff firmly with polyester fiberfill.

Cut two circles of fabric equal to the diameter of the hose, plus a ½-inch seam allowance. Insert the tube into the covering. Set a circle aside for the tail and stitch the other to the open end of the head to hold the stuffing in. Sew to one end of the fabric-covered tube.

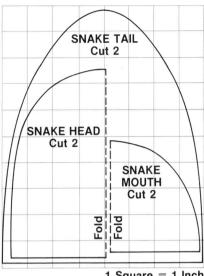

SNAKE TAIL
Cut 2

SNAKE HEAD
Cut 2

SNAKE MOUTH
Cut 2

Fold Fold

1 Square = 1 Inch

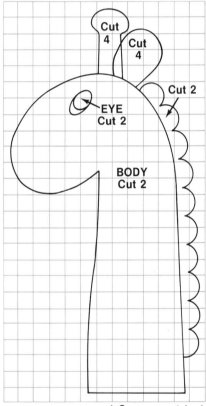

Cut 4

Cut 4

Cut 2

EYE
Cut 2

Cut 2

BODY
Cut 2

1 Square = 1 Inch

Stitch the tail pieces together, with right sides facing. Turn, stuff with fiberfill, and stitch closed with the remaining circle of fabric. Pin and stitch the tail to the open end of the fabric tube, compressing the dryer vent to fit, if needed.

Hobby Giraffe

shown on page 29

Materials

⅓ yard green cotton fabric; ¼ yard yellow cotton fabric; scraps of white and blue felt; scraps of quilt batting; 2 feet of ¼-inch cording; broomstick or 1-inch-diameter dowel; yellow paint; 1½ yards of yellow ribbon for reins.

Instructions

Enlarge the pattern (left), adding ½-inch seam allowances to all pieces. Cut the giraffe head and ears from green fabric, the horns and scalloped mane from yellow fabric, and the eyes from white and blue felt in the amounts indicated on the diagram. Also cut a dozen hearts in varying sizes from white felt.

Machine-appliqué the eyes and a scattering of hearts to each head piece.

Next, sew the horns together, in pairs, leaving the bottoms open. Clip the seams, turn, press, and stuff the horns lightly. Sew ears together with a single layer of batting, leaving an opening for turning at the base of each ear. Clip seam allowances, turn, press, and topstitch around each ear ¼ inch, ½ inch, and ¾ inch from the outside edge of the ear.

Stitch the mane, right sides together, leaving the long, straight edge open. Clip seams, turn, and press.

To assemble the giraffe, pin the mane, ears, and horns to the right side of a head piece; point them in toward the center of the piece. Pin the other head piece on top with the right side facing and stitch the pieces together, leaving the bottom open. Clip the seams and turn. Roll the lower edge up 1 inch for the hem, and stitch.

Cut a bias strip of green fabric 1½x18 inches long. Turn under the raw edges, and pin and stitch the strip ¾ inch above the lower edge of the head to make a casing for the cording. (The ends of the casing should meet at the back of the neck seam.) Thread the cord through the casing.

Sand the dowel lightly. Then paint the dowel yellow and allow it to dry.

Stuff the head firmly. Insert one end of the dowel at least 6 inches into the neck, pull the cording snug, and tie tightly. Tack ribbon reins around nose as shown in the photograph.

continued

33

Country Bear

shown on page 29

Materials

⅜ yard light brown velour; scraps of blue and white felt and red print cotton fabric; black embroidery floss; two ⅝-inch-diameter buttons; fiberfill; graph paper; dressmaker's carbon paper.

Instructions

Enlarge the patterns (right) onto graph paper. (Patterns include ¼-inch seam allowances.)

Cut the pieces from fabric as follows: two body pieces from velour; one shirt from white felt; one overalls front, one overalls back, one overalls strap, and a 1½x2-inch rectangle for a pocket from blue felt; 7x7x10-inch triangle for a bandanna from red print cotton fabric.

To make the body: Transfer the face onto the body front with dressmaker's carbon paper. Using two strands of floss, embroider the eyes and nose with straight stitches and the mouth with running stitches.

With right sides facing, stitch the body pieces together, leaving an opening along one leg for turning. Clip the curves and trim the seams. Then, turn the body right side out, stuff firmly, and slip-stitch the opening closed.

To dress the bear: Make a neck opening on the shirt by slashing along the top fold line between the Xs. Slip the shirt onto the bear.

Pin the underarm edges together, overlapping the edges slightly. Stitch. To make cuffs, fold over ½ inch of the sleeve edges, and tack in place.

Center the rectangular pocket on the front of the overalls and pin in place. Fold a ½-inch square of red fabric in half and tuck it under one side of the pocket. Stitch the pocket to the overalls front along the sides and bottom, catching the red fabric in the stitching.

On the overalls front and back, slash along the fold line from the bottom up to the X. This will define the legs.

Overlapping the raw edges slightly, pin the overalls front to back along the sides, then topstitch together with red thread. Match each leg front to back along the inner legs; topstitch together.

To attach the overalls strap, tuck ½ inch of the squared end of the strap inside the overalls back. Topstitch together with red thread. Slip the overalls onto the bear, then bring the overalls

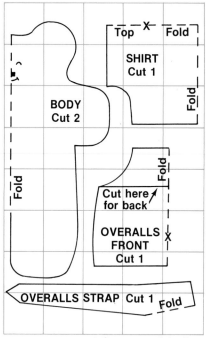

1 Square = 2 Inches

straps over the bear's shoulders to the front. Position a button at the pointed end of each strap and sew in place through the strap and overalls front.

Tie the red bandanna around the bear's neck and tack it in place.

Freckle-Faced Poppet

shown on page 30

Materials

½ yard muslin; fiberfill; two ¾-inch-diameter and two 1-inch-diameter buttons, each with four sewing holes; sport-weight yarn for hair; button thread; long needle (3 to 4 inches); beeswax; glue; powdered rouge; ¼ yard each of bloomer, blouse, and skirt fabric; black felt for shoes; scraps of lace and eyelet trim; ½-inch-wide grosgrain ribbon; pair of infant stockings; two small buttons; snaps; small beads; short lengths of ⅛- and ¼-inch-wide elastic.

Instructions

Enlarge the patterns (above, right) and transfer to the appropriate fabrics.

Note: Except where indicated, do *not* cut pattern pieces from fabric. Instead, trace the pattern outline onto the

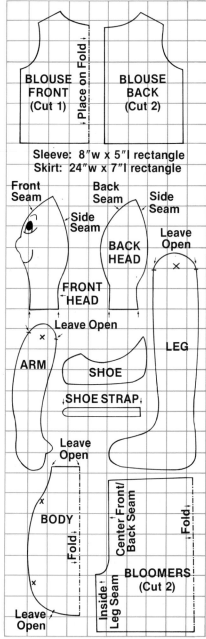

Sleeve: 8"w x 5"l rectangle
Skirt: 24"w x 7"l rectangle

1 Square = 1 Inch

wrong side of the doubled fabric, stitch along the drawn line, then cut out ¼ inch beyond the stitching.

To make the head: Trace the front and back sections onto doubled muslin. Stitch the front seam (nose) of the front sections and the back seam of the back sections. Cut out the sections ⅛ inch beyond the stitching line and *on the drawn line* for the side seams.

Turn the back section right side out. Slip the back section into the front section, right sides together, matching seams. Stitch the side seams; leave neck open. Turn, and stuff firmly.

For the body: Trace the body shape, stitch (leaving the top and bottom open), trim, and turn. Turn under the top opening of the body ¼ inch; slip the body over the neck of the head, matching side seams. Blindstitch the head and body together. Stuff the body, and gather the opening at the bottom of the body and pull closed, causing the bottom of the body to taper.

For arms and legs: Trace patterns, stitch (leaving tops open), trim ⅛ inch from seam line, turn, and press. Stuff the arms and legs to within 1½ inches from the top of each piece.

Rub button thread across the beeswax to strengthen the cord; use the button thread to sew a ¾-inch-diameter button to the inside of each arm and a 1-inch-diameter button to the inside of each leg on side nearest the body, as indicated on the patterns. Stitch through the holes diagonally, so that the sewn thread makes an X on the right side of the fabric. Finish stuffing the arms and legs; turn under the top edges and slip-stitch closed.

To assemble the body: Use waxed, doubled button thread and a long needle. Stitch through the X on arm (made by sewing on the button); do *not* sew through fabric on arm. Run needle through the body, pulling tightly, through the X on the other arm, and back through the body again, pulling tightly. Repeat several times. Fasten thread. Repeat for legs.

Lightly pencil the features on the face. Using two strands of embroidery floss, outline-stitch the eyes, mouth, and eyebrows. Satin-stitch the pupils of the eyes; make small French knots for the doll's freckles. Use powdered rouge to lightly color the cheeks.

For hair: Cut 100 strands of yarn, each 24 inches long. Center the yarn on a 1½x6-inch strip of body fabric and stitch in place, using thread to match the color of yarn. Glue the yarn to the head; braid and tie ends with ribbon.

For clothing: Enlarge the patterns to size; transfer them to the appropriate fabrics and cut out the pieces.

Pin and stitch together the pieces for the bloomers. Add lace trim to the legs and ¼-inch elastic to waistband.

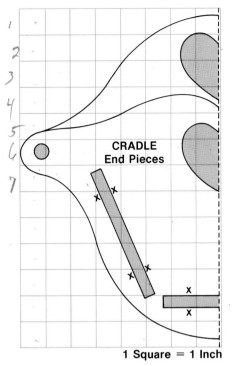

CRADLE End Pieces

1 Square = 1 Inch

Cut 5x8-inch rectangles to use as the sleeves for the blouse. Gather one long side of each rectangle and sew a casing for ⅛-inch elastic on the other end for cuffs. Add lace trim to the cuffs, and thread elastic through the casing; stitch to secure. Make double ½-inch hems at blouse center back. Assemble blouse; trim the neckline with lace.

Cut a 7x24-inch piece of fabric for the skirt. Join the short ends in a ⅜-inch seam, stopping 2½ inches from the top. Press the seam open and top-stitch around the center opening. Gather the skirt top to fit the doll's waist.

Cut a 1½-inch-wide waistband to equal the doll's waist, plus 1 inch. Pin and stitch the waistband to the gathered skirt, binding the raw edge. Turn in the raw edges on the band ends; stitch and add a snap. Cut and stitch ribbon for shoulder straps to the skirt. Add small buttons to the strap fronts at the waistband. Hem the skirt.

For the doll's socks, slip an infant sock on a foot, wrong side out. Pull the excess fabric to the bottom of the foot; pin. Remove the sock, and stitch a seam along the pins, trim away the excess, and turn. Repeat for other sock.

Finally, cut pieces for the shoes and straps from black felt. Stitch the pieces together to make each shoe, and sew the strap to the instep of the shoe. Add small beads to the outer edge of each shoe for a "button."

Wooden Cradle

shown on page 31

Materials

Baltic birch plywood in the following dimensions: ½x17x24 inches, two pieces ½x5¼x24 inches, and one piece ½x4½x24 inches. Also, two 24-inch-long, ½-inch-diameter wooden dowels; twelve 1-inch-long, ¼-inch-diameter dowels for pegs; drill with ½-inch bit; jigsaw or saber saw; sandpaper; graph paper; wood stain or latex paint in desired shade; polyurethane.

Instructions

Enlarge the pattern (left) onto graph paper. The pattern pieces are for the two ends of the cradle—the 12½-inch-high headboard and the 9½-inch-high footboard. The shaded areas on the pattern indicate the areas that are to be cut out with the jigsaw.

Cut the patterns from the graph paper and trace them onto the appropriate pieces of birch plywood. With a jigsaw or saber saw, cut along the outline for each of the cradle pieces.

Cut out the hearts and the rectangular areas for the side and bottom slats. Drill a hole in the area to be cut out to insert the saw blade to begin cutting.

Drill holes for the side dowels with a ½-inch drill bit.

On the ends of each slat, drill two ¼-inch-diameter holes, each positioned 1 inch in from the side and ¼ inch in from the end for the side dowels.

Sand all of the edges and surfaces of the cradle smooth.

To assemble the cradle, feed the slats through the openings until they extend ½ inch beyond both ends of the cradle. Insert a peg through each hole in the slats to anchor each of the pieces.

Fit the side dowels into the holes until they extend ½ inch beyond the surfaces of the headboard and footboard.

Secure the side dowels with glue and nails and secure the pegs with glue.

To finish, stain the cradle with the desired shade, or paint the cradle with latex paint in an appropriate color. Coat with polyurethane as a protective finish, if desired.

Fashion Accessories for the Whole Family

These simple-to-make accessories are sure to add a touch of class to any ensemble. They're little gifts that will mean a lot to the fashion-savvy friends on your gift list.

♦ The demure—and detachable—lace jabot (left) turns a simple silk blouse into an instant Victorian heirloom. And it's a snap to make from either pieced and gathered lengths of purchased lace or scraps of antique lace and trims.

♦ For a dash of country chic, stitch squares of floral-printed fabric into a dainty drawstring purse (right). Trim with a flounce of eyelet and add satin cords to tie.

Instructions for these, as well as the other fashion-wise accessories on the following pages, begin on page 44.

Fashion Accessories for the Whole Family

Strikingly original and absolutely stunning, this designer-look jewelry is made with relative ease from dime store findings and thrift shop materials.

♦ The carefree clothes of summer call for accessories with spirit and impact, like this bold bead necklace (left). These imaginative marbleized beads add a touch of pizzazz to anything from a light and lacy blouse to a plain-and-simple summer sundress.

To create a knockout necklace of your own, just color plain, unfinished wooden beads with an easy-to-do, dip-and-dye technique that uses a combination of oil paints and water to create a marbleized effect.

Once the beads are colored and have dried, spray them with a protective glossy finish. Then just slip the marbleized beads onto a coordinating silk or cotton cord, making a simple overhand knot between each of the beads to hold them in place.

Why not experiment with a variety of sizes and shapes of beads for different effects. You might even wish to try your hand at marbleizing simple wooden bangle bracelets to match.

◆ For an entirely different look, decoupage wooden beads with colorful scraps of gift wrap, like these brightly patterned baubles (below).

First, sand the wood lightly. Then cover each bead with cut-to-size bits of patterned paper, using a solution of watered-down white glue.

Protect the beads with varnish and, after they dry, string them on a silken cord, separating beads of different shapes and sizes with simple knots in the cord or with plastic spacers for added textural interest.

◆ Fashioned from old buttons, tiny glass beads, bits of lace, and assorted oddities, these "antique" brooches (left) are every bit as pretty as the real thing—but they cost only pennies to make.

Use metal button forms or padded cardboard shapes as a base, then cover with an elegant velvet or satin fabric and embellish with a thrift-shop assortment of buttons, beads, and lace. To finish, glue a pin back in place and *voilà*—an almost instant heirloom that has truly special appeal.

Fashion Accessories
for the Whole Family

If you've got a knack for knitting and crocheting, these snuggly accessories should top your list of gifts to make for yourself or others.

♦ The handsome pair of his and hers weskits (left) are tailor-made for those with fashion flair. With classic cable styling and traditional watch pockets, these versatile knit vests fit under a sport coat or over a ruffled blouse with ease.

And because the pattern is sized for small, medium, and large, and designed for both men and women, you can easily knit a vest for just about everyone on your gift list—from fashion-conscious teens to time-honored traditionalists.

♦ Even if you're just a novice at knitting, you can easily make this perky vest (left) for a little girl in no time at all. Select yarns in shades to coordinate with her favorite blouse or school dress, and it's sure to be a much-worn favorite.

Delight her by knitting several, in a variety of color combinations, to provide her with a colorful selection of fashion accessories that will keep her warm in winter.

♦ For a shortcut to high style, transform an ordinary store-bought crewneck sweater with a quick-crochet collar and matching hat.

Both the hat and the cowl collar (above) are worked with a size J crochet hook, using small amounts of textured yarns in a variety of colors. To achieve the thick and thin striped effect, simply change color at random as you work.

Fashion Accessories
for the Whole Family

A wonderful time-saver for the busy gift-maker is the "buy basic and embellish" philosophy. To get your thinking going along these lines, take a look at what we've done with four store-bought basics.

♦ First, we stitched on a scattering of bead and sequin bouquets to dress up an ordinary purchased pullover (left).

Next, we used rows of sparkly beads, sequins, and tiny seed pearls to turn a daytime sweater into a nighttime dazzler (right). To make one like it, purchase a Fair-Isle yoked sweater, then use elasticized thread to tack a variety of spangles and beads in patterns along the knitted design.

♦ To add snap and punch to a plain summer hat, we "planted" a fresh bouquet of painted flowers along the brim (below, left). Just pick a pretty floral design and trace it onto the brim of any unfinished natural straw hat.

For design ideas, look for floral patterns elsewhere in this book, or in other stitchery books. Then, paint the design using artist's acrylics mixed with water.

♦ Finally, we transformed a plain oxford-cloth shirt into a frilly blouse (below, right) by stitching diagonal rows of eyelet ruffles to the front and back. A pretty strip of flat lace sewn on the placket, a row of seed pearls, and a frill of eyelet attached to the collar and cuffs complete the transformation.

43

Lace Jabot

shown on page 36

Materials

4½ yards of white or ecru 2-inch-wide, pregathered lace; ½ yard of white nylon net; 2 small snaps.

Instructions

First, cut a 9½x16-inch oval from the white nylon netting. Trim away a 4-inch-deep arc from one short end of the oval to form the neck edge.

Next, cut two 22-inch lengths of lace (measuring along the gathered edge). Clip stitching and unruffle the gathers on one of the lengths of lace. Then, stitch the unruffled edge to the bottom (ungathered) edge of the second 22-inch strip, making a 4-inch-wide strip that is ruffled along one edge. Stitch the gathered edge of this strip to the oval of netting, 3 inches in from the outer edge.

To form the center panel of the jabot, ungather the edges of two 9-inch lengths of lace. Stitch the two strips together along the ungathered edges. Center this flat, 4-inch-wide strip on top of the netting, with outer edges of the center panel overlapping gathered edges of the ruffle.

Stitch the center panel in place, carefully hemming the raw edges along the center bottom of the strip. Carefully trim the netting away from behind the center panel.

Finally, stitch a 36-inch length of gathered lace to the outer edge of the netting. Cut a 15-inch length of lace, ungather it, and stitch it to the neck edge to make a high collar. Hem the ends of the collar and attach two small snaps to the ends for a closing. Trim with a strip of ribbon and an artificial flower, if desired.

Drawstring Purse

shown on page 37

Materials

Two 9-inch squares of floral-print cotton fabric with center medallion pattern (as shown); two matching squares of lining fabric; 1¼ yards of 1-inch-wide ruffled eyelet trim; 1½ yards of satin cording.

Instructions

Pin and baste lace along three sides of one print square, with ruffles pointing in toward the center of the square. Then, stitch the lace in place, ¼ inch in from the edge of the fabric.

With right sides together, pin the second print square on top. Stitch the squares together around three sides, leaving a ½-inch seam allowance. Trim seams, turn right side out, and press.

Stitch the lining squares together around three sides (½-inch seams); turn and press. Slip the lining inside the purse, turn under raw edges, and slip-stitch lining in place. Next, turn under the raw edges of the opening, stitching a strip of lace around as you go.

Make loops of thread around the top of the purse, just below the ruffle of lace, to slip cording through. Cut the cording into two pieces; slip cords through loops, and knot ends.

Note: If center medallion fabric is not available, appliqué contrasting fabrics together to form a medallion square.

Marbleized Beads

shown on page 38

Materials

Natural-colored wooden beads in graduated sizes; artist's oil paints in primary colors; turpentine or paint thinner; disposable plastic containers; 3 small glass jars with lids; wooden stirring sticks; cookie sheet lined with waxed paper; stiff wire; toothpicks; newspaper and paper towels; gloss spray finish; small cardboard box (such as a shoe box); jewelry clasp; silk or cotton cord.

Instructions

First mix 1½ teaspoons of turpentine and ½ teaspoon of paint in a glass jar. Cover and shake until thoroughly mixed. Repeat with two additional colors of paint—each in a separate jar.

Cover the work surface with newspaper, and fill a plastic container with cold water. Float a few drops of two or three of the premixed colors on top of the water; gently swirl them together with a toothpick.

Make a hook from a short length of wire and slip a large bead onto it (use a toothpick to dip smaller beads). Dip each bead straight down into the floating paint mixture, then pull the bead straight up. Slip the bead off the hook or toothpick and lay it on a cookie sheet covered with waxed paper to dry.

Periodically clean the water by laying a sheet of paper on it. Remove paper and repeat paint step.

Make a rack to hold beads for spraying by stringing a wire across the inside of the cardboard box. Suspend the wire on slits cut in the sides of the box. When paint on beads is dry, string them onto wires so that they are not touching. Spray beads lightly with gloss finish; let the beads dry and spray again. When the beads are dry, string them on cord, tying a simple overhand knot between each one. Add clasp.

Decoupage Beads

shown on page 39

Materials

Patterned gift wrap; wooden beads in a variety of shapes and sizes; decorative cording; white plastic rings (optional); white glue; soft paintbrush; varnish; small, sharp scissors.

Instructions

Lightly sand beads to remove any varnish that may be on them.

Cut gift wrap paper into narrow strips and apply strips to a bead with a solution of watered-down white glue. (Add enough water to the glue to make it the consistency of light cream.)

Paper strips should be long enough to extend approximately ¼ inch into the hole of the bead on either end. Small beads can be covered with a single piece of paper cut slightly larger than the bead.

For the striped beads, alternate narrow strips of paper with uncovered strips of raw wood on the bead. Smooth out any wrinkles in the paper with a thumbnail; tuck ends of paper inside center hole.

Allow beads to dry thoroughly and then protect them with several thin coats of clear varnish.

String beads on cord cut to desired length. Use plastic rings or knots tied in the cord as spacers between beads.

"Antique" Brooches

shown on page 39

Materials

Metal button forms (available at notions counters); cardboard; scraps of velvet and/or satin fabrics; pieces of lace doilies and edgings; lightweight quilt batting; assorted buttons and beads; small pliers; beading needle; embroidery floss in assorted colors; white glue; pin backs; epoxy cement.

Instructions

Design pins according to available materials—the size and shape of your lace motifs and selected buttons. Slip-stitch a small lace motif to a piece of satin or velvet fabric. Outline the shape with clusters of beads or embroidery stitches (such as French knots), using several strands of floss.

Center beaded lace motif on an appropriate-size button form or a piece of cardboard cut to size.

If using a button form, use pliers to remove the button shank from the metal backing piece. Then cut appliquéd fabric slightly larger than the form, stretch the fabric gently around the form, pull it to the back, and snap the metal backing in place.

For a cardboard form, first cover the cardboard with a thin layer of quilt batting. Then center the appliquéd fabric on the batting, pull raw edges to the back, and glue to wrong side of cardboard. Cover raw edges on the wrong side of the pin with a patch of fabric stitched or glued into place.

To mount small antique buttons on a brooch, remove the button shank with small pliers and glue button in place.

To edge the brooch with rows of beads, slip four or five beads onto a beading needle, backstitch through the fabric, and then stitch through the last bead in the row again to secure. Continue beading all the way around the rim of the brooch. For an extra flourish, glue a row of ruffled lace or fabric around the edge of the brooch, before adding the backing fabric.

Finally, glue pin backs in place using epoxy cement.

Man's Cable Knit Vest

shown on page 40

Directions are for size Small (36-38); changes for sizes Medium (40-42) and Large (44-46) follow in parentheses. (See the note below on the finished measurements.)

Materials

Coats & Clark Red Heart Sport Yarn (3-ounce balls): 4 (4, 5) balls of No. 846 skipper blue; size 5 (6, 7) knitting needles, or size to obtain gauge given below; cable needle; four ¾-inch-diameter buttons.

Abbreviations: See pages 218-219.
Gauge: With size 5 needles over overall cable pat, 6 sts = 1 inch; 7 rows = 1 inch. With size 6 needles over overall cable pat, 11 sts = 2 inches; 13 rows = 2 inches. With size 7 needles over overall cable pat, 5 sts = 1 inch; 6 rows = 1 inch.
Finished measurements: When garment is buttoned, chest = 41 (45, 48½) inches.

Instructions

Note: All sizes are worked with the same number of sts. Different size needles are used for each size to obtain the measurements given. Take care to see that your gauge accurately matches that given above.

Back: Beg at lower edge with size 5 (6, 7) needles, cast on 126 sts.

Row 1 (right side): K 7, * p 2, k 8. Rep from * across, ending with k 7.

Row 2: P 7, * k 2, p 8. Rep. from * across, ending with p 7.

Row 3-4: Rep Rows 1 and 2.

Row 5 (cable row): K 7, * p 2, *sl next 4 sts onto cable needle and hold in back of work, k next 4 sts, k the 4 sts from cable needle—cable twist made;* p 2, k 8. Rep from * across, ending with k 7.

Row 6: Rep Row 2.

Rows 7-14: Rep Rows 1 and 2. Rep Rows 5-14 for pat until total length from beg measures 13 (13½, 13½) inches, ending with a wrong-side row.

Armhole shaping: *Rows 1 and 2:* Cast off the 1st 7 sts; complete row in pat. Keeping to pat, dec 1 st at each end on the next row and every other row thereafter until 96 sts rem. Work even in pat until the total length past the 1st row of

the armhole shaping measures 9½ (10, 10½) inches, ending with a wrong-side row.

Shoulder shaping: *Rows 1-4:* Keeping to pat as established, cast off 1st 10 sts; complete row.

Rows 5-6: Cast off 1st 11 sts; complete row. Cast off rem 34 sts for back of neck.

Pocket lining (make 2): Beg at lower edge with size 5 (6, 7) needles, cast on 28 sts. Work in st st for 22 rows, ending with a p row. Sl sts to a holder to be worked later.

Left front: With size 5 (6, 7) needles, cast on 2 sts. *Row 1:* K. *Row 2:* P.

Row 3: Cast on 4 sts at beg of row, inc 1 st in each of next 2 sts—8 sts.

Row 4: P.

Row 5: Cast on 4 sts at beg of row, k across to last 2 sts, inc 1 st in each of last 2 sts—14 sts.

Row 6: Rep Row 2.

Row 7: Cast on 4 sts at beg of row, k 3, p 2, k 7, inc 1 st in each of last 2 sts—20 sts.

Row 8: P 1, k 2, p 8, k 2, p 7.

Row 9: Inc 4 sts at beg of row, k 7, p 2, k 8, p l, inc 1 st in each of last 2 sts—26 sts.

Row 10: P 3, (k 2, p 8) twice; k 2, p 1.

Row 11: Cast on 4 sts at beg of row, k 1, p 2, k 8, p 2, make cable twist over next 8 sts, p 2, k 1, inc 1 st in each of last 2 sts—32 sts.

Row 12: P 5, (k 2, p 8) twice; k 2, p 5.

Row 13: Cast on 4 sts at beg of row, k 5 (p 2, k 8) twice; p 2, k 3, inc 1 st in last 2 sts—38 sts.

Row 14: P 7 (k 2, p 8) 3 times; k 1.

Row 15: Cast on 4 sts at beg of row, p 1, k 8, (p 2, k 8) twice; p 2, k 5, inc 1 st in last 2 sts—44 sts.

Row 16: K 1, (p 8, k 2) 4 times; p 3.

Row 17: Cast on 4 sts at beg of row, work in pat as established to last 2 sts, inc as before—50 sts.

Row 18: P 1, (k 2, p 8) 4 times; k 2, p 7. Mark end of row for side edge.

Row 19: Work in established pat to last 2 sts—inc as before—52 sts.

Row 20: Work even in pat as established, being careful to keep to pat, and working cables every 10th row as for back. Rep last 2 rows worked until there are 60 sts on needle, ending with a wrong-side row.

continued

Next row: Inc 1 st at front edge; complete row in pat. Work even in pat as established across the 61 sts for 11 rows, ending at side edge.

Pocket placement: *Next row:* Work in pat across 1st 19 sts, sl next 28 sts to holder to be worked later for pocket border. With right side of lining facing, work across the 28 sts of 1 pocket lining as follows: (K 8, p 2) twice; k 8, complete row. Continue in cable pat across the 61 sts on the needle until total length from side marker measures 13 (13½, 13½) inches, ending at the side edge.

Armhole and neck shaping: *Row 1:* Cast off 1st 7 sts, work in pat across, dec on st at front edge for beg of neck shaping.

Row 2: Work even.

Row 3: Dec 1 st at both ends, work in pat across.

Row 4: Rep Row 2.

Row 5: Rep Row 3. Continue in pat, dec 1 st at armhole edge on every other row 6 times more *and at the same time* dec on st at front edge every 4th row 4 times—39 sts. Keeping armhole edge straight, continue to dec 1 st at neck edge every 4th row until 31 sts rem. Work even in pat until total length past 1st row of armhole shaping measures 9½ (10, 10½) inches, ending at armhole edge.

Shoulder shaping: *Row 1:* Cast off 1st 10 sts; complete row in pat.

Row 2: Work even.

Rows 3-4: Rep Rows 1-2. Cast off rem sts.

Pocket band: Sl the 28 sts from holder to a size 5 (6, 7) needle. With right side facing, join yarn. Work in k 1, p 1 ribbing for 1 inch. Cast off in ribbing. Sew ends of band and free edges of pocket lining in place.

Right front: With size 5 (6, 7) needles cast on 2 sts. *Row 1:* K.

Row 2: P.

Row 3: Inc 1 st in each st, cast on 4 sts at end of row, 8 sts.

Row 4: P.

Row 5: Inc 1 st in each of 1st 2 sts, k across, cast on 4 sts at end of row—14 sts.

Row 6: Rep Row 2.

Row 7: Inc 1 st in each of 1st 2 sts, k 7, p 2, k 3, cast on 4 sts at end of row—20 sts.

Row 8: P k, k 2, p 8, k 2, p 1.

Row 9: Inc 1 st in each of 1st 2 sts, p 1, k 8, p 2, k 7, cast on 4 sts at end of row—26 sts.

Row 10: P 1, k 2 (p 8, k 2) twice; p 3.

Row 11: Inc 1 st in each of 1st 2 sts, p 1, k 2, make cable twice over next 8 sts, p 2, k 8, p 2, k 1, cast on 4 sts at end of row—32 sts.

Row 12: P 5, (k 2, p 8) twice; k 2, p 5.

Row 13: Inc 1 st in each of 1st 2 sts, k 3, (p 2, k 8) twice; p 2, k 5, cast on 4 sts at end of row—38 sts.

Row 14: K 1, (p 8, k 2) 3 times; p 7.

Row 15: Inc 2 sts as before, k 5, (p 2, k 8) 3 times, p 1, cast on 4 sts at end of row—44 sts.

Row 16: P 3, k 2, (p 8, k 2) 3 times; p 8, k 1.

Row: 17: Inc 2 sts as before, k 7 (p 2, k 8) 3 times; p 2, k 3, cast on 4 sts at end of row—50 sts.

Row 18: P 7, k 2 (p 8, k 2) 4 times; p 1.

Row 19: Inc 2 sts as before, complete row in pat—52 sts. Mark end of row for side edge.

Row 20: Work even in pat. Being careful to keep to pat as established, and working cable every 10th row as for back, rep last 2 rows until there are 60 sts on needle, ending on wrong side.

Next row: Inc 1 st at front edge; complete row in pat. Work even in pat over the 61 sts for 11 rows, ending at front edge.

Pocket placement: Work in pat across 1st 14 sts, sl next 28 sts of rem pocket lining as follows: (K 8, p 2) twice; complete row in pat. Complete to correspond to left front.

Pin to measurements; dampen and leave to dry.

Back lower border: With right side facing and size 5 (6, 7) needles, pick up and k 114 sts evenly spaced along lower edge of back. Work in k 1, p 1 ribbing for 8 rows. Cast off in ribbing.

Back neck border: With right side facing and size 5 (6, 7) needles, pick up and k 32 sts along neck edge of back and work in k 1, p 1 ribbing for 8 rows. Cast off in ribbing.

Right front border: With right side facing, join yarn at side edge. With size 5 (6, 7) needles, pick up and k 32 sts evenly along lower edge to st at point, place a marker on needle, pick up and k next st for center of point, place another marker on needle, pick up and k 25 sts along rem lower edge and 108 sts along front edge.

Row 1: Work in k 1, p 1 ribbing to 1 st before next marker, inc 1 st in next st, sl marker, p 1, sl marker, inc 1 st in next st; complete the row in ribbing.

Row 2: Work even in ribbing across, being careful to k the st bet markers. (*Note:* Always sl markers.) Rep last 2 rows until 8 rows have been completed. Cast off in ribbing.

With pins, mark position of 4 buttons evenly spaced on right front border, having 1st pin in last inc row on front edge and last pin in line with beg of neck shaping.

Left front border: Beg at shoulder, work ribbing to correspond with opposite border until 3 rows of ribbing have been worked.

Next row: (Work in ribbing to next pin, cast off 3 sts) 4 times; complete row.

Following row: Work in ribbing, casting on 3 sts over each grp of cast-off sts.

Next 3 rows: Complete as for right front. Cast off in ribbing. Sew shoulder seams.

Armhole border: With right side facing and size 5 (6, 7) needles, pick up and k 114 sts along entire armhole edge and work in k 1, p 1 ribbing for 6 rows. Cast off in ribbing.

Sew up the side seams, including the borders. Sew on buttons. (*Optional:* With crochet hook and wrong side facing, sl st around outer edges of ribbing to stabilize.)

Woman's Cable Vest

shown on page 40

Directions are for size Small (8-10); changes for sizes Medium (12-14) and Large (16-18) are in parentheses. (See note below on finished measurements.)

Materials

Coats & Clark Red Heart Super Sport Yarn (3-ounce balls): 3 (4, 4) balls 819 blue jewel; size 5 (6, 7) knitting needles, or size to obtain gauge given below; cable needle, four ½-inch-diameter buttons.

Abbreviations: See pages 218-219.
Gauge: With size 5 needles over overall cable pat, 6 sts = 1 inch; 7 rows = 1 inch. With size 6 needles over overall

cable pat, 11 sts = 2 inches; 13 rows = 2 inches. With size 7 needles over overall cable pat, 5 sts = 1 inch; 6 rows = 1 inch.

Finished measurements: When the garment is buttoned, the bust equals 33 (36, 40) inches.

Instructions

Note: All sizes are worked with the same number of sts. Different size needles are used for each size to obtain the measurements given. Take care to see that your gauge accurately matches that given above.

Back: Beg at lower edge with size 5 (6, 7) needles, cast on 100 sts.

Row 1 (right side): K 5, * p 2, k 6. Rep from * across, end with p 2, k 5.

Row 2: P 5, * k 2, p 6. Rep from * across, ending with p 5.

Rows 3-4: Rep Rows 1-2.

Row 5: K 5, * p 2; *sl next 3 sts onto cable needle and hold in back of work, k next 3 sts, k the 3 sts from cable needle—cable twist made.*

Row 6: Rep Row 2.

Rows 7-14: Rep Rows 1-2. Rep Rows 5-14 for pat until total length from beg measures 10 (10½, 11½) inches, ending with a wrong-side row.

Armhole shaping: *Rows 1 and 2:* Cast off 1st 6 sts; complete row in pat. Keeping to pat, as established dec 1 st at each end on next row and every other row until 78 sts rem. Work even in pat until total length past 1st row of armhole shaping measures 9 (9½, 10) inches, ending with a wrong-side row.

Shoulder shaping: *Rows 1-4:* Keeping to pat as established, cast off 1st 7 sts; complete row.

Rows 5-6: Cast off 1st 8 sts; complete row. Cast off rem 34 sts for back of neck.

Pocket lining (make 2): Beg at lower edge with size 5 (6, 7) needles, cast on 22 sts. Work in st st for 21 rows, ending with a k row, sl sts to a holder to be worked later.

Left front: With size 5 (6, 7) needles, cast on 2 sts.

Row 1: K 2.

Row 2: P 2; cast on 4 sts—6 sts.

Row 3: P 2, k 4; cast on 4 sts—10 sts.

Row 4: K 2, p 6, k 2, cast on 4 sts—14 sts.

Row 5: K 4, p 2, cable twist over next 6 sts, p 2; cast on 4 sts—18 sts.

Row 6: P 4, k 2, p 6, k 2, p 4; cast on 4 sts—22 sts.

Row 7: P 2, (k 6, p 2) twice; k 4; cast on 4 sts—26 sts.

Row 8: (K 2, p 6) 3 times; k 2; cast on 4 sts—30 sts.

Row 9: K 4, (p 2, k 6) 3 times; p 2, cast on 2 sts—32 sts.

Row 10: P 2, (k 2, p 6) 3 times; k 2, p 4; cast on 9 sts—41 sts.

Row 11: Mark beg of row for side edge; k 5, (p 2, k 6) 4 times; p 2, k 2, cast on 2 sts—43 sts.

Row 12: P 4, (k 2, p 6) 4 times; k 2, p 5.

Row 13: K 5, (p 2, k 6) 4 times; p 2, k 4; cast on 2 sts—45 sts.

Row 14: (P 6, k 2) 5 times; p 5.

Row 15: K 5, (p 2, cable twist over next 6 sts, p 2, k 6) twice; p 2, make cable twist over next 6 sts; cast on 2 sts—47 sts.

Row 16: K 2, (p 6, k 2) 5 times; p 5.

Rows 17-24: Work even in pat as established.

Row 25: K 5, (p 2, cable twist over next 6 sts, p 2, k 6) twice; p 2, cable twist, p 2. Pat is now established.

Rows 26-30: Work even in pat.

Pocket placement: *Next row:* Work in pat across 1st 15 sts, break off yarn, sl next 22 sts to a holder to be worked later for pocket border. Attach ball of yarn and work in pat across last 10 sts.

Following row: Work in pat across 10 sts, pick up a pocket lining, and with p side facing, work across sts of lining as follows: (P 6, k 2) twice; p 6; complete rem sts in pat. Continue in cable pat across the 47 sts on needle until total length from side marker measures 10 (10½, 11½) inches, ending at side edge.

Armhole and neck shaping: *Row 1:* Cast off 1st 6 sts; complete row.

Row 2: Work even. Now dec 1 st at beg and end of next row and every other row until 31 sts rem. Keeping armhole edge straight, continue with established decs at neck edge until 22 sts rem. Work even until armhole measures same as for back, ending at armhole edge.

Shoulder shaping: *Row 1:* Cast off 7 sts at beg of row.

Row 2: Work even.

Rows 3-4: Rep Rows 1 and 2. Cast off rem sts.

Right front: With size 5 (6, 7) needles, cast on 2 sts.

Row 1: K 2; cast on 4 sts—6 sts.

Row 2: K 2, p 4, cast on 4 sts—10 sts.

Row 3: P 2, k 6, p 2; cast on 4 sts—14 sts.

Row 4: P 4, k 2, p 6, k 2; cast on 4 sts—18 sts.

Row 5: K 4, p 2, cable twist over next 6 sts, p 2, k 4, cast on 4 sts—22 sts.

Row 6: K 2 (p 6, k 2) twice; p 4; cast on 4 sts—26 sts.

Row 7: P 2, (k 6, p 2) 3 times; cast on 4 sts—30 sts.

Row 8: P 4, (k 2, p 6) 3 times; k 2, cast on 2 sts—32 sts.

Row 9: K 2, (p 2, k 6) 3 times; p 2, k 4; cast on 9 sts—41 sts.

Row 10: Mark beg of row for side edge; p 5 (k 2, p 6) 4 times; k 2, p 2; cast on 2 sts—43 sts.

Row 11: K 4, (p 2, k 6) 4 times; p 2, k 5.

Row 12: P 5, k 2, (p 6, k 2) 4 times; p 4; cast on 2 sts—45 sts.

Row 13: (K 6, p 2) 5 times; k 5.

Row 14: P 5, (k 2, p 6) 5 times; cast on 2 sts—47 sts.

Row 15: (P 2, cable twist, p 2, k 6) twice, p 2, cable twist, p 2, k 5.

Rows 16-30: Work even in pat as established, working 3 cables on Row 25.

Pocket placement: *Next row:* Work in pat across 10 sts, break off yarn, sl next 22 sts to a holder to be worked later for pocket border; then attach ball of yarn and work in pat across last 15 sts.

Following row: Work in pat across 15 sts, pick up pocket lining, and with p side facing, work across sts of lining as follows: (P 6, k 2) twice, p 6, work across rem 10 sts in pat. Work next 2 rows even in pat. Now continue to work even in pat, working 3 cable twists on next and every 10th row as established until the total length of the side edge equals that of the back, ending at the side edge.

Armhole, neck, and shoulder shaping: Complete to correspond to the other side.

Pin to measurements; dampen and leave to dry.

Pocket border (make 2): Sl sts from holder to size 5 (6, 7) needles and work k 1, p 1 ribbing for 6 rows. Cast off in ribbing.

Lower back border: With right side facing and size 5 (6, 7) needles, pick up and k 90 sts. Work as for the pocket border.

continued

Back neck border: With right side facing and size 5 (6, 7) needles, pick up and k 33 sts along back neck edge. Work as for pocket border.

Right front border: With yarn, mark positions for making 4 buttonholes on ribbing along right front edge. With right side facing and size 5 (6, 7) needles, and beg at lower edge, pick up and k 29 sts along lower edge of front to point, place a marker on needle, pick up and k 1 st, place a marker on needle, pick up and k 26 sts along lower edge to front, pick up and k 110 sts along entire front edge to shoulder—166 sts.

Row 1: Work in k 1, p 1 ribbing to within 1 st before marker, inc 1 st in this st, sl marker, p 1, sl marker, inc in next st; complete row in ribbing.

Row 2: Work even in ribbing, being careful to k the st bet markers.

Row 3: Rep Row 1.

Row 4: (Working in ribbing to buttonhole marker, cast off 3 sts) 4 times; complete row.

Next row: Work in ribbing, casting on 3 sts over each group of cast-off stitches.

Following row: Work even. Cast off in ribbing.

Left front border: Work to correspond to right front border, eliminating buttonholes. Sew shoulder and front border seams.

Armhole border: With size 5 (6, 7) needles, pick up and k 110 sts along entire armhole edge. Work as for pocket border.

Sew the side seams, including the borders; sew down the pocket linings and borders; sew on the buttons. (*Optional:* With crochet hook and wrong side facing, sl st around the outer edges of the ribbing to stabilize it.)

Child's Knitted Vest

shown on page 41

The instructions given below are for size 4; changes for a child's size 6 follow in parentheses.

Materials

Tahki Creole cotton yarn (100-gram skeins); 2 (2) skeins each of No. 707 white and No. 708 pink; sizes 7 and 9 knitting needles, or size to obtain gauge given below; size H aluminum crochet hook; 4 buttons.

Abbreviations: See pages 218-219.
Gauge: With larger needles over st st, 7 sts = 2 inches; 5 rows = 1 inch.
Finished measurements: Chest = 23½ (25) inches.

Instructions

Back: With purple and smaller needles, cast on 41 (43) sts. Work in k 1, p 1 ribbing for 2 inches. Change to larger needles, and follow pattern from chart (above, right); work in white and pink sts as indicated. Begin pattern at point A for size 4 and at point B for size 6.

After 10 rows of chart have been completed, work even with purple until total length measures 9½ (10½) inches. Mark ends of last row with small safety pins for underarm. Work even until total length from beg measures 13 (14) inches, ending with a wrong-side row.

Neck and shoulder shaping: *Next row:* Work across 15 sts and sl to holder for right shoulder. Cast off next 11 (13) sts for back neck; work across rem 15 sts for 7 (9) rows more for left shoulder. Cast off on right side. Sl 15 sts from holder onto needle, attach yarn and work same as for left shoulder.

Right front: With purple and smaller needles, cast on 21 (23) sts. Work pink and white pat as for back, beg at point C for size 4 and point B for size 6. Work same as for back until 13 (15) rows past underarm marker have been worked. Cast off 4 sts at beg of next row, then 1 st every other row at neck edge 2 (4) times—15 sts. Work even until total length of the piece equals that of back.

Left front: Work same as for right front until 13 (15) rows past underarm marker have been worked, ending with a right-side row. Cast off 4 sts at beg of next row, then 1 st every other row 2 (4) times—15 sts. To complete, follow directions for right front, given above.

Finishing: Sew shoulder seams; sew side seams. With crochet hook and pink, work 1 row sc around entire inside edge of sweater. Fasten off.

Attach white and work 1 sc around, working in 4 buttonholes along front edge (right front for girls; left front for boys) as follows: Sc, ch 1, sk 1 sc, sc in next sc. Fasten off. Work 1 more row with pink. Fasten off.

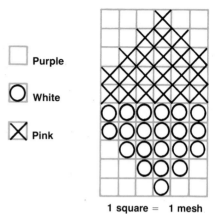

□ Purple
○ White
⊠ Pink

1 square = 1 mesh

Sew buttons in place. Attach pink to underarm opening and work 2 rnds sc around. Fasten off. Attach white and work 1 more rnd of sc.

Crocheted Hat and Turtleneck

shown on page 41

Hat instructions are for size Small (21-inch-circumference head); changes for sizes Medium (22-inch-circumference head) and Large (23-inch-circumference head) follow in parentheses.

Materials

Stanley Berocco Dju-Dji *or* Merabella (50-gram skeins): small amounts of various colors equal to 3 skeins for the hat; small amounts equal to 2 skeins for the collar; size J aluminum crochet hook, or size to obtain gauge given below; crew-neck sweater.

Abbreviations: See pages 218-219.
Gauge: 3 sc = 1 inch.

Instructions

Note: Change colors randomly for striped effect. Work hat brim in a single color, as shown in the photograph.

Hat brim: With 1 strand of yarn, ch 11. *Row 1:* Sc in 2nd ch from hook and in each ch across; ch 1, turn. *Row 2:* Sc in back lp of 1st sc and in back lp of each sc across; ch 1, turn. Rep Row 2 until 63 (66, 69) rows are worked. Secure last row worked to beg ch to form a lp large enough to fit around head.

Hat crown: Attach yarn at joining of brim, sc evenly along end of each row, working 1 sc for each row—63 (66, 69) sc; sl st to beg sc, ch 1.

Next rnd: Sc in same st as joining, sc in each sc around, sl st to beg sc; ch 1. Rep last row, changing colors randomly, until 20 rnds have been completed.

Dec row: Mark st directly opposite joining st on last rnd. ***Insert hook through sc, yo, draw up a lp, insert hook through next sc, yo, draw up a lp, yo and draw through all 3 lps on hook—dec made.*** Rep twice more, work even to 6 sc before marker, make 3 decs over next 6 sc, sl marker, make 3 decs over next 6 sc, work even to within last 6 sc of rnd, make 3 dec over last 6 sc of rnd; join to beg of rnd with a sl st.

Next rnd: Work even. *Following rnd:* Rep dec rnd. *Next rnd:* Work decs in each pair of sc around. Flatten hat crown so that last rnd forms a seam from front of head to back of head; sew or sl st seam tog. Fasten off.

Cowl neck: Fold neckline ribbing of sweater under; tack in place. With a tape measure, measure circumference of resulting neck opening. With 1 strand of yarn, ch to this measurement, having 3 ch per inch; sl st to form ring. Sc in each ch around; join to 1st sc at beg of rnd. Changing colors randomly, rep this rnd until total length measures 4 inches.

Inc rnd: Working as before, work 2 sc in 5 sc, evenly spaced around. Keeping to pat, work even until total length from beg measures 8½ inches.

Picot edging: * Sc in 1st sc, ch 3, sl st in 1st sc, sc in next sc. Rep from * around. Fasten off.

Beaded-Bouquet Sweater

shown on page 42

Materials

Purchased, finely knit sweater; assortment of small beads; beading needle; thread; crewel yarn or embroidery floss in assorted colors; embroidery needle (optional).

Instructions

Plan the positioning of several 4-inch-diameter circles across the front and shoulders of the sweater. Distribute the circles in an asymmetrical pattern (see photograph, page 44). Thread the beading needle, knot the thread,

and draw the thread up from the wrong to the right side of the sweater.

Thread a small bead onto the needle and return the needle to the wrong side of the fabric, close to where it was brought up. (To secure a larger bead, or a sequin or spangle, bring the needle to the right side, thread on a larger bead or sequin, then thread a smaller bead. Return the needle to the wrong side of the fabric through the hole in the larger bead; the smaller bead will hold the larger one in place.)

Work around the outside of the circle first, stitching down various colors and styles of beads randomly. Then work to fill in the centers of the circles.

If you prefer, embroider each flower in the bouquet, using beads only on centers of flowers. Make a cluster of five or six small lazy daisy stitches for each flower using No. 8 pearl cotton embroidery floss or a single strand of crewel yarn. Then stitch a small bead to the center of each embroidered flower.

Beaded-Yoke Sweater

shown on page 43

Materials

Purchased Fair-Isle sweater; fine elasticized thread; assorted small beads and seed pearls; beading needle.

Instructions

Use the colors and patterns of the Fair-Isle yoke as inspiration. With elasticized thread, stitch rows of beads and pearls along the rows of the pattern. Use a single stitch to secure each bead and ensure even spacing.

If elasticized thread is too heavy to go through the beads you have selected, work with regular beading thread, but stitch no more than 10 or 12 beads in a row before tying the thread off and beginning with a new strand. This is to preserve the shape and elasticity of the knit fabric.

Painted Hat

shown on page 43

Materials

Summer hat or sun visor in natural, unfinished straw; simple floral design of your choice; graphite paper; artist's acrylic paints and fine, soft brush; acrylic spray (optional).

Instructions

First, choose an appropriate floral design from a pattern within this book, or from another book of needlework designs. If you wish, the flowers may be sketched freehand using real flowers as an inspiration.

Transfer the outlines of the floral pattern onto the brim of the hat, using graphite paper or dressmaker's carbon.

Then, paint the design, using acrylic paints diluted with water to consistency of light cream to ensure that the paint can easily cover the texture of the straw hat. Be careful not to overload the brush with paint; stroke excess paint onto a paper towel before working on the hat. When the paint has dried, protect the design with several coats of clear acrylic spray, if desired.

Eyelet-Ruffled Shirt

shown on page 43

Materials

Purchased oxford-cloth shirt; approximately 1½ yards of 3-inch-wide ruffled eyelet, 3 yards of 1½-inch-wide ruffled eyelet, 1 yard of 1-inch-wide eyelet (for collar and cuffs), ⅔ yard of 1½-inch-wide flat eyelet (for the shirt placket); small seed pearls; thread and beading needle (optional); water-erasable pen.

Instructions

Using a water-erasable pen, mark the position of the uppermost ruffle on the shirt. Carefully sketch a western-style curve from about ⅔ of the way down the front of the shirt, up over the pockets, and across the shoulders, forming a curved yoke in the back. Stitch a row of 1½-inch-wide eyelet along this line.

Space a second row of 1½-inch-wide eyelet beneath the first ruffle, and then stitch a ruffle of 3-inch-wide eyelet in place (study the photograph on page 45 for placement).

Next, trim the placket of the shirt with flat eyelet lace. Restitch the buttonholes, if necessary. Finally, add a ruffle of narrow eyelet along the collar and cuffs of the shirt and trim the ruffle with a row of seed pearls.

49

Children's Playtime Favorites

Family Pets and Farmyard Friends

Soft and comfortable as a mother's hug, stuffed animals will always be among the most cherished companions of childhood. And no child ever seems to get enough of them.

So if you're looking for a sure-to-please present for a youngster, you can't go wrong with the cuddlesome creatures pictured here and on the following pages.

♦ Our plush, family-size pooch (left) is so lifelike, he even manages to fool a visiting litter of playful pups. He and a tiny tyke are bound to become fast friends in no time—and best of all, this puppy is completely house-trained!

♦ Stitch and stuff a sassy cat pillow (above) to keep your preschooler company. With its bright calico "fur" and big Cheshire-cat grin, our plump, oversize kitty creates a cozy, child-size corner in any room in the house. The features are machine-appliquéd to the body, and the comfortable cat is softly stuffed with fiberfill.

Instructions begin on page 56.

51

Family Pets and Farmyard Friends

Imagine the tales of travel and adventure this family of storybook bears (opposite) will inspire among the nursery set. Stitched of soft brown felt and made with movable arms and legs, Mama and Papa Bear are each about 12 inches tall. Baby Bear—when standing on his hind paws and stretching a bit—is close to seven inches tall.

All three bears are decked out in splendid felt finery trimmed with ribbons and laces and snippets of embroidered fabric. Add a silk flower or two and bits of costume jewelry to complete the bears' outfits.

♦ Cozy cat pillows (above) have the look of simple outline embroidery. But they're actually even easier to make, because the "stitchery" is nothing more than carefully sketched lines drawn on muslin with permanent markers. And their bright eyes and heart necklaces are painted on with special fabric paints.

Family Pets and Farmyard Friends

When it comes to winning a youngster's affection, dogs and cats and fuzzy brown bears are the perennial favorites. But you'll find that lots of other animals can rival these traditional stuffed toys.

For example, these down-on-the-farm animals will surprise and amuse every child who is lucky enough to receive them as gifts.

♦ The woolly lambs (below) and their stout mother sheep are just the thing for a child to cuddle. Stitched from soft acrylic fleece (so they are washable) and lightly stuffed, they have bright button eyes, shiny black hooves (made from polished cotton), and floppy ears lined in pink. Bells tied with pretty ribbons adorn the trio.

Mother is a hefty two feet long and 18 inches high, and her babies each measure about 12 inches from the tips of their little pink noses to their plump tails.

♦ The amusing geese (right) are two more friends from the farm that kids will adore. They're easy to stitch from sturdy white fabric and they have separately stitched wings that are securely attached.

Their perky eyes are appliquéd so they're safe for even the smallest of children, and their spiffy attire gives them a certain charm that even teens will love.

Dress the pair in coordinating outfits. The goose has a lace-trimmed apron and bonnet made from polka dot fabric and tied with contrasting grosgrain ribbon. Her pretty flower is a simple roll of felt tacked to the underside of her hat.

The gander sports a smart little vest and tam, and the white collar and gingham tie complete his outfit. You might want to fashion the clothes so they are removable and create alternate wardrobes for hours of fun.

You'll find that all the animals in this section make unusually lovable toys—fit companions for all the other animal friends in your youngster's collection.

Floppy Dog

shown on page 50

Materials

60-inch-wide fake fur in the following amounts and colors: ⅞ yard dark brown short nap, ⅜ yard shaggy white, ⅜ yard tan medium nap, ⅜ yard shaggy tan; scrap of black leather; fiberfill; two ¾-inch-diameter glass buttons with eyelet backs; buttonhole cord.

Instructions

Enlarge patterns (below); pieces include ⅜-inch seam allowances.

Note: The tail is made from three separate sections stitched together. Cut the tail pattern into three sections along the solid lines. Add ⅜-inch seam allowance on the cut end of each piece, then cut the three pieces from fabric.

When cutting the pieces from fake fur, pin and cut out one piece at a time. Lay the pieces on the fabric so that the nap always runs in the same direction, and remember to turn the pattern pieces over so that right sides will match when you stitch.

Cut pieces from fur as follows: *From dark brown:* two ears, upper third of the tail, head sides, top side head pieces, and upper body pieces. *From shaggy white:* head center top, head front, and lower third of tail. *From tan:* underbody pieces. *From shaggy tan:* two ears, under head, lower front paws, and center tail section.

Letter the backs of the pieces as they appear on the pattern to prevent confusion when assembling the pieces.

With fake fur, make invisible seams by pushing the pile away from each seam as you stitch. Practice on a scrap of fabric before you begin.

For the head: Stitch the darts at the crown of the side top pieces. With right sides together, pin the curved edge of the center top piece to the side top pieces, matching the A notches to make head top. Stitch; clip curves.

With right sides together, pin the head top section to the head front along seam B. Stitch. Along the fold line, fold the head front together, right sides facing, and stitch from point E to point F. Clip curves.

With right sides together, fold the head front along the wedge cutout, matching point E to point C. Pin and stitch along the lines indicated on the pattern, forming a horizontal ridge across the head front.

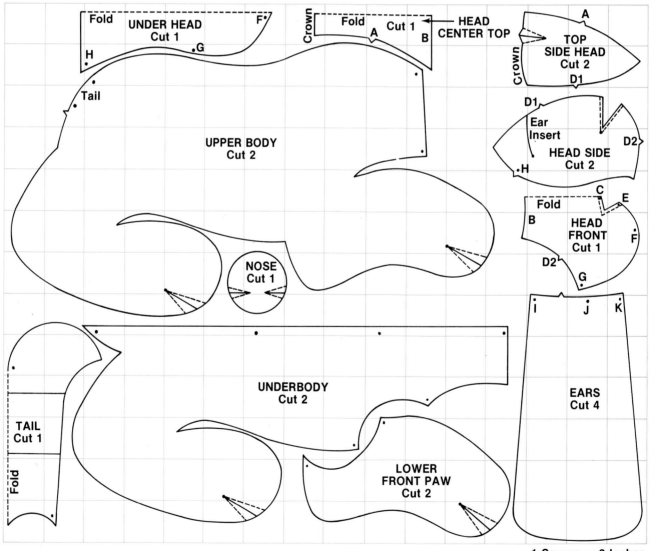

1 Square = 2 Inches

Stitch the darts on the head side pieces. Slash along the ear insert lines.

Matching raw edges and with right sides facing, pin the ear pieces together, pairing each dark brown piece to a tan one. Stitch from point I to K along the sides and bottom. Clip curves, trim the seam, and turn right side out.

On each ear, fold I over to J and stitch across the top. Insert ⅜ inch of the top of the ears through the ear insert slashes on the head side pieces so the dark brown side of the ears and the right side of the head side pieces are facing up. Using a ¼-inch seam allowance, stitch, easing the top of each ear around the corner so that point K matches point D1.

With right sides together, pin the head top and front section to one head side piece from points D1 to D2. Repeat for the other side.

Pin the under head to the rest of the head, right sides facing and matching points F, G, and H along each side. Stitch and clip curves.

For the tail: Stitch the three sections together. Fold along fold line, right sides together; stitch from dot to dot, leaving an opening at one end. Clip curves and turn. Stuff lightly, turn raw edges to the inside, and stitch closed.

For the body: Stitch the darts on all paws. With right sides together, stitch the two upper body pieces together from the top dot on the neck edge, along the dog's back, and around to the notch on the back paw, leaving an opening between the dots for the tail.

With right sides together, pin the two underbody pieces together along the long straight (center) edge. Stitch, leaving open between center dots. With right sides together, pin the lower front paw pieces to the underbody, matching dots. Stitch and clip curves.

With right sides together, pin the underbody to the upper body. Beginning at the neck, stitch all around, leaving the neck edge open. Double-stitch over all corners, then clip curves. Do not turn right side out.

Turn the head right side out and insert it into the body through the neck. Match raw edges and position the head so that the under head seam meets the underbody center seam, and the center crown matches the center back seam. Pin around neckline and stitch. Clip curves and turn right side out through the opening on the underbody.

Stuff firmly, using the blunt end of a knitting needle to reach the paws. Stuff the paws, the head, the tail area, and the body. Blindstitch the opening on the underbody closed.

Insert the end of the tail into the tail opening on the body; stitch tail firmly in place.

For the nose: Cut a nose from black leather. Stitch the darts, then turn under ¼ inch around the edge of the nose and gather until it forms a pouch. Do not knot your thread.

Stuff the nose lightly with fiberfill, shaping as you go. When the nose is the desired shape, gather closed and knot to secure. Pin the nose in place so that the flat (darted) side is on top. Stitch securely with buttonhole cord.

For the eyes: Using a double thread of buttonhole cord, sew one eye in place along seam of head front and side top,

and about 1 inch from top of head. Do not cut thread. Instead, push needle through head front to the spot where the other eye will be. Sew on the other button. Knot your thread and go back through the head to the first button. Tie a secure knot and cut your thread.

For the mouth: With one strand of buttonhole cord, satin-stitch over the vertical seam from the bottom of the nose to the underbody.

Cushy Cat Chair

shown on page 51

Materials

3 yards red dotted fabric; 1 yard navy-and-red calico; ¼ yard white eyelet fabric; 2½ yards muslin; scrap of black fabric; 1½ yards fusible webbing; *continued*

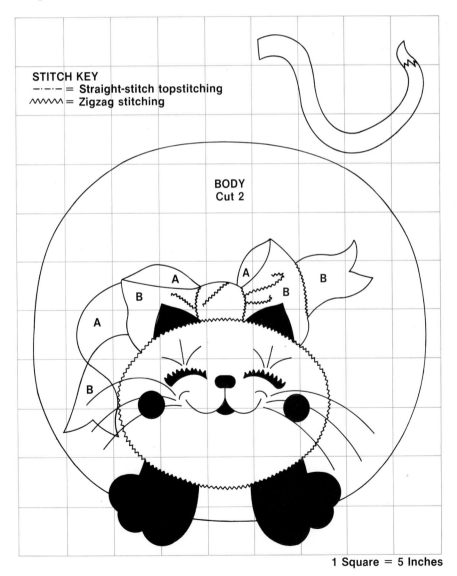

STITCH KEY
–·–·– = Straight-stitch topstitching
∿∿∿∿ = Zigzag stitching

BODY
Cut 2

1 Square = 5 Inches

57

⅓ yard quilt batting; polyester fiberfill; black embroidery floss; dressmaker's carbon paper; nylon fastening tape; graph paper.

Instructions

Enlarge the pattern on page 57 onto graph paper, transferring all the design lines as a guide for cutting and appliquéing. Adding ½-inch seam allowances all around, cut two body pieces, four ears, and four feet from the red dotted fabric.

The remaining pieces will be machine-appliquéd and need no seam allowances. Cut them as follows:

From red dotted fabric: an oval for the cat's face.

From calico: a tail, and the A pieces in the bow.

From eyelet: two cheeks, the B pieces in the bow, and the tip of the tail.

From black fabric: a nose, a tongue, and two eyelashes.

To make the cat's face, first transfer the outlines of the eyelashes, nose, cheeks, and tongue to the face piece, using dressmaker's carbon paper. Using a machine zigzag stitch, appliqué these pieces to the cat face.

To the front foot and ear pieces, transfer the topstitching lines using dressmaker's carbon paper. If desired, embroider a ladybug atop a topstitching line on one foot piece. Then pin a square of batting to the wrong side of each foot and ear piece; baste. Trim batting ¼ inch from the edges.

With right sides facing, stitch together the ears and feet, leaving an opening at the top of each foot and the bottom of each ear. Stitch again to reinforce. Clip curves, trim seams, and turn. Without turning under the raw edges, baste the openings closed.

Press the feet and ears lightly. Then, along the lines indicated on the pattern, topstitch the feet and ears through all layers.

Referring to your master pattern for positioning, pin the bow pieces in place on the right side of the body front; appliqué with machine zigzag stitching. Then, along the lines indicated, topstitch with zigzag stitches.

Pin the face to the right side of the body front. Tuck raw edges of the feet and ears under the face; pin in place. Zigzag-stitch around face's edge, catching the feet and ears in the stitching. The feet and ears will be loose.

With three strands of black embroidery floss, outline-stitch the whiskers, mouth, and eyebrows, referring to the pattern for positioning.

On the right side of the body back, center the tail appliqué; pin in place. Position the eyelet tip of the tail over the tail piece; pin. Zigzag-stitch the pieces in place.

From muslin, cut two pieces the same size as the body. Stitch them together, using a ½-inch seam allowance and leaving an opening for stuffing. Turn right side out, stuff lightly, and stitch the opening closed.

Along 25 inches of the bottom of the cat pillow front and back, press under ½ inch along the seam allowance. Cut a 25-inch strip of nylon fastening tape. Stitch one strip to each edge.

With right sides facing, pin the cat front and back together, matching the nylon fastening strips. Stitch, using a ½-inch seam allowance and leaving the seam open along the strips. Stitch again to reinforce. Grade seams, clip curves, turn, and press.

Slip the muslin pillow into the cat, then press the strips to close.

Storybook Bears

shown on page 52

Materials

⅓ yard of brown felt; ¼ yard of peach felt; matching sewing thread; No. 5 pearl cotton *or* 6-strand embroidery floss in black, light green, and medium brown; black carpet thread; jet buttons and black beads for eyes; brown shirt buttons for shoulder and hip joints; white glue; polyester fiberfill; small silk flowers; small buttons; various laces and trims; costume jewelry brooch; tissue paper.

Instructions

Note: Bears shown on page 52 are worked in felt, with ⅛-inch seam allowances. Patterns may be adapted for use with woven fabrics or fake furs by increasing seam allowances to ⅝ inch.

For bear bodies: Enlarge the body patterns (opposite) and transfer them to tissue paper. Cut out all body pieces except foot pads from brown felt. Cut foot pads from peach felt. Mama and

Papa Bear bodies are identical except for the snout piece and front sections of Papa Bear's body. All pattern pieces include ⅛-inch seam allowance.

For each body, stitch two body fronts together from A to B. Sew two body backs together from A to B. (The straight seams fall along the midline of the torso.) Place front and back together, right sides facing; stitch around, leaving neck edges open. Stuff body firmly with fiberfill.

For each arm, place two pattern pieces right sides together and stitch from A to B. Turn right side out, stuff, and slip-stitch closed.

Topstitch foot pads to each foot piece, using peach pearl cotton and tiny running stitches. Then place two leg pieces right sides together and stitch from A to B. Turn right side out, stuff, and whipstitch a foot piece to the open end of each leg.

For adult heads, stitch two head pieces from A to B to form head front. Repeat for head back. Place right sides together and stitch around, leaving neck edges open. Turn.

Stitch Mama and Papa snouts as indicated on patterns. Turn right side out. Stuff snouts and pin each in position, centering along the front seam of the head. Topstitch in place using brown pearl cotton and small running stitches.

For the baby's head, sew head parts together from A to B. Align the back head gusset (marked "Back of Head"); pin in place and stitch from C to D on both sides.

For each bear, stitch two ear pieces together with brown pearl cotton and running stitches. Whipstitch ears to tops of heads.

Stuff heads. Stitch on small jet buttons for Papa's and Mama's eyes; use black beads for Baby's eyes. Embroider nose in satin stitches and mouth lines in outline stitches, using black floss. Study the photograph for placement of features. Slip-stitch head to body.

To assemble bodies: Use four brown shirt buttons for each bear. Each button must have four holes. With button thread, sew a button to the inside center of the right and left arms about ½ inch down from top seam. Stitch buttons in place with Xs; clip threads.

Rethread needle and tie end of thread around the cross-stitch on the left arm button. Run needle through

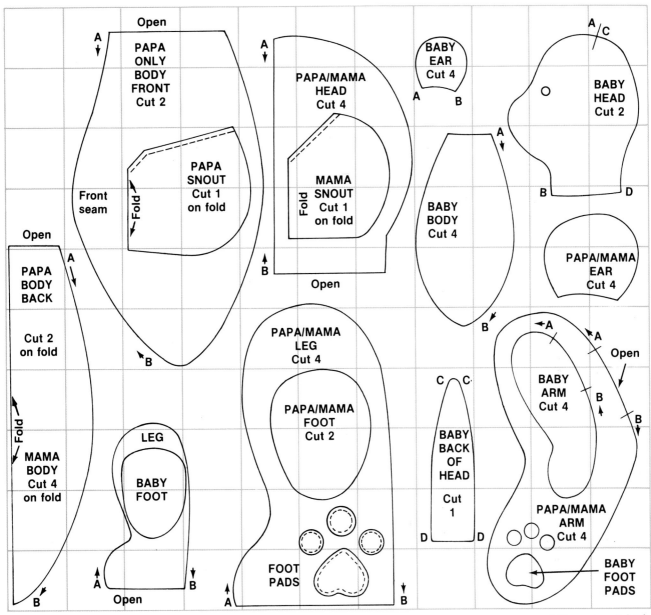

Open
A
PAPA
ONLY
BODY
FRONT
Cut 2

Front
seam

Fold

PAPA
SNOUT
Cut 1
on fold

A

PAPA/MAMA
HEAD
Cut 4

Fold

MAMA
SNOUT
Cut 1
on fold

B

Open

BABY
EAR
Cut 4

A   B

A

BABY
BODY
Cut 4

A/C

O

BABY
HEAD
Cut 2

B   D

PAPA/MAMA
EAR
Cut 4

Open
PAPA
BODY
BACK

A

Cut 2
on fold

B

Fold

MAMA
BODY
Cut 4
on fold

LEG

BABY
FOOT

A   B

B   Open

PAPA/MAMA
LEG
Cut 4

PAPA/MAMA
FOOT
Cut 2

FOOT
PADS

A   B

B

C   C

BABY
BACK
OF
HEAD

Cut
1

D   D

B

A   A
Open
BABY
ARM
Cut 4
B
B

PAPA/MAMA
ARM
Cut 4

BABY
FOOT
PADS

1 Square = 1 Inch

body at shoulder height to opposite shoulder. Pass needle several times around cross-stitch on the right arm button. Squeeze arms to body slightly, and draw thread tight. Wrap thread around button and knot; run needle back through middle of body and clip.

Repeat this step for both legs.

For Papa Bear's costume: Fashion a dickey and high collar out of white felt. Next, cover a piece of white felt with embroidered fabric for a fancy vest; add beads for buttons.

Finally, cut a sleeveless coat from a double thickness of peach felt (an elongated oval with holes cut out for the arms). Sandwich lace edging between the two layers and secure with tiny running stitches in pearl cotton. Add a scrap of lace for an ascot, and trim the jacket with a small silk flower.

For Mama Bear's hair and clothing: To make Mama's curls, thin white glue with water to the consistency of light cream. Dip an 18-inch length of No. 3 or No. 5 brown pearl cotton into the glue and wrap around a pencil. Pat off excess glue with paper toweling. Let glue dry, moving curls a few times while drying so that floss doesn't ad-

here to pencil. Make eight or 10 rolls of curls and tack to Mama's forehead. Add a few silk flowers to hair.

Next, make a simple sleeveless dress out of peach felt and trim with bands of lace, ribbon, and embroidered trim. Embellish with a decorative button or a small piece of costume jewelry.

Cut a bonnet from a double layer of felt and trim with lace.

For Baby's costume: Cut a high collar from peach felt and stitch around Baby's neck. Add a bow of grosgrain ribbon and a perky little flower.

continued

59

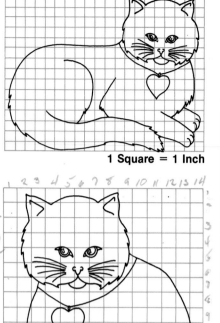

1 Square = 1 Inch

1 Square = 1 Inch

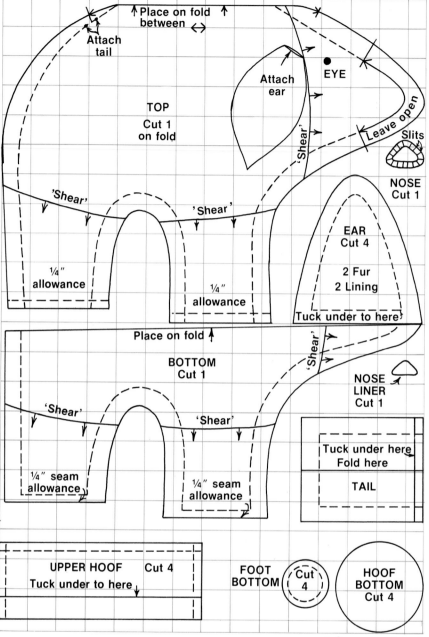

1 Square = 1 Inch

Within the sheep pattern image:
Place on fold between ↔
Attach tail
Attach ear
EYE
'Shear'
Leave open
Slits
NOSE Cut 1
TOP Cut 1 on fold
'Shear'   'Shear'
EAR Cut 4
2 Fur
2 Lining
Tuck under to here
¼" allowance
¼" allowance
Place on fold ↑
BOTTOM Cut 1
'Shear'
NOSE LINER Cut 1
'Shear'   'Shear'
Tuck under here
Fold here
TAIL
¼" seam allowance
¼" seam allowance
UPPER HOOF   Cut 4
Tuck under to here ↓
FOOT BOTTOM
Cut 4
HOOF BOTTOM Cut 4

Muslin Cats

shown on page 53

Materials

¾ yard of muslin for each cat; yellow, red, and fine-tip black permanent markers; 2 pounds of fiberfill for each cat; brown paper.

Instructions

Enlarge patterns (above) and transfer to brown paper. Pin a piece of muslin over each of the cat patterns and trace with black fine-tip marker. Use smooth, even strokes so that ink does not bleed. Remove pattern.

Place a scrap of paper under eyes and heart before coloring. Color eyes yellow and heart red. Heat-set colors by ironing on wrong side of fabric.

Pin front and back (untraced) pieces of muslin together, right sides facing. Pencil lightly around the edge of the cat shape 1⅝ inches outside the traced image, allowing extra fullness at neck and paw curves to avoid sharp angles. Cut along pencil line.

Leaving an opening at bottom, stitch front and back together, using ⅝-inch seam allowance. Clip curves; turn. Stuff firmly with fiberfill, beginning with ears. Slip-stitch opening closed.

Sheep

shown on page 54

Materials

60-inch-wide white fleece fabric: 1 yard for mother sheep and ½ yard for each lamb; scraps of black felt, satin, or cotton for hooves; scraps of pink felt, satin, or cotton for ear linings and nose; polyester fiberfill; two black ball buttons for eyes for each sheep; small bells; decorative ribbons; powdered rouge; corsage pins; extra-long sewing needle (1¾ inches); clear nail polish (optional); tissue paper.

Instructions

Enlarge pattern pieces (above) onto tissue paper. (*Note:* Scale is 1 square = 1 inch for lambs and 1 square = 2 inches for the mother.)

Cut bottom and top pieces according to pattern markings. Using tailor tacks, carefully mark eye, tail, and ear positions on right side of fleece fabric.

Beginning at legs, pin top to bottom piece, right sides facing. Continue until the top rear seams meet. Pin these to each other. Using ⅝-inch seams, machine-stitch everything pinned. Remove pins and trim seams to ¼ inch.

Pin bottoms of feet inside legs, right sides facing. Hand-stitch in place.

Turn lamb to right side through opening in head. Stuff with fiberfill, using the blunt end of a pencil to poke stuffing into hard-to-reach places. Tuck in the raw edges of the head opening. Pinch head end flat to form lamb's snout (refer to photograph). Use corsage pins to hold it in place, then hand-stitch opening closed to form flat snout.

Cut nose and liner from pink fabric. Baste liner inside the nose piece, tucking raw slit edges under. Pin nose on face and hand-stitch in place.

Cut hoof bottoms and uppers from black fabric. Pin and stitch hoof bottoms over existing feet. Then pin hoof uppers to hoof bottoms, turning under raw edges and overlapping fabric to form a seam at the back of each leg. Slip-stitch uppers in place.

Cut and sew on ears and tail, following pattern markings. Line ears with pink fabric. Tuck in raw edges, then pin and hand-stitch openings closed. Stitch button eyes in position (a touch of clear nail polish adds appealing sparkle).

To finish, rub a small amount of powdered rouge on nose, into cheeks, and just inside lamb's ears.

Use scissors to shear fleece a bit shorter on lower legs and face. Thread a bell on a length of ribbon and tie it around lamb's neck.

Geese

shown on page 55

Materials

1 yard of 45-inch-wide sturdy white fabric; 5x10-inch scrap of yellow fabric; scrap of black fabric; fusible webbing; fiberfill; scraps of print fabrics for bonnet, apron, vest, and hat; scraps of yellow and green felt; lengths of grosgrain ribbon, gathered eyelet, yellow rickrack, and double-fold bias tape.

Instructions

Enlarge pattern pieces (above, right) and transfer them to brown paper.

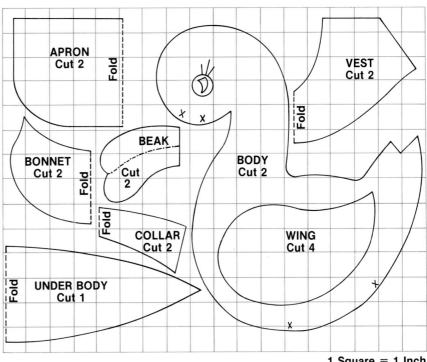

1 Square = 1 Inch

Pieces include ¼-inch seam allowances. (*Note:* Directions below are for one goose body; notes on male and female clothing and accessories follow.)

For each goose, cut out two body and one underbody pieces from white fabric. Cut out two eye pieces from black fabric and fuse to body with fusible webbing. Machine-appliqué eyes to body with satin stitching. Cut out two eye accents from white fabric and fuse one to center of each eye. Embroider eyelashes with straight stitches and double strand of black thread. (*Note:* Make the male's eyelashes shorter than the female's.)

Cut two beaks from yellow fabric. Stitch beaks together, leaving straight edge open. Trim seam, clip, turn, and press. Stuff lightly. Topstitch as pattern indicates. With right sides facing and matching raw edges, pin beak to right side of one body piece.

Pin and stitch body pieces together along top of body, from dot on bird's breast to dot just below tail. Triple-stitch under chin. Pin and stitch underbody between body pieces, leaving an opening between Xs for turning. Trim seams, clip curves, turn, and press.

Stuff, using blunt tool to push fiberfill into small spots. Stuff neck *very* firmly. Slip-stitch opening closed.

Cut four wings from white fabric. With right sides facing, stitch pairs of wings together, leaving an opening for turning. Clip seams, turn, and press. Stuff wings lightly and slip-stitch closed. Blindstitch wings to body. (*Note:* For male, set wings aside until vest is sewed on, then sew on wings.)

To dress the geese: Cut two apron pieces from fabric. Trim one piece with lace and ribbon, then stitch the two pieces together, leaving the straight edge open. Turn and press. Gather the straight edge until it measures 6 inches long; center it on a 25-inch piece of bias tape. Stitch, then tie apron onto goose.

Cut two bonnet pieces. Stitch them together, then turn and press. Gather edge to 5 inches long and stitch it to a 30-inch piece of bias tape. Make a flower from felt and tack it to bonnet.

For the gander, cut two vest pieces and stitch them together, leaving an opening. Turn, press, and slip-stitch closed. Sew vest to goose at center front. Assemble collar and stitch to goose. Fashion a necktie from ribbon, loop it under the collar, and tie. Sew on gander's wings.

For hat, cut two 3½-inch-diameter circles of fabric. From the center of one piece, cut out and discard a 1½-inch circle; stitch ⅛ inch from the inside edge and bind it with bias tape. Stitch hat pieces together around outer edges. Turn, press, and stuff hat lightly. Sew to gander's head.

Places to Play and Things to Ride

Children love to play in imaginary places. With a little time, energy, and imagination of your own, you can make a country cottage dollhouse, a storybook castle, a cozy card table playhouse, or one of the exciting ride-'em toys shown on the following pages for your child.

Best of all, each of these projects is designed to last, so that several generations of children can enjoy the world of fun you've created.

♦ All it takes is a bit of "remodeling" and a quick coat of paint to turn an unfinished wooden cabinet into a delightful dollhouse (left). Just cut out a door and a couple of windows, add a peaked roof (with a flip-down entrance for the attic), and paint in the architectural details.

The result is a dream of a house for a little girl's favorite dolls—or a unique decorative cupboard to house a grown-up girl's best collectibles.

♦ If time and inclination permit, you might populate the dollhouse with a pair of diminutive "homebodies" modeled after the couple shown here (right).

Both dolls are made from one basic pattern, and a simple change of features, hairstyle, and clothing can make either the boy or the girl.

♦ Fill the interior of their cottage cupboard with easy soft-sculpture furniture fashioned from foam rubber and fabric scraps and scaled to match the dainty dolls.

Experiment with the plump flowered sofa and matching easy chair first, then try your hand at designing other household items, using the examples pictured (left) for inspiration.

Check through your scrap bag for tiny prints and small-scale checks suitable for the doll furniture. Look, too, for scraps of lace trims and edgings to use for doilies and finishing details.

You might wish to try these other hints for crafting fast and easy furnishings: Machine-stitch patterns on fabric to simulate architectural details or textures (such as moldings on the fireplace and bricks on the raised hearth).

Use fusible webbing or fabric glue to fix appliqué pieces in place (like the fire in the fireplace). Braid or crochet dollhouse-size "rag" rugs from embroidery floss or lightweight yarn.

Fabric-covered box tops make sturdy tabletops, and small wooden beads make convenient ball feet for a low table or an ottoman.

Just keep thinking small and you're bound to find other things that you can use "as is" or after a little remodeling.

Instructions for the projects in this section begin on page 68.

Places to Play and Things to Ride

Transform an ordinary card table into a make-believe western town with a machine-appliquéd "slipcover" like the one below.

Stitch up the four sides of the cover first, making flaps and zippered openings for doors and inserting rectangles of clear vinyl for the windows. Cut appliqué details from fabric scraps and use iron-on letters to spell out various "points of interest" around town. Then, stitch the sides to the top to make a snug little playhouse—the perfect place for kids to while away a rainy day.

If a western town is not your child's style, use your imagination to come up with another scheme. For example, you might sketch a series of storefronts or the houses in a child's own neighborhood, or even a fanciful version of the New York skyline.

♦ Give your youngsters a taste of romance and fantasy—and inspire them to create hours of fairy-tale play—with this easy-to-make plywood castle and tower bridge (above). A catwalk and working drawbridge add realistic detail and offer endless possibilities for adventure.

Ideal for the beginning wood craftsman and entertaining for those with more experience, this project features a simple design and requires just a few materials and a minimum of basic tools.

Make the royal couple and the ten whimsical knights from scraps of 2x2-inch lumber. The instructions include patterns for the painted figures so you will have as much fun painting the fantasy figures as the kids will have playing with them.

65

Places to Play and Things to Ride

Getting there is *more* than half the fun when kids "travel" in this kind of style.

♦ Our rocking version of the cow that jumped over the moon (left) is sure to delight your favorite toddler. Cut from ½-inch-thick pine and painted in bright acrylics, this nursery-rhyme rocker makes a handsome addition to any child's room. If you want to accommodate a twosome, just make the seat twice as wide as the pattern calls for.

♦ For another variation of the traditional rocking horse, construct an airplane rocker (left) from 2x8-inch pine. Easy to assemble and virtually indestructible, this sturdy little plane should last for several generations of eager aviators.

♦ Junior car buffs will love the sporty little roadster (above). It's built of ½-inch-thick plywood and mounted on metal casters so it can move easily over carpet or concrete for fun indoors and out.

The lift-open trunk in the front has lots of storage space for toys. And the car is a convertible, too, with a roll-down top to make from quilted fabric (not shown).

Doll House

shown on page 62

Materials

Unfinished wooden cabinet with doors (15x27x28 inches or size of your choice); 48-inch length of ¾x7¼-inch pine; pine shelving for gables; two 18-inch squares of ½-inch plywood for the roof; scraps of pine blocks; four metal angles; two small hinges; magnetic latches; bright oil or acrylic paints; paintbrushes.

Instructions

If the cabinet has only one shelf, remove it and change the shelf's position. Then add a second shelf (cut to size from ½-inch pine), to make two evenly spaced floors for the dollhouse.

Cut the doorway and windows in the cabinet doors, referring to the photograph for placement. Then cut the gables, including the attic door, from pine shelving. Attach gables to the top of the cabinet at front and back, using metal angles. Attach the attic door to the front gable with small hinges, positioned so that the door folds outward.

Next, cut and miter the plywood roof, and saw shallow kerfs (indentations) across the roof's surface (as shown) to resemble roofing—or paint on shingles. Attach the roof to house, with pine-block scraps for supports.

Paint the house inside and out, using the photograph as a guide.

Dollhouse Dolls

shown on page 63

Materials

⅓ yard of muslin for each doll; fiberfill; scraps of yarn for hair; fabric scraps, plus bits of trim and lace; beads and small snaps; fabric glue; bias tape; permanent black marker.

Instructions

Enlarge the patterns (above, right). Transfer head and arm pieces to a double thickness of muslin; do not cut out.

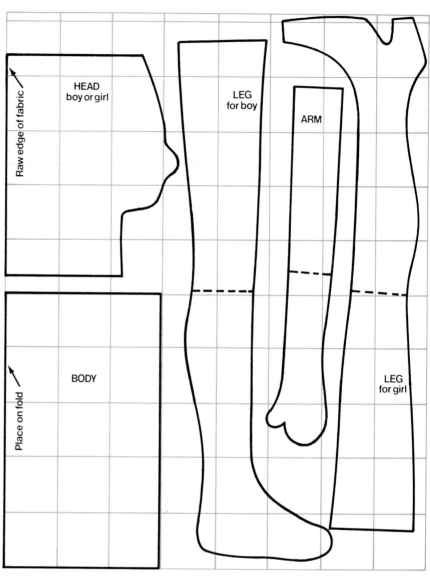

1 Square = 1 Inch

To make the head: Use small stitches to machine- or hand-stitch along the profile and neck front. Trim excess fabric close to stitching; turn and lightly press. Stuff nose and chin, then stuff remainder of head.

Bring the straight edges of the muslin around to the back, forming a tube. Turn under one raw edge ¼ inch and stitch tube closed, leaving the top and bottom open.

Add fiberfill through the top and bottom of the tube until the head is firmly stuffed. Fold excess fabric at the top of the head as you would tuck in the ends of a package; whipstitch closed. (The head will not be perfectly round, but hair will round out the shape.) Leave neck open.

Using the photograph as a guide, pencil in eyes and mouth on each face. Outline eyes with permanent black marker. Color eyeballs using acrylic paints. Embroider mouth with tiny straight stitches. Use powdered rouge or colored pencil for blush on cheeks.

For girl's hair: Wrap a strand of lightweight yarn 70 times around a 12-inch length of cardboard. Remove the yarn from the cardboard and stitch it, centered, to a 1x5-inch strip of muslin; trim away excess muslin under yarn.

Glue the muslin strip to the head, letting stitching form a center or side part. Cut the loops; tie into ponytails.

For boy's hair: Wrap yarn 40 times around a 7-inch length of cardboard. Remove and stitch the yarn to a 1x4-inch strip of muslin; trim muslin and glue to head. Cut loops and trim yarn in random lengths.

To make the body: Stitch and stuff the arms; align seams (for upper arm and underarm); sew the elbow joint. Using colored fabric to simulate stockings, stitch legs; stitch across at knee.

Cut the body from colored or printed fabric to make the shirt or dress bodice. Sew the sides, using ¼-inch seams; leave 1½ inches open on one side for stuffing. Sew the legs to the bottom of body. Gather the top of the body around the neck and blindstitch to neck. Stuff firmly through side opening and blindstitch the opening closed. Tack the arms to the sides of the body.

Make simple clothing from squares, rectangles, and strips of fabric. Refer to the photograph for ideas. Embellish with trims, and gather to fit each doll.

Dollhouse Furniture

shown on page 63

Materials

1-inch-thick foam rubber; fabric scraps in small prints; thread and regular sewing needle; small, curved upholstery needle; quilt batting.

Instructions

Cut foam rubber to the following sizes: 1x4x9 inches for the sofa seat and 1x4x4 inches for the chair seat. Wrap each piece of foam with a thin layer of quilt batting; whipstitch the edges of the batting together.

To make fabric casings, cut two pieces of fabric for each foam block, adding ¾ inch to dimensions of foam *all the way around* (1½ inches total). Sew fronts to backs (¼-inch seams), leaving an opening along one edge. Sew a self-gusset in each corner, following the diagrams (above, right). Pull left side seam and top seam together, forming a triangle in the corner (diagram A). Draw a line 1 inch long from edge to edge and perpendicular to the seam (diagram B); stitch. Trim the fabric ¼ inch beyond the new seam line. Turn and insert the foam piece into the fabric casing; blindstitch the opening closed.

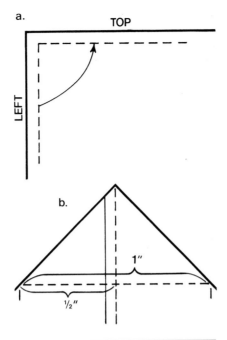

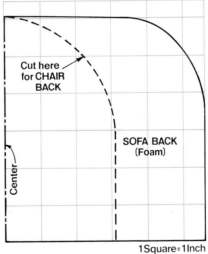

1 Square = 1 Inch

Stitch the fabric-covered pieces together to form chair or sofa.

Enlarge the patterns for the chair and sofa backs (above). Cut pieces from foam, wrap with batting, and cover with fabric casings.

Assemble pieces by blindstitching along the edges. A curved upholstery needle is useful for joining blocks.

For side arms, cut four pieces of foam 1x3x4 inches (two for sofa, two for chair). Wrap with batting and cover with casings. To assemble, blindstitch side arms to bottom of chair or sofa. Then sew back to seat and to side arms.

Stuff loose cushions with fiberfill. Make pillow covers with self-gussets in the corners. Cut two 5½-inch squares for the chair cushion and two 5½x6-inch pieces for the sofa cushion.

Card Table Playhouse

shown on page 64

Materials

5½ yards of 44-inch-wide tan, medium-weight fabric; scraps of solid and print fabric in assorted colors; clear vinyl for windows; iron-on letters, zippers, and trim of your choice.

Instructions

For a 31-inch-square card table, cut a 33x33-inch top for the playhouse from tan fabric, leaving a 1-inch seam allowance. Cut sides of the playhouse to fit the top (33 inches wide) and long enough to fall the height of the table, plus 1 inch each at the top and bottom for seams and hems.

Using the photograph on page 64 and your own imagination as a guide, sketch motifs for the sides of the playhouse. Design western storefronts and other motifs, as shown, or sketch familiar buildings in your neighborhood, or invent fantasyscapes, as desired.

Plan flaps (either zippered or plain) for doors, and clear vinyl windows to let in light on at least two sides.

Cut appliqués for the buildings' motifs from assorted scrap fabrics and stitch into place. Assemble the sides of the playhouse, stitch to the top with 1-inch seams, and hem.

Miniature Fortress

shown on page 65

Materials

4x8-foot piece of ¼-inch-thick plywood; 10 ice-pop sticks (for portcullis); 6-inch-long piece of ¼-inch-diameter dowel (for hinges); ¾-inch wire nails; gray and white paint; 41-inch length of 2x2-inch lumber for figures; bright acrylic paints and artist's brushes; ³⁄₃₂-inch-thick balsa wood for shields.

Instructions

Before cutting plywood, plan a cutting diagram; then cut as follows: For castle towers, cut eight 5x10¾-inch pieces; mark two pieces each A, B, C, and D. Also cut eight 4½x10¾-inch pieces and mark two pieces each A, B, C, and D. For tower floors, cut four 4½-inch-square pieces.

continued

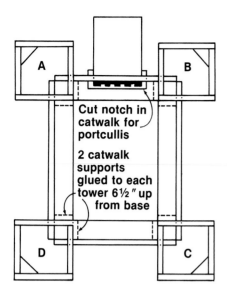

Cut notch in catwalk for portcullis

2 catwalk supports glued to each tower 6½" up from base

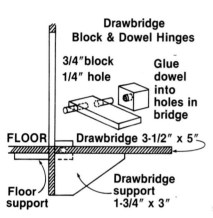

Drawbridge Block & Dowel Hinges

3/4" block
1/4" hole

Glue dowel into holes in bridge

FLOOR

Drawbridge 3-1/2" x 5"

Floor support

Drawbridge support 1-3/4" x 3"

On one piece only, cut away crenelation to connect bridge to castle

FLOOR

←1"→←1"→←1"→

←2-1/4"→←1-1/8"→

2"

Glue floor supports in corner opposite castle wall corner

Catwalk support
Cut from scrap

←2"→
←1-3/4"→

B & D
Cut slots on left side

4-1/2"

A & C
Cut slots on right side

6-1/2"

←4-1/2"→
←5"→

CASTLE TOWERS

←2-1/2"→
←1-3/4"→

4"

←1-1/4"→←1-1/4"→←1"

Cut slots 9/32" wide

DOORWAY
Cut in one end

CENTER

←2-1/4"→

CASTLE FRONT & BACK

Cut 8½x13¾-inch pieces for front and back walls; cut 8½x16¼-inch pieces for sidewalls. For catwalks, cut two 1¾x12¾-inch pieces and two 1¾x10¼-inch pieces.

Cut crenellations in tops of walls and slots for assembly following diagrams (above). (Cut first crenellation and slot on castle sidewalls the same as for the front and back.) Cut out the doorway in the front wall.

From wood scraps, cut catwalk supports and triangular floor supports for towers. To assemble towers, nail together pieces with matching letters (A, B, C, D), as shown (above). Nail floor and catwalk supports (see diagram).

Cut a 4¾x6-inch piece of plywood for the drawbridge. Assemble with block and dowel hinges, as shown (above); omit drawbridge support.

Using ice-pop sticks, assemble the latticelike portcullis by gluing the pieces together. Hang portcullis with small nails behind doorway.

For the bridge, cut four 4½x10¾-inch pieces and four 5x10¾-inch pieces of plywood. On two of the 5-inch pieces, cut away crenellation to connect towers to castle, if desired. Cut 3-inch-wide doorways in the 5-inch pieces, with the base of the doorway 2 inches above the bottom. Cut two floors, each 4½x4½ inches.

Assemble the bridge towers in the same manner as the castle towers. Add small pieces for floor and catwalk supports. Cut a tower catwalk.

Cut drawbridges and supports; assemble tower drawbridges in doorways with block and dowel hinges (see diagram above). Cut two 3½x12-inch ramps and cut ¼-inch notches in corners of one short end on each piece. Position the ramps in the doorways opposite drawbridges.

For figures, cut two 2x2x4-inch pieces for the king and queen. Cut the remaining 2x2-inch wood into 3¼-inch-high pieces for the knights.

Sand and paint the fortress and tower. Paint the king, queen, and knights according to diagrams (opposite).

Rocking Cow

shown on page 66

Materials

4x5-foot piece of ½-inch plywood; 27-inch-piece of 1¼-inch-diameter dowel; acrylic paints, artist's brushes in assorted sizes; nails; glue; sandpaper.

Instructions

Note: The finished rocker is approximately 30 inches long, 24 inches high, and 13 inches wide.

Enlarge the pattern (opposite) and transfer to the sheet of plywood. Cut out the cow-shaped sides from the plywood. From the remaining wood, cut a 16x12½-inch back, a 10x12½-inch seat, an 8x12½-inch leg support, and a 2½x12½-inch footrest. Cut two 12½-inch lengths of dowel for the handlebar (front brace) and the back brace.

Using the photograph on page 66 as a guide, assemble the cow so that back brace is just inside the cow's hindquarters. Nail and glue the seat to the back at a slight angle, so the seat is 9¾ inches below top of back. Attach a leg support to front end of the seat, then attach

70

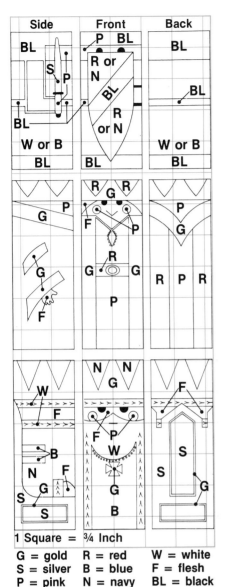

Side	Front	Back

1 Square = ¾ Inch

G = gold   R = red   W = white
S = silver   B = blue   F = flesh
P = pink   N = navy   BL = black

1 Square = 2 Inches

a footrest to the lower end of the leg support. Position the seat between the rocker's sides; nail and glue into place.

Nail and glue 1x¾-inch braces beneath the seat and leg supports. Add the handlebar about 9 inches in from the cow's nose.

Sand the rocker thoroughly, then transfer the enlarged design for the cow's details to the plywood with carbon paper. Paint with latex paints or acrylics, using the photograph as a guide for colors. Protect the finished piece with several coats of clear polyurethane, if desired.

Kiddie Car

shown on page 67

Materials

Two 4x8-foot sheets of ½-inch plywood (good on both sides); 8 feet of 1x12-inch lumber for wheels, lights, bumpers, and cleats; 42-inch length of 2x4 lumber; three pairs of 3-inch T hinges; thirty-six ¼-inch-diameter No. 7 flathead wood screws for hinges; four plate-type furniture casters; 2-inch-diameter wood cabinet pull for hood; three 1¼-inch-diameter wood cabinet pulls for dashboard; three 1¼x20-inch wood dowels; paint; wood putty; nails; white glue.

For convertible top: 1⅝ yards of medium-weight fabric; 22x58 inches of quilt batting; four heavy-duty snaps.

Instructions

Using the diagram on page 72 as a guide for measurements, cut out all pieces; sand lightly until smooth.

Follow the diagram to assemble the car. First construct the framework for the car using 2x4s and 1x2s. Glue and nail the hood, seat, and trunk sections to the frame. Next, glue and nail the sides of the car to the car body. Position the dowels at the top and back; add dashboard details to the interior.

Attach the coasters to the bottom of the chassis. Assemble the plywood disks into wheels and attach them to the car slightly above the floor's surface, using glue and nails so the coasters are able to move.

Add headlight and taillight details and attach the hood and doors with hinges. Make the door handles from small scraps of lumber and dowel.

Paint car, referring to the photograph for colors and details.

For the rollback fabric top (not shown in photograph), cut two 22x58-inch pieces of heavyweight fabric or canvas. With right sides facing and batting on top, sew three sides together with a ½-inch seam. Turn, press, and stitch the remaining side closed. Quilt the top, if desired.

Sew one half of each of the snaps to the underside of the canopy 5½ inches from the front, and the other half to the edge of the canopy. Staple the other end of the fabric top to the lower dowel. Stretch the fabric canopy over top two dowels and snap in place around the front dowel.

continued

Rocking Airplane

shown on page 67

Materials

13 feet of 2x8-inch pine; scraps of 1-inch pine; 33 inches of ⅜-inch-diameter dowel for pegs; 33 inches of ¾-inch-diameter dowel for front and back stabilizers; jigsaw or saber saw; drill and drill bits to match the diameter of the dowels; glue; sandpaper; brown paper; stain and varnish.

Instructions

Enlarge the pattern pieces for the airplane from the diagram (below, right) onto brown paper. Cut out the paper pattern pieces and trace them onto the lumber. Then cut out the parts with a jigsaw or a saber saw.

Drill ⅜-inch holes for the assembly pegs (⅜-inch dowels), which will hold the pieces together; drill ¾-inch holes for the stabilizers (¾-inch dowels), which fit between the rockers, as indicated on the diagram (below, right).

Carefully sand all the pieces until smooth, rounding off any hard edges or sharp corners.

Assemble the pieces of the airplane with wood glue and the ⅜-inch dowels

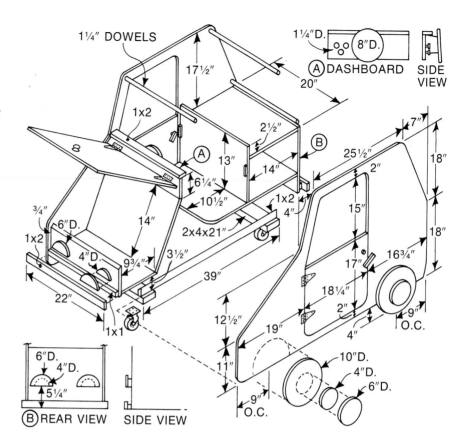

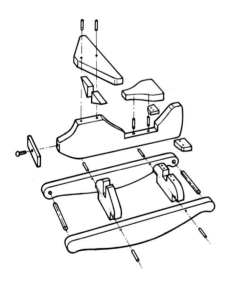

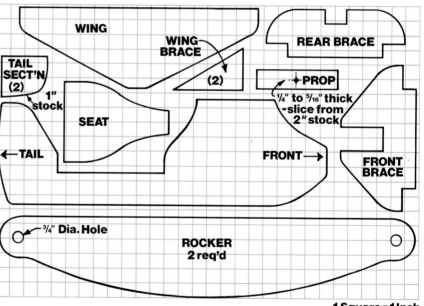

1 Square = 1 Inch

cut to size, using the assembly diagram (above) for reference.

Finish the airplane with a stain or varnish. Then, if desired, apply several coats of clear polyurethane (sanding lightly between coats) for a durable, protective finish.

For a different look, you might consider painting the airplane with a bright, high-gloss enamel. Or paint it a conventional "airplane gray" and decorate it with traditional airplane logos such as a white star within a blue circle for a realistic effect.

How to Enlarge, Reduce, and Transfer Designs

Successful completion of a craft project often begins with accurately enlarging (or reducing) a pattern. And changing the size of a pattern is easy when you use a grid. Here are some tips to help you enlarge or reduce the patterns in this book, plus some suggestions for transferring the designs to fabric and other materials.

Patterns with grids

Many patterns appear on grids—small squares laid over the design. Enlarge these patterns by drawing a grid on tissue or brown paper, using the scale indicated on the pattern. For example, if the scale is "one square equals 1 inch," draw a series of 1-inch squares on your pattern paper to enlarge the drawing to the recommended size.

When enlarging a design, be sure to choose paper that can accommodate all of your finished pattern. Or, tape small pieces of paper together to get a piece large enough for the full-size pattern. Preprinted graph paper also can be used for the pattern. Mark off the paper in squares that correspond to the scale called for in the original design.

To form a working grid, count the number of horizontal and vertical rows of squares on the original pattern. With a ruler, mark the same number of horizontal and vertical rows of larger squares on the pattern paper.

Number the horizontal and vertical rows of squares in the margin of the original pattern. Then transfer these numbers to corresponding rows on your pattern.

Begin by finding a square on your grid that corresponds to a square on the original. Mark your grid with a dot wherever a design line intersects a line on the original. (Visually divide every line into fourths to gauge whether the design line crosses the grid line halfway or somewhere in between.)

Working one square at a time, mark each grid line where it is intersected by the design. Mark several squares, then connect the dots, following the contours of the original as shown in the diagrams (right). Work in pencil so you can easily erase any errors.

Patterns without grids

Even if the pattern for a project has no grid, you can enlarge it if you know any one of the dimensions of the final pattern. Draw a box around the design. Then draw a diagonal line between two of the corners on the grid.

On pattern paper, draw a right angle; extend the bottom line to the length of the new pattern. Lay the original in the corner; using a ruler, extend the diagonal. Then draw a perpendicular line between the diagonal and the end of the bottom line (see diagram, right).

Divide the original and the new pattern into quarters and draw a second diagonal between corners. Number the sections, and transfer the design as explained above.

Designs also may be enlarged by photostating. Just take the pattern to a blueprint company and have it enlarged to the needed size.

Transferring designs

Dressmaker's carbon paper: Use dressmaker's carbon (not typist's carbon paper) as close as possible to the color of the fabric you intend to mark (yet still visible). Place it facedown between fabric and pattern. Trace design lines using a tracing wheel or pencil and just enough pressure to transfer design lines to the fabric.

Hot transfer pencil: Keep the transfer pencil sharp so design lines do not blur. Lightly trace outlines of the design onto back of pattern. Then iron the transfer in place. (Test the transfer pencil on scrap fabric before you begin because color deposited on the fabric does not always fade when the article is washed or dry cleaned.)

Blue lead pencil: Use this on light-colored, lightweight fabrics. Tape the pattern to a window; then tape the fabric over it. Trace the pattern, marking dotted lines instead of solid ones.

Washable marking pen: Draw or trace directly onto light-colored fabric (use a light touch), then work your design. When you are finished, simply dampen the fabric and the blue lines will disappear. Look for this pen in needlework, fabric, and quilt shops.

Basting: Use this method on dark, soft, highly textured, stretchy, or sheer fabrics—whenever other methods suggested above will not work.

Draw the pattern on tissue paper and pin it to fabric. Hand- or machine-baste around design lines. Tear away the tissue paper and proceed with the project. Remove basting stitches when you've finished working.

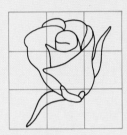

The original design

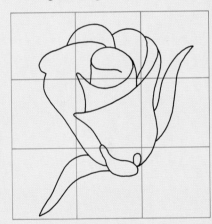

The enlarged design

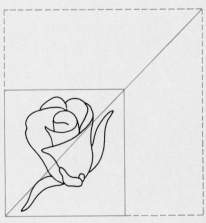

Enlarging without a grid

Special-Interest Gifts & Wraps

Presents with a Personal Twist

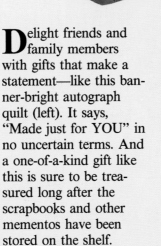

Delight friends and family members with gifts that make a statement—like this banner-bright autograph quilt (left). It says, "Made just for YOU" in no uncertain terms. And a one-of-a-kind gift like this is sure to be treasured long after the scrapbooks and other mementos have been stored on the shelf.

♦ Chenille letters, scripted names, and sports patches add personality to plain purchased canvas totes and duffles (above).

♦ And for a designer look that teens will love, use permanent markers or machine embroidery to transform a favorite jacket or ordinary sweatshirt into a "signed" original (above).

Instructions for projects begin on page 82.

Presents with a Personal Twist

Surprise a fellow craft enthusiast with a gift that caters to *her* (or his) particular passion.

♦ Anyone interested in needle arts would welcome a custom-designed work basket like the one pictured (opposite). To make one like it, outfit a purchased wicker basket with clear plastic and quilted fabric pockets, each made for a favorite tool or small stock of essential supplies.

Bulky materials and projects in progress tuck right inside the basket, and the whole mini-workshop totes from one place to another with a minimum of fuss.

Select the basket with an eye to the kinds of materials to be stored in it, and modify the size and shape of the plastic pockets accordingly.

This handy basket was designed for a dedicated stitcher, with pockets sized for thimble and threads, scissors, packets of needles, pins, tape measure, and embroidery marking pens.

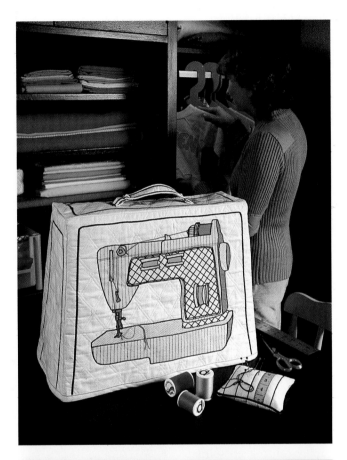

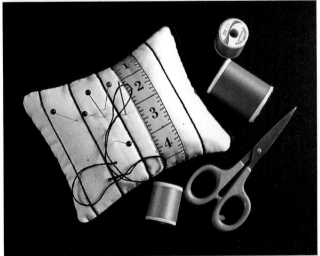

♦ Sewing enthusiasts will love the clever cover-up (left). A mere flick of the wrist, and this handsome dust cover transforms an unsightly machine into a work of art. It's a perfect present for a stitcher who keeps her trusty portable set up and ready to stitch at a moment's notice.

If you're handy with a sketch pad, use the appliquéd cover-up idea to create other gifts. Design covers for a gourmet cook's food processor, for that portable TV in a soap opera lover's kitchen, or for other bulky but indispensable items.

♦ The pincushion (below, left) makes a thoughtful memento for anyone who sews—from reluctant menders to professional seamstresses—and it's simple to make using muslin, embroidery floss, and decorative tape.

Presents with a Personal Twist

For the gardeners you know, choose gifts inspired by nature. Ever-blooming flowers, fruits, and vegetables will perk up even the dullest winter days.

These colorful designs have all the sparkle and freshness of a day in May—and each offers a gentle salute to a gardener's labors and his or her bountiful rewards.

♦ To craft the cheerful set of place mats and matching apron (right), just paint stylized tiger lilies on muslin, outline the designs with black felt markers (for a stained-glass look), and trim with bias tape.

♦ Flower-bedecked containers like this charming collection (below) bring a welcome touch of spring to any setting. Graced with delicately sculpted clay motifs, these pretty pots and pitchers can be used to hold fresh flowers or breakfast juice with equal elegance.

♦ For the person who takes pride in tilling the soil to produce a bumper crop of vegetables, needlepoint this wall hanging of familiar produce (opposite) to keep spirits bright until spring planting time rolls around.

If you haven't the time to work the whole project, you might consider picking a pair of favorite vegetables to give. Stitch individual patterns into comfortable pillows. Gardeners will love them as rainy-day and cold-weather reminders of a favorite pastime.

Presents with a Personal Twist

For anyone who enjoys a spirited game of tennis or racquetball, or a leisurely summer picnic, these warm-weather gifts are perfect companions. And they're a breeze to make, using simple machine stitchery techniques.

♦ The "strings" of the tennis and racquetball racquet covers (above) are styled by couching embroidery floss to the fabric with zigzag stitches. To quilt the covers, pad the outer fabric with layers of polyester fleece before couching.

♦ For the family with everything, the checkered picnic cloth (right) is a useful gift solution.

The kids will be delighted by the colorful machine appliqués of their favorite picnic foods, including a platter of corn on the cob and a tantalizing chocolate cake! And Mom will love the drawstring cord that easily turns the cloth into a tote bag for transporting picnic plates and food.

Refer to the appliqués in the photograph for inspiration, then decorate your cloth with a different feast of favorites. If you like, use leftover fabric for matching napkins and accessories.

Autograph Quilt

shown on pages 74-75

Materials

1 yard each of hot gold, light orange, navy, dark red, hot pink, and light blue 45-inch-wide polished cotton; matching threads; 5⅓ yards of 44-inch-wide polyester fleece; 5 yards of 45-inch-wide fabric for lining; permanent markers; zigzag sewing machine.

Instructions

This quilt is about 84 inches square—suitable for a double bed. For a twin- or bunk-size mattress, alter the size of the squares, or reduce the number of autograph squares.

Cut each yard of polished cotton into six 12x22-inch blocks. Cut fleece into 36 matching blocks.

Ask friends to autograph the cotton blocks using permanent markers. Then pin and baste one fleece block to the back of each autographed block. Set zigzag machine at widest satin stitch and embroider over the signatures with contrasting thread.

For fabric appliqués on the blocks (such as the heart), cut shapes from contrasting fabrics. Pin in place and satin-stitch around raw edges.

To assemble the quilt, arrange 32 blocks in four rows of eight blocks each (four across, eight down). Place light-colored blocks next to dark-colored blocks in random, checkerboard style. With right sides facing, use ½-inch seams to join each vertical row of eight blocks. Then join the resulting strips together lengthwise. Press seams open.

To line quilt, stitch two 2½-yard lengths of lining fabric together lengthwise to make a 90-inch square. With wrong sides facing, center the lining on the quilt top (lining should extend beyond edges of quilt top on all sides). Pin and baste all three layers together. Machine-quilt along seam lines between all blocks, if desired. Or, hand-tuft the quilt at the corners of each block. Fold edges of lining over edges of quilt top to make a 1-inch-wide border; trim excess lining. Topstitch in place.

Stitch any remaining autographed blocks into pillows; back with contrasting fabric and stuff with fiberfill.

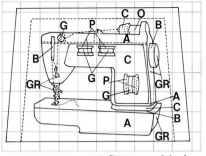

1 Square = 2 Inches

Color Key:
A — Striped Print
B — Dotted Print
C — Square Pattern
O — Orange
P — Peach
GR — Gray
G — Gold

Sewing Machine Cover-Up

shown on page 76

Materials

¾ yard of 45-inch-wide ecru quilted fabric; scraps of black and white fabric prints; ½ yard of fusible webbing; peach, gold, and orange fabric scraps; 4 yards of black soutache braid; 1¾ yards of off-white wide bias tape; black and orange embroidery floss; black thread; two 1-inch "D" rings.

Instructions

Note: Cover-up fits a basic portable sewing machine. Adjust size and shape as necessary. Enlarge pattern (above); ½-inch seam allowance is included.

From quilted fabric, cut basic cover-up pieces. Use outer line of pattern for front and back; cut two. Cut two end pieces (14 inches high, 7 inches wide at top, sloping to 11 inches wide at bottom), and a 6x17½-inch strip for top. For handle, cut one 2x7-inch strip and two 2x2½-inch strips.

For appliqué designs, cut shapes from fabric scraps and fusible webbing. Fuse appliqués to front. Satin-stitch around raw edges with black thread.

Machine-couch six-strand black embroidery floss along dotted lines on pattern (for couching directions, see instructions for pincushion, below). Machine-couch black soutache braid 1 inch from all raw edges of cover-up front, back, ends, and top.

With right sides facing, assemble cover-up, using ½-inch seam allowances. Clip corners and turn. Bind raw edges along bottom with bias tape.

For handle, trim long edges of strips with soutache braid, couching it in

place ½ inch from edges. Fold under raw edges and hem with zigzag stitches. Slip "D" rings onto ends of the long strip, loop ends, and stitch across raw edges to lock rings in place on handle ends. Loop short strips through opposite sides of each "D" ring, matching raw edges. Zigzag over raw edges of short strips to fasten them to the cover-up at center of top.

Pincushion

shown on page 77

Materials

Two 5x6-inch pieces of quilted ecru fabric; 6 inches of decorative trim or scrap of tape measure; black embroidery floss; black piping; black thread; box of birdcage grit.

Instructions

To make the top of the pincushion, machine-couch black floss along ecru fabric's quilted lines (see photograph). To machine-couch, set the zigzag stitch width slightly broader than the embroidery floss to be fastened down; set stitch length at medium. Hold floss against the fabric surface and fasten in place with machine zigzag stitches.

Topstitch decorative trim or tape 2 inches from one end of the top; stitch black piping ¼ inch from raw edges.

With right sides facing, sew pincushion back to front along previous stitching line. Leave an opening. Turn, press, fill with grit, and sew opening closed.

Workbasket

shown on page 76

Materials

Woven wicker basket, approximately 15 inches in diameter; ¼ yard of clear plastic; fabric scraps; 6½ yards of extra-wide, double-fold white bias tape.

Instructions

Cut rounded pockets to fit sewing tools. For each pocket, cut one shape from plastic and second (2 to 3 inches longer) from fabric. Bind top of each plastic pocket with bias tape. Bind plastic and fabric pockets together, using bias tape; topstitch. Leave top of fabric piece unbound.

Make enough pockets to house tools and other materials; trim fabric tops of pockets evenly. Line up pockets side by side, aligning top edges. Encase top raw edges in a bias tape tie-on strip about 2 yards long; fold tape in half and machine-stitch in place. Tie pockets to basket with bias tape strip.

Vegetable Garden Wall Hanging

shown on page 79

Materials

1¼ yards of 36-inch-wide No. 10-count interlock needlepoint canvas; 3-ply Persian wool yarn in colors and amounts noted on color· key (page 84); No. 18 tapestry needle; 4½ yards of 2-inch-wide rug binding; 1¼ yards of white felt; masking tape; black waterproof marking pen; 10-squares-per-inch graph paper; wide seam binding.

Instructions

Note: Finished hanging is about 34x35 inches. Use full 3-ply strands of yarn throughout. Work background in basket-weave stitches; work designs in continental stitches. All borders are *single* rows unless otherwise noted.

Begin by enlarging patterns (page 84) onto graph paper. (One square equals one stitch. Each square is 76x76 mesh, excluding borders.)

Bind canvas edges with masking tape. Mark center of canvas by locating center horizontal and vertical canvas threads. Stitch a one-row, 326-mesh-square border in forest green yarn around center point. All 16 squares fall within this border.

Divide square into fourths by stitching a double row of green borders horizontally and vertically, making four equal-size squares within the larger square.

Next, work the beet pattern in the upper left-hand corner. Begin with a one-row, 78-mesh, white square border so that it is adjacent to two sides of the green border. Then work a one-row, green border inside the white border. Complete the beet design, following the charted pattern.

Next, stitch the zucchini square the same way, so pattern is outlined by a green border, a white border, and another green border. (The double row of green stitches will provide border for right-hand side of zucchini square.)

When first row of motifs is finished, begin second row along left-hand side. Repeat until all squares are complete.

When motifs are finished, work outer border: Begin with a four-row white border around the original 326-mesh square, leaving corners unstitched. In each corner work a 6x6-mesh red square. Finally, add one row of green, two rows of white, one row of green, and two rows of white; end with six rows of green.

Block canvas and let it dry thoroughly. Mount finished canvas on stretchers, in a frame, or over plywood, or simply bind raw edges and back with felt or other sturdy backing fabric. Hang as appropriate to backing.

Flowered Containers

shown on page 78

Materials

Crockery container; ovendrying clay (such as Sculpey); small, sharp knife; acrylic or oil paints; toothpicks; paintbrush; graph paper.

Instructions

Make flowers by shaping, baking, and painting clay petals, leaves, and stems. The pattern (above, right) is for the wild roses shown on the middle lower crock in the photograph. For other flowers, follow the same general instructions.

To form the flowers: Knead clay until it is soft and pliable. With a rolling pin, roll it out to the thickness of a piecrust. Trace the shape of the petals and leaves onto the clay. Cut out shapes using a small, sharp knife.

Work edges of petals between your fingers to make them thin and supple. Cup petals slightly and press them firmly in place on the ceramic container. For texture, poke the center of the flowers with a toothpick.

For stems and branches, roll the clay between your fingers to make spaghetti-like strands. Arrange them as desired on the crock, using a toothpick to press them to the flowers where desired.

Pinch and ripple edges of leaves. Press leaves onto the container, then lightly "draw" veins on each leaf with the tip of your knife.

Bake the container in a preheated oven according to the manufacturer's instructions. The clay may be soft when

1 Square = 1 Inch

you take it out of the oven, but it will harden as it cools. If a baked piece of clay breaks off, just glue it back in place. Clay may be rebaked if you wish to add more shapes to your design.

Paint flowers with oils or acrylics. Paint dark colors first; add highlights later. If desired, thin the paint so it will flow into cracks and crevices.

To make the rose: Enlarge the pattern (above). Cut out pieces, arrange on the container, and bake. Paint the flowers light yellow with black shading and white highlights; paint centers, leaves, and stems light yellow mixed with black; for small blossoms use blue mixed with white.

Day Lily Apron and Place Mats

shown on page 79

Materials

For apron and four mats: 1 yard of 54-inch-wide natural-color duck canvas; 3 packages of wide black bias tape; black, yellow-green, golden yellow, vermilion, and orange-yellow acrylic paints; fine-point brushes; black permanent marking pen; thread; dressmaker's carbon paper.

Instructions

Enlarge designs (page 85) and transfer to canvas, using dressmaker's carbon. Paint the motifs, using acrylic *continued*

83

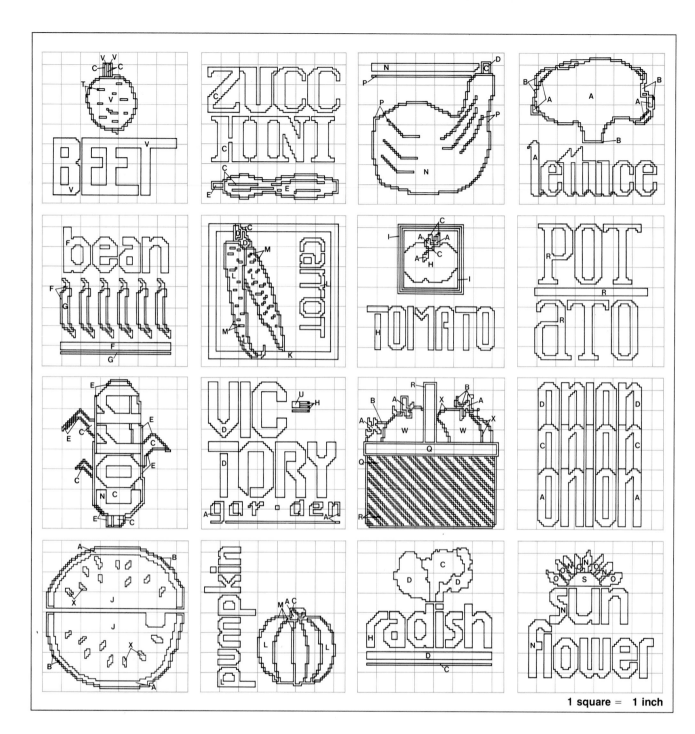

1 square = 1 inch

		Yards
A	Lime Green	45
B	Green	38
C	Kelly Green	32
D	Forest Green	255
E	Dark Green	7
F	Olive Green	8
G	Light Olive Green	7
H	Red	28

		Yards
I	Red-Brown	7
J	Dark Red	15
K	Light Orange	22
L	Orange	24
M	Dark Orange	5
N	Gold	52
O	Yellow-Gold	3
P	Dark Gold	3
Q	Tan	14

		Yards
R	Brown	24
S	Dark Brown	3
T	Navy Blue	3
U	Royal Blue	2
V	Maroon	20
W	Dark Purple	9
X	Black	4
Y	White or Off-White	670

1 square = 3 inches

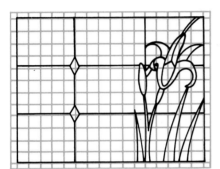

1 square = 1 inch

paints thinned with water to the consistency of light cream. When paint is dry, outline shapes with black marker. Heat-set colors and marker lines by ironing on the wrong side.

Bind edges of apron and mats with bias tape. Sew 17-inch ties and a 20-inch neck loop of bias tape to apron.

Racquet Covers

shown on page 80

Materials

For one cover: ⅔ yard of fabric; scrap of fabric for ball; black double-fold bias tape; black embroidery floss; polyester fleece; 12-inch zipper; black thread; thread to match fabric for ball.

Instructions

To make a pattern, trace around the racquet onto paper; add ½-inch seam allowance all around. Draw an arc to mark the "rib" at the top of the handle (base of strings), then draw a grid of lines ⅜ inch apart to simulate the racquet strings. Transfer pattern to cloth. Pin fleece to the wrong side of fabric.

Machine-couch three strands of floss along the string lines, clipping floss along the line for the rib. Then cover ends of floss along the rib with a strip of bias tape. Appliqué a circle of fabric for the ball.

To make a lining, pin a piece of fabric beneath the fleece layer. Stitch ⅛ inch from the racquet outline through all layers, leaving the bottom open. Clip curves, then zigzag-stitch the seam allowances through all layers.

Finish the base of the top (below the rib) by trimming the fleece and turning under raw edges ½ inch; topstitch.

Assemble the back of the racquet cover by tracing the shape, pinning it to the fleece and lining fabric, and stitching close to the outline.

To make a boxing strip for joining front to back, cut fabric 1½ inches wide and long enough to fit along one side and across the top of the racquet cover. Leave 12 inches free on the opposite side for the zipper. Turn under ¼ inch on long raw edges and stitch.

Sew bottom of zipper (closed end) to one short end of strip, right sides facing. With *wrong sides facing,* pin zipper and strip to cover front and back, aligning the open end of zipper with base of cover. Stitch, using ½-inch seam. Stitch bias tape over exposed seams.

Picnic Cloth

shown on page 81

Materials

3 yards of 45-inch-wide blue plaid fabric for cloth; 3 yards of red plaid fabric for lining and napkins; 1 yard of fusible webbing; ¼ yard *each* of yellow and green fabric; ⅛ yard *each* of orange, rust, gold, yellow check, and "watermelon print" fabric; scraps of pink, brown, light blue, black, navy, yellow polka dot, and unbleached muslin fabrics; 6 yards of white double-fold bias tape; 5 yards of sturdy cord; white floss; thread to match fabrics; 32 extra-large grommets.

Instructions

The finished cloth is approximately 54 inches square.

Note: Use fusible webbing to anchor smaller pieces of the design before machine-appliquéing them in place. Cut shapes from fusible webbing at the same time you cut shapes from fabrics.

To keep iron from picking up stray wisps of webbing, lay a paper towel atop pieces to be fused before pressing.

To construct cloth: Cut and piece a 54-inch square of blue plaid fabric. Mark four "place settings" on the right side of the cloth. From matching fabric, cut four 12-inch circles for the plates and one 13-inch circle for a center platter.

Bind edges of circles with white bias tape, then machine-couch a length of white embroidery floss 1 inch in from the edge of each plate or platter to define the shape. Stitch plates and platter to tablecloth, using the photograph as a guide. (Use remaining blue plaid fabric to make napkin rings and a silverware bag, if desired.)

For appliquéd feast: Refer to the photograph for design ideas. Then, from fabric scraps, cut out food, flower, and accessory appliqués *without* seam allowances but *with* matching pieces of fusible webbing. Position appliqués on the background; iron in place. Machine-satin-stitch around all raw edges with matching or contrasting thread.

Before appliquéing some design elements to the cloth, add topstitching details (see mushrooms on shish-kabobs, grill marks on ham steaks, and shaping of chocolate cake).

For shish-kabobs, first couch a 12-inch length of six-strand embroidery floss with machine stitches to simulate a skewer stretched at an angle across each plate. Then fuse and machine-appliqué skewer handle and fruit and vegetable pieces in place.

To complete: First center and baste a 48-inch-diameter circle on the face of the cloth to indicate line for placement of grommets.

Next, cut and piece a 54-inch square of red plaid fabric for the lining. (Cut and hem remaining red plaid fabric to make a set of 17-inch-square napkins.)

With right sides together, pin and stitch lining to cloth top (¾-inch seams). Leave a 12-inch opening for turning. Trim corners, turn, and press. Topstitch ½ inch in from edges.

Following manufacturer's instructions, attach grommets at 5-inch intervals along basted circle. Remove basting stitches. Thread cord through eyelets and knot ends together to complete drawstring tote.

85

Plain and Fancy Package Wraps

Even a modest gift becomes something truly special when it's imaginatively presented.

♦ The colorful paper posies (right) add a welcome touch of spring to any package, whatever the time of year. Combine twigs with simple paper sculptures, made with scraps of colored paper, to transform any plain package into a garden of flowery delights.

♦ Here are more creative ways to turn plain, glazed papers into imaginative and elegant gift wraps (opposite).

Stitch real lace and narrow satin ribbons right onto the paper. Print (or stencil) designs on colorful tissue, using paper doilies, shells, pressed ferns, and other feathery leaves. Add a splash of paint and a sprinkling of glitter, or even a host of pretty stick-on butterflies.

Then wrap your gift so the lid can be removed without destroying your creation. That way, the pretty box can be reused—an added bonus, and a gift in itself.

Instructions for these wraps begin on page 92.

86

Plain and Fancy Package Wraps

Delight your favorite young animal lover with a gift done up in one of these whimsical animal wraps.

Choose from five friendly animals in the mini-menagerie at right—a lion, a tiger, an elephant, a monkey, and a rascally rabbit.

The patterns can be enlarged or reduced to any dimension to suit the size of the gift box, and all of the animal heads can be cut on the fold or mounted on folded stock to serve as gift cards as well as package decorations.

Once you've experimented with these designs, use the same principle to devise animal wraps of your own. Just copy the pattern for an animal's head from a coloring book or cartoon illustration, enlarge it, and execute in construction paper.

For a very special birthday party, use our animal wraps as the basis for your party decorating scheme.

For example, decorate several gifts—or a batch of empty boxes—with variations of these packages and stack them together for a centerpiece.

Extend the animal theme with a pin-the-tail-on-the-elephant (or lion or tiger) game you make yourself. Use one of the animal heads glued to a simple body shape drawn on paper as the target animal.

Make small animal-head cards for invitations or place cards, and hand out little boxes of animal crackers as party favors.

Plain and Fancy Package Wraps

A trio of old-fashioned furniture finishing tricks turn dime store kraft and shelving papers into the country-fresh package wraps shown here.

With the simple techniques of combing, stamping, and sponge painting, you can create prettily patterned papers quickly—and at a fraction of the price of purchased gift wraps.

♦ A cardboard comb drawn across water-thinned paints yields the subtle combed patterns (left). Whether you opt for rhythmic waves of color or random sweeps and swirls, this no-fail technique yields spectacular results every time.
♦ To print your own papers, select an interesting novelty stamp for the repeat images and spell out words or phrases with letters from a child's printing set. Or, have special stamps made to order for a modest fee at the local printer's or at an office supply shop.

Print on plain paper, or create unique designs on scraps of subtly patterned purchased wraps.
♦ Sponge painting is another nearly foolproof technique that turns plain paper into yards of handsome gift wrap in next to no time. Taking our cue from an antique spongeware bowl, we dabbed brown and white papers with blue and brown acrylics, sometimes alternating or overprinting the two colors.

Once you've mastered these simple techniques, use them on small wooden boxes to make reusable gift containers, such as the comb-painted gift boxes on page 160.

Flower Wraps

shown on page 86

Materials

Wrapping paper in solid colors; construction paper in various colors; bits of colored tissue paper; white glue; compass; variety of boxes; green felt-tip pen; graph paper.

Instructions

General directions: Cover the lids and the bottoms of the boxes with colored wrapping paper. Center the box top or bottom on the paper and trim so there is sufficient paper to cover each of the sides as well as wrap over the edge and into the box. Carefully fold the paper up over the box sides and secure with transparent tape.

For a more finished gift box, you may wish to line the inside with a contrasting paper. Measure the inside of the box and cut the lining paper to the proper dimensions. Glue in place with a thin coat of white glue.

Enlarge the patterns (right) onto graph paper. Vary the size of the flowers and leaves by adjusting the grid scale when you enlarge the patterns.

Score all dotted lines with the pointed tip of a compass, making sure you do not tear through the paper.

Make the leaves and flowers as instructed below, then arrange them on the box and glue them in place. For accents, add small twigs tucked under the flowers.

If you wish to incorporate a ribbon into the flower design, wrap the ribbon around the package and tie it into a bow before adding the flowers.

Tulips (shown on the white box in the photograph): Each tulip has three petals, a sepal, and several leaves. Cut the petals from pink or purple paper, the sepals from light green, and several leaves from light and dark green, adjusting the sizes for variety.

On one petal for each tulip, score along the dotted lines on each edge. This will be the center petal. On the right petal, score along the right side only, and on the left petal, along the left side only. Pinch the petals along the score lines to cup them slightly.

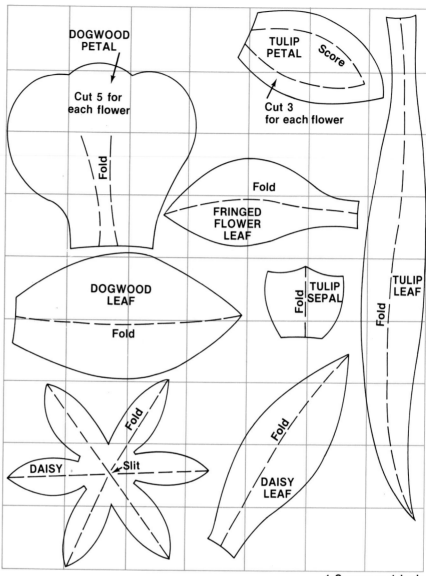

1 Square = 1 Inch

For the sepals, score each along the dotted line and fold slightly. Score the leaves along the line indicated.

Cut a narrow, straight or curved piece of green paper for each stem. Then arrange all the pieces on the box, first laying down the stems, then the side petals, the center petal, the sepals, and the leaves. When arranged as desired, glue in place.

To make the stamens shown peeking out above the petals, cut long triangles of yellow paper, then fringe one edge of each and tuck them inside the petals. Glue in place.

Fringed flowers (shown on the purple box): To make the petals for each flower, cut a 3-inch-diameter circle from yellow and a 2-inch-diameter circle from white. On each, make a slit from the edge to the center of the circle. Overlap the cut edges, causing the circle to cup. Glue edges together.

Fringe the edges of each cupped circle, then glue the white circle inside the yellow one.

Cut several leaves from light and dark green papers and score them along the lines indicated. Fold slightly along the score lines.

Arrange the leaves and flowers on the package, placing the flowers atop the leaves. Glue in place.

Add centers to the flowers by rolling up bits of red tissue paper into tiny balls; glue one to each flower.

Dogwood flowers (shown on the pink box): For each flower, cut five petals from white paper. Score along the lines indicated, then pleat each petal by folding the left scored line over to the right one. Glue in place.

Cut three leaves from light green paper and score along the line indicated. With a green marking pen, draw vein lines on each leaf.

Arrange the leaves on the box, then add the petals, overlapping the edges. Glue in place.

Cut narrow strips of pink paper for stamens and roll up bits of yellow tissue paper into several balls to glue into the center of the flower.

Daisies (shown on the yellow box): For each flower, cut one daisy shape from blue or lavender paper. Score and fold the petals along the dotted lines, and make a slit where indicated.

To make the stamens, cut a 2-inch-diameter circle from paper in a contrasting color; cut the circle in half. Fringe the curved edge, then roll the half-circle into a tube and insert the center point down through the slit in the daisy. Glue in place. Cut a tiny circle of paper and glue it in the center of the fringed stamens.

Cut several leaves from light and dark green papers and score along the lines indicated. Arrange the leaves on the box, then add the flowers; glue in place. If desired, curl thin strips of paper into tendrils and glue them at random among the flowers.

Elegant Wraps

shown on page 87

Materials

Glazed paper in assorted colors; paper doilies; pastel-color tissue paper; assorted acrylic spray paints; artist's acrylic paints; assorted laces and ribbons; white glue; glue stick; silver felt-tip pen; paintbrush; sponge; silver glitter; purchased butterfly stickers.

Instructions

General directions: The package wraps are all made with glazed papers. Always work on the glazed side, making the design large enough to wrap the package you have in mind.

Snowflake paper: Lay paper flat, glazed side up, on a stack of newspapers or piece of cardboard. Position paper doilies at random on the paper, then secure them by sticking pins through the paper and into the newspapers or cardboard.

Spray several light coats of spray paint onto the paper. (We sprayed pink paper with white paint and white paper with lavender and pink paint.)

Allow the paint to dry, then remove the doilies, revealing the original color of the paper below.

Pastel-flower paper: Cut a petal pattern from a piece of cardboard. Then, on tissue paper, trace around the pattern and cut out five petals for each flower. Cut out the petals along the traced lines or gently tear them along the lines for a ragged edge.

Mix a small amount of water with white glue to make a thin, creamlike consistency. Lightly paint the glue mixture onto one side of a tissue paper petal. Then lay the petal, glue side down, on the glazed paper. Pull up the petal from the paper; it will leave a colored print. Don't worry if the color does not print evenly; the inconsistencies add texture to the paper's surface.

To complete a flower, repeat this process with the other four petals, overlapping each of the petals slightly as you go. Cut or tear out a tissue paper circle to use for printing the center of the flower. Then repeat the entire process to make other flowers across the surface of the wrapping paper.

When the flower designs are dry, outline them with a silver felt-tip pen or use a small brush and silver paint to make free-form outlines.

Shell paper: Cut a sponge into a simple clamshell shape. Pour white paint in a pie tin and dip the sponge into the paint. Dab the sponge on a piece of scrap paper to remove excess paint. Then press the sponge onto the paper in a random design. Let dry.

Rinse the sponge and repeat the process with silver paint. Let dry.

Rinse the sponge again and dip it into a mixture of white glue and water. Print at random again, but before the glue dries, sprinkle with silver glitter.

Fern and butterfly paper: Spread green artist's acrylic paint in a pie tin or onto a piece of glass. Then press a frond of fern (asparagus, maidenhair, and Boston ferns all work well) into the paint. Lay the fern, paint side down, on white paper and press the edges of the fern to make an even print.

Re-ink the fern and press it on the paper again. Repeat until the paper is entirely printed. Apply butterfly stickers to the paper at random.

Ribbon and lace paper: With a glue stick, spot-glue strips of lace and ribbon in a striped pattern across glazed paper. Using thread in contrasting colors, zig-zag-stitch the laces and ribbons to the paper surface.

Animal Wraps

shown on page 89

Materials

Pink, gray, orange, yellow, and white wrapping paper; white, yellow, orange, and brown lightweight poster board; black, pink, red, orange, and beige construction paper; rubber cement; white pompon; grosgrain ribbon; graph paper; black marker.

Instructions

Decorate the packages by wrapping them in colored papers, then gluing on paper and poster board trims. In several instances, the animal design doubles as a gift tag.

To make the animals, first enlarge the patterns on page 94 onto graph paper, transferring all the design lines. These will be your master patterns for cutting and positioning the pieces. You can adapt the designs for smaller or larger packages or for invitations or place cards by altering the scale when enlarging the patterns.

For the elephant: Wrap a large package with gray paper. Trace the outline of the elephant's head onto white poster board; cut out. Referring to the photograph, cut the head and trunk from pink paper, the collar from red paper, and the stars from gold. Cut the tusks and eyes from white, the eyelids from red, and an ear from light pink.

Glue the pieces to the poster board head. Then outline the features and the collar with black marker.

continued

93

← TIGER

←LION

← RABBIT

ELEPHANT

MONKEY

1 Square = 2 Inches

To turn the elephant's head into a gift tag, cut a white poster board rectangle that is smaller than the head. Tape the top of the rectangle to the back of the head, then tape them both to the package.

Cut a tail from white poster board and pink paper. Glue to the package and add a red bow.

For the tiger: Wrap the package in yellow paper. Fold in half a piece of yellow poster board that is twice the size of the tiger's head. Placing the tips of the tiger's ears on the fold, cut out the face through the two thicknesses. This will form a folding card.

Cut the cheeks, nose, and eyelids from orange paper, the tip of the nose and tongue from red, the eyes from white, and the stripes from black. Glue them in place.

With black marker, outline the face and all the features; add freckles, whiskers, eyelashes, and pupils. Cut black strips to wrap around the package; glue the head to the package front.

For the lion: Wrap the package in orange paper. Cut the head from yellow poster board, placing the top of the mane on the fold to create a gift tag.

Cut a mane, nose, and eyelids from orange paper, a tongue and tip of the nose from red, and eyes from white. Glue in place.

With the black marker, outline the features; add pupils, mouth, freckles, and whiskers. Glue the back of the gift tag to the package.

To make the lion's tail, cut a leaf shape from orange paper. Add black lines, then attach the tail to the end of a ribbon wrapped over the package.

For the rabbit: Wrap a small package in pink paper. Cut the head from white poster board. From pink paper, cut out the cheeks, nose, and eyelids, and glue them in place on the poster board cutout.

With black marker, outline the features; add the mouth, teeth, freckles, whiskers, and pupils.

Cut a white poster board rectangle that is smaller than the rabbit's head. Tape the top of the rectangle to the back of the head to create a gift tag, then glue the back of the tag to the top of the package.

Glue a white yarn pompon to the package for a rabbit tail.

For the monkey: Wrap a package in white paper. Cut the basic body shape from brown poster board, and cut the face and underside of the monkey from beige paper. Glue the paper to the poster board cutout.

With a black marking pen, outline the features and body; add eyes, nose, and mouth.

Glue the monkey to the package and attach a ribbon bow atop its head.

Comb-Painted Wraps

shown on page 90

Materials

Shelf paper or plain-color glazed gift wrap; Liquitex acrylic gloss medium; acrylic paint in desired colors; large brush; scraps of cardboard or mat board; scissors.

Instructions

To begin, cut sturdy cardboard or mat board scraps into 3x4-inch pieces.

With sharp scissors, cut small triangular notches into one edge to create a cardboard rake or comb.

Tape a piece of the shelf paper or the glazed wrapping paper onto a flat work surface.

Pour into a container a sufficient amount of gloss medium to cover the paper. Add a dab of acrylic paint in the desired color and mix thoroughly.

With a large brush, quickly cover the entire surface of the paper with the acrylic-and-gloss-medium solution. Before the paint dries, pull the notched cardboard comb across the surface of the paper to scrape away the paint.

Experiment by combing with different patterns or designs. Stripes, wavy lines, or scallops are effective patterns. Or, use your imagination to create other patterns that you think will make an unusual gift wrap.

Allow the paper to dry thoroughly, then remove it from the workboard.

Wrap the gift box as desired, then embellish it with ribbons, twine, or other country accents.

Stamped Gift Wrap

shown on page 90

Materials

Assorted solid-color papers, including shelf and brown wrapping papers; decorative stamps (either use purchased rubber stamps or carve your own from gum erasers, potatoes, or linoleum blocks); inked stamp pads, acrylic paints, or marking pens in assorted colors.

Instructions

Print wrapping papers in random patterns or create small scenes or geometric designs. Refer to the photograph on page 90 for design ideas.

To print with acrylic paints, first thin paint with water to the consistency of light cream. Use a small paintbrush to ink the stamp with a thin, even coat of paint.

Experiment with first, second, and third impressions to determine the right amount of paint or ink to use and to observe different effects.

Whether you use paints, stamp pads, or colored pens to ink the stamps, be sure to clean each stamp gently but thoroughly with soap and water, and then allow the stamp to dry before switching colors. To keep the rubber stamps from becoming clogged or drying out, clean them thoroughly at the end of a stamping session.

Sponged Wraps

shown on page 91

Materials

Shelf paper or brown paper; assorted natural and household sponges; acrylic paint.

Instructions

Dilute paint with water to a thin consistency. Dip a sponge in paint and dab onto scrap paper to remove excess paint. Then, referring to the photograph for design ideas, dab the sponge onto the paper. Let dry. Rinse the sponge and repeat with another color of paint, if desired.

Experiment with different color combinations and a variety of sponges to create a new look for each paper.

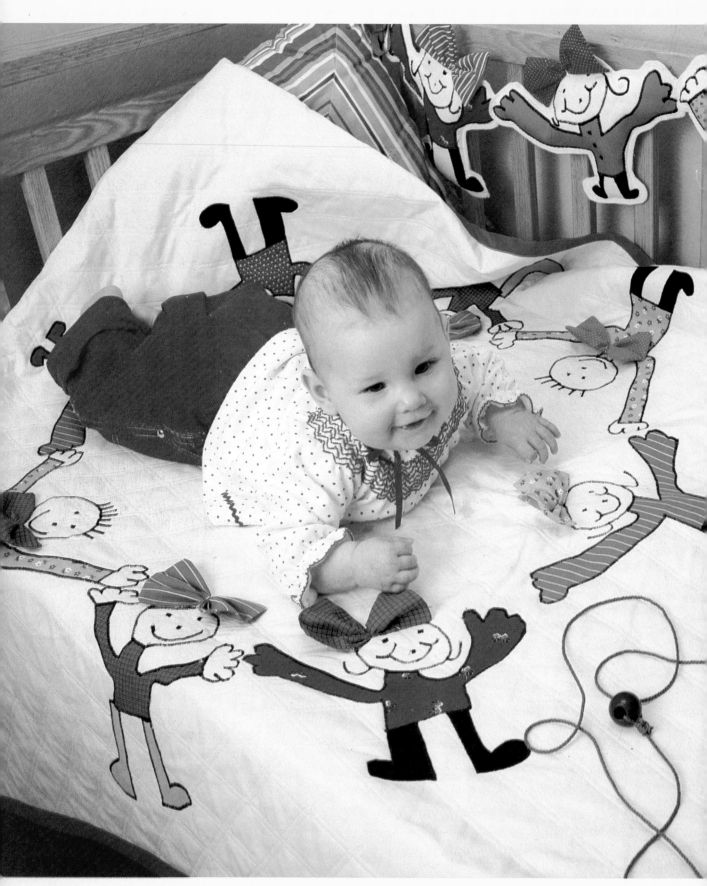

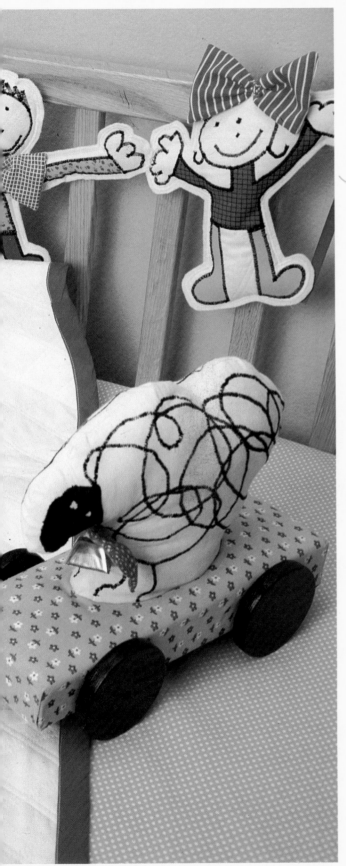

Quilts, Toys, and Infants' Accessories

You'll find this chapter full of exciting ideas for the newborns and toddlers on your gift list, and some for their parents as well.

♦ For example, why not let older children share in the fun of designing special presents for a new brother or sister? To make a crib-size circle-of-friends quilt like the one shown here, just trace children's drawings onto prequilted muslin. The crisp calico bows and the brightly colored machine-appliquéd clothing are sure to capture the baby's attention.

♦ Make a matching crib toy for the baby to play with using a second set of appliquéd figures.

Strung across the crib, these cheery dancing figures will entertain the smallest tot for hours.

♦ The softly sculptured pull toy in the foreground also is a fabric translation of a child's drawing.

Machine stitchery turns a whimsical sheep, complete with bow and bell, into this fanciful plaything. The same technique works equally well for toys based on drawings of the family dog or cat, or even imaginary animals.

How-to instructions for the quilt and baby toys begin on page 102.

Quilts, Toys, and Infants' Accessories

When thinking of gifts for babies, don't overlook presents for parents, too. For example, a brand-new mother (or mother-to-be) would be thrilled to receive this sweet needlepoint bunny bag (left). With this hand-stitched tote she can carry baby's paraphernalia in style.

♦ This colorful carryall measures a roomy 12x3x18 inches—just the right size for packing up a bottle, a toy, and an extra diaper or two when mother takes baby on an outing.

Make the bag from bright red corduroy, as shown, or use any sturdy fabric of your choice. Line the tote with a cheerful cotton calico, or if you prefer a wipe-clean lining, choose lightweight oilcloth or a plastic-coated fabric.

Needlepoint the bunny pocket and tulip-trimmed strap on No. 10 mono canvas, using continental stitches for the bunnies and blossoms. Fill the background with quick-to-stitch bargello in a pattern of your choice.

A practical plus: The stylish tote fits comfortably over the shoulder and under the arm, leaving Mom's hands free to care for baby.

♦ Even a first-time cross-stitcher can make this birth announcement (above) in short order. If you're eager to begin, stitch the carrousel and outline the canopy, base, and horses while awaiting baby's arrival. Then, embroider the pertinent details after baby is born. That way you'll have your gift finished by the time baby's home from the hospital.

We've included an "It's a girl" canopy and an alphabet so you can stitch any name, and much of the design can be worked with leftover embroidery threads.

Cross-stitch the announcement on 18-count Aida cloth with No. 5 pearl cotton. The finished design fits a standard 8x10-inch frame.

Quilts, Toys, and Infants' Accessories

For a baby gift with lots of bounce, make a set of squeezable blocks for baby to play with. Each block is made of six 3-inch crocheted squares stitched together and stuffed with fabric-covered cubes of nonallergenic foam.

♦ Both the felt picture book (right) and the cheerful, crib-size quilted comforter (below) feature simple appliqué

motifs adapted from children's coloring books and other sources.

♦ Make the easy cut-and-paste picture book for a child who is just learning his ABCs. To illustrate each letter, choose easily recognizable pictures, and the book quickly will become a bedtime favorite.

♦ And what better way to herald a baby's arrival than with a one-of-a-kind quilt? The comforter's design is simplicity itself—alternating squares of appliquéd and patterned fabric. Your choice of motifs gives it a truly personal touch.

Almost from their very first moments, babies seem to be intrigued by color, shape, and movement. So mobiles are wonderful entertainment for a newborn.

♦ The marvelous clown mobile (above) will delight a child for hours and encourage his interest in the world around him. This merry troupe of acrobatic circus clowns is an easy-to-assemble project that you can put together in just an afternoon.

Use heavy-duty pipe cleaners to form the clowns' limber bodies, and fashion their heads from fabric-covered plastic foam balls. Add wisps of yarn for hair and a tiny red pompon for a nose. Embroider the eyes with black cotton floss. Their tiny costumes are stitched from scraps of gingham and trimmed with collars of ruffled white eyelet.

Adjust the number of dolls and the height and width of the mobile to suit the space you have available for hanging.

♦ Accomplished crocheters can make the striped layette (above) in just a couple of evenings. The pants feature a comfortable drawstring waist, and the striped top has a simple squared neckline to slip easily over little heads. (For the instructions for the crocheted outfit, look in the following chapter on page 122.)

101

Crib Quilt and Toy

shown on page 96

Materials

1⅓ yards of off-white prequilted fabric; ½ yard *each* of red, yellow, blue, and green calicos; ¼ yard of white felt; 5½ yards of red bias tape; 8 ounces of polyester fiberfill; water-soluble transfer pen; black and white thread; fusible webbing; graph paper.

Instructions

Ask your child to draw pictures (approximately 8 inches high) of boys and girls in a circle (see photograph). Using the drawings as master patterns, cut the figures' clothing from bright-colored calicos. The heads and facial details will be outlined with machine zigzag stitching.

For the quilt: Cut a 36x45-inch piece of prequilted fabric. Arrange the clothing for eight figures in a circle; pin to fabric. With the transfer pen, draw the figures' heads and hands in place. Then, using black thread, zigzag-stitch along edges of appliqués and over the drawn lines.

For bows, cut twenty-four 2x4½-inch rectangles from calico scraps. For each bow, stitch two rectangles together, leaving an opening. Turn, press, and sew the opening closed. Gather the bow at the center and tack it to a figure's collar or hair.

Bind the edges of the quilt with red bias tape.

For the crib toy: Position the figures' clothing on prequilted fabric. Appliqué in place, then zigzag-stitch the heads and hands as for the quilt, above.

Trim away the quilted fabric ¼ inch from the outer edges of each figure. Pin the figures on white felt and, with white thread, zigzag-stitch the edges of the quilted fabric to the white felt background, leaving an opening for stuffing.

Stuff the figures lightly, then zigzag-stitch them closed. Trim the felt ¼ inch beyond the stitching. Join figures by tacking the hands together.

Make bows; add lengths of ribbon to the ends and tie to the crib.

Animal Pull Toy

shown on page 97

Materials

¼ yard *each* of muslin and calico; fabric scraps; polyester fiberfill; scrap of hardboard; four 3-inch-diameter wooden wheels; scrap lumber; four metal washers; two 5¼-inch-long, ¼-inch-diameter dowels; drill with ¼-inch-diameter drill bit; jigsaw; nylon cording; wooden bead.

Instructions

Read through the instructions carefully before you begin.

Trace the outline of a child's animal drawing onto muslin. (To allow for the hardboard support, the base should be wider than the top of the drawing.) Add ½-inch seam allowances; cut two pieces. On the right side of each muslin piece, zigzag-stitch and appliqué any details desired. With right sides facing, sew the pieces together; leave the bottom open. Clip seams, turn, and press.

Trace around the shape of the animal onto the hardboard, adding ½ inch to the bottom edge. With a saw, cut out the shape and slip it inside the muslin animal. Stuff with fiberfill.

From wood scraps, build a 4x11-inch frame for base. Cut a 4x11-inch wood rectangle; make a slit in center for the hardboard. Glue and nail rectangle to frame. Drill two holes on each long side of frame for wheels. Drill a hole in the center front for string.

Push the bottom edge of the hardboard into the slit. Glue the bottom raw edges of the muslin to the wood.

Pad the base with batting; cover with calico, cutting an oval for the animal. Turn under and glue edges of calico.

Cut fabric at holes and push dowels through the holes to create axles for the wheels. Slip a washer onto each end of the dowels. Attach wheels to dowels and glue in place. Knot pull cord through hole in front of frame.

Needlepoint Tote Bag

shown on page 98

Materials

1½ yards of red corduroy; 1 yard of yellow calico; yarn in colors listed in color key, below; ½ yard of No. 10 needlepoint canvas; 1⅔ yards of white piping; 2½ yards of cording; cardboard; tapestry needle.

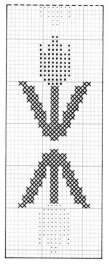

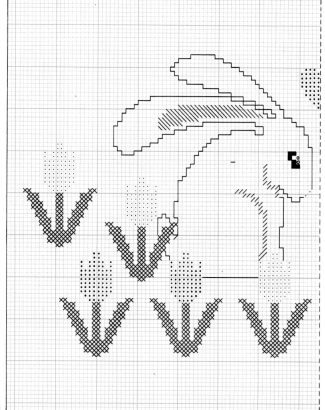

COLOR KEY
- ⊠ Green
- ⊡ Pink
- ⊙ Red
- ⊚ Turquoise
- ⊘ Gray
- ⊠ Light Pink
- ■ Black
- ⊟ White
- ☐ Yellow

1 Square = 1 Stitch

Instructions

For the needlepoint: Cut a 13x18-inch piece of canvas for the pocket and two 4x27-inch strips for the strap. Following the diagrams, opposite, stitch the needlepoint designs, flopping them along the dotted lines.

Work nine tulips on each strap. Use continental stitches for the design and bargello for the background. When completed, block and steam-press.

To assemble the bag: Cut the pieces for the bag from fabric as listed below. (*Note:* Measurements include ½-inch seam allowances.)

From corduroy: Two 2x13-inch strips, one 2x15-inch strip; two 13x19-inch pieces, one 4x19-inch piece, 2½ yards of 3-inch-wide bias strip.

From calico (for the lining): Two 13x19-inch pieces, two 4x25-inch strips, one 4x19-inch strip, and one 11x16-inch piece.

To make the pocket: Stitch white piping to the edges of the needlepoint pocket front between the first and second rows of needlepoint stitches.

To attach pocket lining, pin the 11x16-inch piece of calico to the needlepoint, right sides facing. Sew across top edge only, checking to see that piping is flat. Trim seam and turn; press. Baste raw edges together.

To make the bag front: With right sides facing, pin and stitch the 2x15-inch corduroy strip to the bottom edge of the pocket. Stitch the two 2x13-inch strips to the sides of the pocket and bottom strip. Trim seams; press.

With right sides up, lay pocket atop one 13x19-inch corduroy rectangle, matching bottom and side raw edges. Beginning at one top edge, sew through all thicknesses just outside piping.

To join bag front to bottom and back, pin bottom edge of front to one long edge of 4x19-inch corduroy strip, right sides facing. Stitch. Then pin one long edge of the other 13x19-inch corduroy piece to the remaining long edge of the bottom strip. Sew; trim seams.

To make the strap: With right sides facing, pin the two needlepoint strips together on one short edge. Sew between the first and second rows of needlepoint stitches.

Cover the cording with bias corduroy strips. Then stitch the cording to the seam line on both long sides of the strap and to the top edge of the bag front and back.

With right sides together, stitch the ends of the strap to the ends of the bottom piece. Then, with right sides facing, pin each side of the front to the sides of the strap. Stitch. Repeat for the back. Turn right side out and set aside.

To make the lining: Join the two 13x19-inch pieces and the 4x19-inch strip as for the bag. This will make the lining front, back, and bottom.

With right sides facing, stitch the two 4x25-inch strips together along one short edge. Stitch this strap lining to the lining bottom, front, and back following the instructions for the bag. Slip lining inside the corduroy bag.

Cut pieces of cardboard the size of the front, back, and bottom of the bag, and slip them between the lining and bag to add shape and strength. Turn under the raw edges of the lining and the bag, and hand-stitch them together along the sides of the strap and the top edge of the bag.

Birth Announcement

shown on page 99

Materials

14x18 inches of 18-count Aida cloth; one skein of No. 5 pearl cotton embroidery thread in the following colors: black, red, blue, kelly green, yellow, and orange; embroidery needle; graph paper; colored pencils.

Instructions

Work the design using the chart on page 104. Substitute the "It's a Girl!" canopy, if desired, and graph out the baby's name along the carrousel base using colored pencils and graph paper.

To begin stitching, draw vertical and horizontal lines along the center of the design. With regular sewing thread, baste lines vertically and horizontally in the center of the fabric. Using these lines as reference points, cross-stitch the design in the colors indicated.

Embroider the baby's weight and birth date on the horses' flanks, using tiny straight stitches.

Crocheted Blocks

shown on page 100

Materials

Small amounts of four-ply yarn in white and pastel colors; size G aluminum crochet hook, or size to obtain gauge below; 3x3x3-inch foam rubber cubes; scraps of white fabric to cover cubes. (*Note:* Each pair of squares requires approximately 4 yards of yarn; each block requires two squares each of three colors.)

Gauge: One square is 3x3 inches.
Abbreviations: See pages 218-219.

Instructions

Block A: Ch 5, sl st to form ring.

Rnd 1: 8 sc in ring.

Rnd 2: Working in top lps only throughout, * sc, 3 sc in next st (corner made). Rep from * around. (Corners are formed with 3 sc group in center st of 3 sc group in preceding rnd.)

Rnd 3: Sc in each of next 2 sts, 3 sc in next st, (sc in next 3 st, 3 sc in next st) 3 times.

Rnd 4: Sc in next 4 sts, 3 sc in next st, (sc in next 5 sts, 3 sc in next st) 3 times.

Rnd 5: Sc in next 6 sts, 3 sc in next st (sc in next 7 sts, 3 sc in next st) 3 times.

Rnd 6: Sc in next 8 sts, 3 sc in corner st, (sc in next 9 sts, 3 sc in next st) 2 times; sc in next 9 sts, join with sl st. End off.

Joining: Make six crocheted squares (two of each color) to place opposite each other for each block.

With white yarn, join squares into a cube with sc sts in top lps of edges. Leave two sides of one square open; insert a foam cube that has been covered with white fabric. Stitch the remaining two sides of the cube closed with sc. End off yarn.

Block B: Ch 4, sl st to form ring.

Rnd 1: Ch 3, work 2 tr in ring, (ch 2, 3 tr in ring) 3 times, ch 2 join with sl st to top of ch-3.

Rnd 2: Sl st to 1st ch-2 sp, ch 3, in same sp work 2 tr, ch 1 and 3 tr, * ch 2 in next ch-2 sp, work 3 tr, ch 1 and 3 tr. Rep from * 2 times; ch 2, join with sl st. End off.

Joining: Follow the instructions given above for Block A.

continued

KEY =
- ☒ -black
- · -red
- ○ -blue
- ● -kelly green
- ◢ -yellow
- ■ -orange

Alphabet Book

shown on page 100

Materials

½ yard of 72-inch-wide green felt; scraps of felt in assorted colors for appliqués; scissors and pinking shears; thread; nontoxic white glue; waterproof marking pen.

Instructions

Cut twenty-six 6x6-inch pages for the book from green felt. You will need a simple appliqué motif to illustrate each of the letters. Use children's coloring books for simple designs. Cut motifs from felt scraps and glue to pages. Add details with a nontoxic, waterproof marking pen. Cut out letters freehand or use letter stencils. Glue in place.

To assemble, stack pages in pairs (cover/A, B/C. . . XYZ/back cover). Stitch each pair together ¼ inch from edge. Trim edges with pinking shears.

With a paper punch, make two holes along the left-hand side of each page. Assemble the book with ribbons.

ABC Quilt and Pillow

shown on page 100

Materials

½ yard each of pink, light blue, and yellow print fabrics; 1½ yards of white cotton; 1¾ yards of solid yellow fabric; ¼ yard *each* of solid pink and blue fabrics; ¼ yard *each* of blue, yellow, and pink gingham; 6 yards of 1½-inch-wide white lace; 32x40 inches of quilt batting; fiberfill; thread; graph paper.

Instructions

The finished quilt measures 33x41 inches.

Enlarge patterns (opposite) onto graph paper.

To piece the blocks: Cut 9-inch squares from the following print fabrics: three yellow, three blue, four pink, and 10 white. From gingham and solid-color fabrics, cut the enlarged appliqués as desired. In addition to the appliqués shown, cut out initials and a 2-inch-diameter circle for the ball.

To appliqué: Referring to the photograph, pin appliqués to white blocks. With a medium-wide zigzag stitch and 20-24 stitches per inch, machine-zigzag-stitch the motifs to the blocks.

104

1 Square = 1 Inch

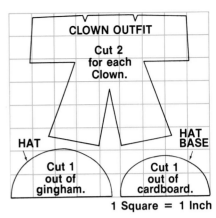

CLOWN OUTFIT
Cut 2
for each
Clown.

HAT
Cut 1
out of
gingham.

HAT
BASE
Cut 1
out of
cardboard.

1 Square = 1 Inch

Clown Mobile

shown on page 101

Materials

For each clown: ¼ yard of gingham; ⅛ yard *each* of white knit and white cotton fabric; red pompon; two white pompons; 1½-inch-diameter plastic foam balls; yarn scraps. Also, 12-inch-long pipe cleaners; 1½ yards of eyelet; three 9-inch-long and one 18-inch-long piece of ¼-inch-diameter dowel; fabric glue; cardboard; monofilament; black embroidery floss.

Instructions

Cut a 7-inch length of pipe cleaner; insert end through a foam ball and secure. Bend to make one leg. Attach a 3½-inch pipe cleaner for the other leg. Wrap a 5-inch pipe cleaner around body for arms. Repeat for all clowns.

Smooth a 4-inch square of white knit fabric over each ball; secure with a rubber band. Embroider eyes with black floss. Glue on red pompon for nose, and yarn scraps for hair.

Enlarge patterns (above). Cut hat base from cardboard and gingham for each clown. Tape cardboard base into a cone; cover with fabric. Glue to head; add white pompon to top of hat. Cut suit from gingham; stitch together, leaving open at neck. Turn right side out and slip over pipe cleaners. Stitch eyelet around neck.

From white cotton, cut a 3x4-inch rectangle for each foot and a 2-inch square for each hand. Gather, and stuff each with fiberfill. Stitch in place. Turn under raw edges and sew on eyelet cuffs. Add a pompon to each suit.

Paint dowels; suspend the clowns from them. Bend clowns as desired.

To assemble the blocks: Refer to the photograph for placement of colors. Sew the squares into rows. Press seams and stitch rows together, matching corners. Press. Cut yellow fabric same size as quilt top for backing.

To add the lace trim: With right sides together, pin and stitch lace to quilt top so straight edge of lace extends ¼ inch beyond quilt edge. Lay the top flat, right side up. On top, put

the back right side down, then the batting. Pin together. Stitch on three sides; leave top open. Clip corners, turn right side out, and press. Stitch opening closed. Lay quilt flat and pin layers along seams of blocks. Stitch along seam lines.

To make the pillow: Cut two 9x14-inch pieces of desired fabric. Trim edges of front with lace. Sew front to back, right sides together, leaving opening. Turn, stuff, and stitch closed.

105

Clothes and Coverlets
to Knit and Crochet

What could be more fun than giving a newborn a handcrafted treasure made just for him or her? If you look forward to knitting and crocheting for the babies (and their parents) on your gift list, you're sure to find just the right project in this enchanting collection of infants' clothes and accessories.

Traditional soft pinks and blues are always appropriate for babies. But don't be afraid to experiment with bolder, brighter colors, as well as classic white and the full range of wonderful greens, yellows, and lavenders. Or blend several different shades for a cheerful knitted or crocheted baby blanket.

♦ The intricately patterned ecru christening gown (*below*) is an exquisite example of knitted lace—and a delightful challenge for the accomplished knitter.

♦ Expert crocheters, on the other hand, might opt to make the handsome filet crochet gown (left). The dress features a stylized tulip on the bodice and skirt panels, and the design is enhanced by a simple, square neckline and demure, wrist-length sleeves.

To enhance the delicate patterns of each of the christening gowns, line them with a contrasting pastel fabric.

♦ A lacy flower medallion and an interwoven grosgrain ribbon accent the christening pillow (opposite). It's easy to crochet in rounds, and it makes a sweet addition to a crib or cradle.

Instructions for these projects, as well as all those that follow, begin on page 114.

Clothes and Coverlets
to Knit and Crochet

ere is a picture-per-fect his *or* hers out-fit and pair of accessories you can complete long before baby's arrival.

♦ Knitted-in tree and bird motifs in blue and pink trim the pullover sweater and matching trousers (right). The sweater is knitted in one piece, with a three-but-ton front closure and ribbing accents.

The pull-on trousers feature identical styling in the front and back, with a comfortable elas-ticized waistband. The pattern is sized for ba-bies six to 12 months old.

♦ Let baby dress up for dinner in a precious cro-cheted party bib (oppo-site). Copied from an heirloom pattern, this special bib features a lacy picot edging woven with ribbons. Add a tiny rosette made of satin rib-bon as a finishing touch.

♦ Confectionery colors sweeten a snuggly and easy-to-do crocheted crib blanket (far right). Choose from a palette of pastel yarns for each granny square. (It's a wonderful way to use up odds and ends of pretty baby yarns.) Use borders and bands of white to join the squares into a harmonious whole.

For Baby...

Clothes and Coverlets
to Knit and Crochet

Classic styling, simple shaping, and subtle textural details enhance the quick-to-knit infant garments pictured here.

Each is worked in soft yarns that feel comfortable next to baby's sensitive skin, yet still provide the washable, easy-care features that new mothers appreciate.

♦ The handsome pull-on overalls (below) work up in a jiffy and fit perfectly into any occasion—from picnics to dressy parties. The overalls feature a textured bib in reverse cable-stitch, ribbed shoulder straps that cross and button in the back, and gently elasticized ankles to keep pants legs from riding up. Sized for three-, six-, and nine-month-old babies, these pants are easy to put on and take off and can be worn with or without a shirt, depending on the weather.

♦ For slip-on ease, make this delightful one-piece romper suit (left and below, opposite). Knitted in speedy stockinette stitch (knit one row, pearl one row), the suit has snugly fitting, ribbed shoulder straps, and a front pocket accent. It's sized for babies six, nine, and 12 months of age.

♦ Both mother and child will be on Cloud Nine when baby's all dressed up in a sweet little sky-blue suit (opposite, far right). Sized for babies three to six months old, the bibbed trousers and cozy cardigan are worked in stockinette stitch and then embroidered with bird and cloud motifs.

Though all the outfits pictured here have been knitted in varying shades of traditional baby-blue yarn, any of the garments would look adorable in almost any pastel shade of your choice. Picture the rompers in a cheerful raspberry color, for example, or stitch the overalls in a sunny yellow or soft lavender. For an entirely different effect, work the ribbing

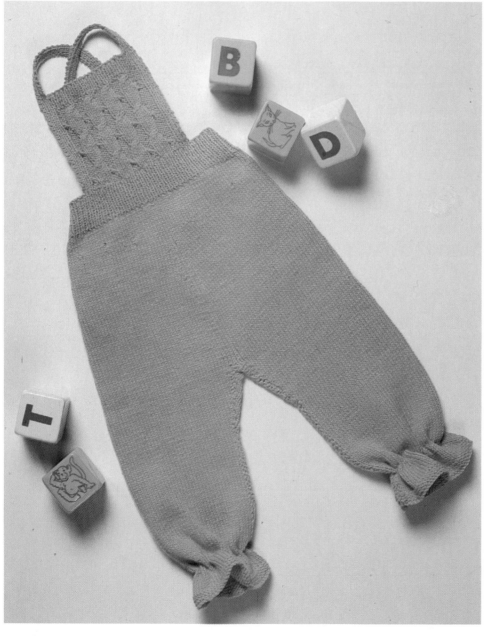

and straps in a contrasting color.

All the garments are suitable for year-round wear and are sure to be saved for other family additions.

And because each pattern is classically styled, you might make an extra pair of overalls or a sweater or two—while you're in the knitting mood—to have on hand for future gift giving.

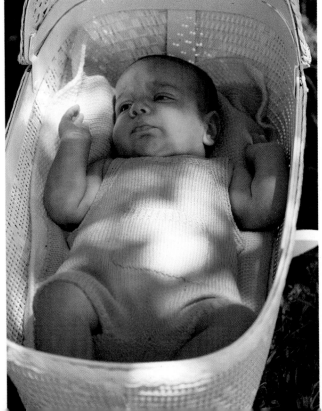

111

Clothes and Coverlets
to Knit and Crochet

Smart-looking baby outfits don't have to be made in pastels.
♦ Blend scraps of bright-colored yarns with strands of white to create an unusual baby blanket (left). Knit each five-inch square in quick-and-easy garter stitch, using double strands of yarn. Then stitch the squares together and border with white.

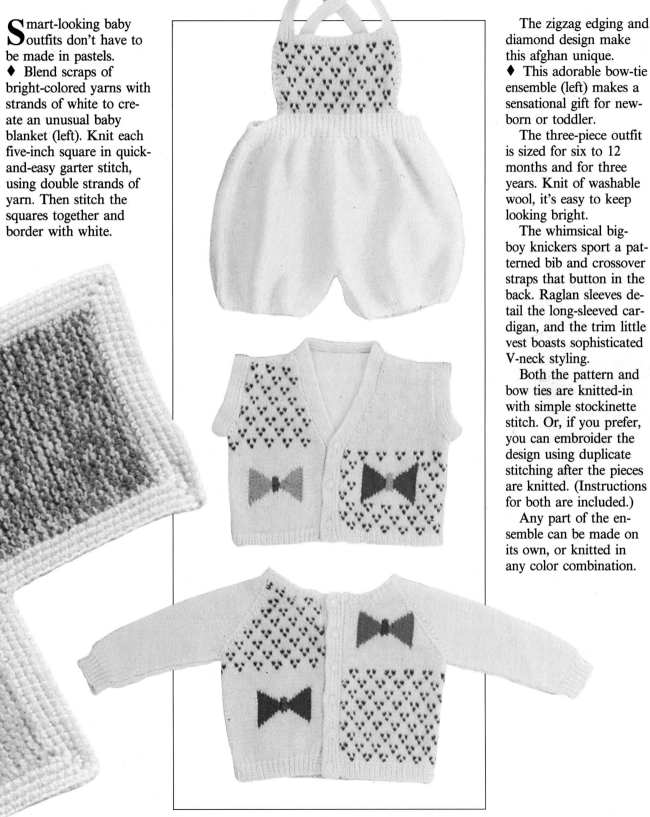

The zigzag edging and diamond design make this afghan unique.
♦ This adorable bow-tie ensemble (left) makes a sensational gift for newborn or toddler.

The three-piece outfit is sized for six to 12 months and for three years. Knit of washable wool, it's easy to keep looking bright.

The whimsical big-boy knickers sport a patterned bib and crossover straps that button in the back. Raglan sleeves detail the long-sleeved cardigan, and the trim little vest boasts sophisticated V-neck styling.

Both the pattern and bow ties are knitted-in with simple stockinette stitch. Or, if you prefer, you can embroider the design using duplicate stitching after the pieces are knitted. (Instructions for both are included.)

Any part of the ensemble can be made on its own, or knitted in any color combination.

113

Crocheted Christening Gown

shown on page 106

Materials

Unger Cruise (1.4-ounce balls), or a suitable substitute: 6 balls white; Size B aluminum crochet hook; 5 buttons.

Gauge: 15 dc = 2 inches.

Instructions

Cluster (cl): (Yo, insert hook, pull up lp) 3 times—7 lps; yo, pull through 6 lps, yo, pull through rem 2 lps.

V-stitch: (Dc, ch 1, dc) in same st.

Note on working from chart: For each block (squares with dotted centers), work 1 dc in bet 2 dc; for each space, work ch 1 bet 2 dc. For bodice beg at bottom and work Rows 1-10; for skirt, beg at top and work entire chart.

Bodice front: Ch 54 for foundation ch; sc in 2nd ch from hook and in each ch across—53 sc; ch 1, turn.

Row 2: Sc across; turn. *Row 3:* Sl st in each of last 6 sc of Row 2; ch 3, dc in 42 dc; ch 4, turn—5 sc each end for underarm tabs.

Row 4: Sk 1st 2 dc, dc in dc, (ch 1, sk dc, dc in dc) 19 times; ch 1, dc in turning ch—21 sps; ch 3, turn.

Row 5 (Row 2 of chart for front): Dc in 1st sp, (dc in dc, ch 1) 6 times; (dc in dc, dc in sp) 7 times; (dc in dc, ch 1) 6 times; dc in dc, dc in next 2 ch; ch 3, turn. *Rows 6-13:* Beg with Row 3 of chart, work motif (see note on working from chart, above). At end of Row 13, ch 3, turn.

Row 14: Sk dc, dc in 2 dc, (ch 1, dc in dc) 8 times; (ch 1, sk dc, dc in dc, ch 1, dc in dc) twice; (ch 1, dc in dc) 7 times; dc in last dc and in turning ch; ch 3, turn. *Row 15:* Sk dc, dc in 2 dc, (ch 1, dc in dc) 5 times; ch 4, turn. (Rem sts are for neck and 2nd shoulder.)

Row 16: (Dc in dc, ch 1) 4 times; dc in last 2 dc and in turning ch; ch 3, turn. *Row 17:* Sk dc, dc in 2 dc, (ch 1, dc in dc) 4 times; ch 1, sk 1 ch, dc in next ch; ch 4, turn. *Row 18:* Rep Row 16. Fasten off.

Second shoulder: Attach thread in turning ch of Row 14; ch 3, dc in next 2 dc and work as for 1st shoulder.

Bodice back: *Row 1:* Ch 31, sc in 2nd ch from hook and each ch across—30 ch; ch 1, turn. *Row 2:* Sc across; ch 3, turn. *Row 3:* Sk 1st sc, dc in 24 sc; ch 3, turn. (Last 5 sc are unworked for underarm tab.) *Row 4:* Sk dc, dc in 2 dc, (ch 1, sk dc, dc in dc) 9 times; dc in last 3 dc and in turning ch; ch 3, turn.

Row 5: Sk dc, dc in next 4 dc, (ch 1, dc in dc) 9 times; dc in last dc and in turning ch; ch 3, turn. *Row 6:* Sk dc, dc in 2 dc, (ch 1, dc in dc) 9 times; dc in last 3 dc and in turning ch; ch 3, turn.

Rows 7-15: Rep Rows 5-6 alternately until there are 12 rows of sps; ch 3, turn. *Row 16:* Sk dc, dc in 2 dc, (ch 1, dc in dc) 5 times; ch 4, turn. (Rem sts are for neck.) *Row 17:* (Dc in dc, ch 1) 4 times; dc in last 2 dc and in turning ch; ch 3, turn. *Row 18:* Sk dc, dc in 2 dc, (ch 1, dc in dc) 4 times; ch 1, sk 1 ch, dc in next ch. Fasten off.

Work other bodice back similarly; sew shoulder seams.

Finishing armhole: *Row 1:* With bodice right side facing and armhole at top, attach thread in 4th sc from end of underarm tab, dc at dc at end of Row 3; working along side of bodice, (2 dc in side of next row, dc in side of next row) 6 times; 2 dc in side of next 4 rows, 2 dc at shoulder seam, 2 dc in side of next 4 rows, (dc in side of next row, 2 dc in side of next row) 6 times; dc in same place as last dc on Row 3, sl st in 4th sc from end of underarm tab—56 dc. Sl st in next 2 sc of underarm, turn.

Row 2: Dc in 56 dc across, sl st in 2nd sc from end of underarm; sl st in end sc, turn.

Row 3: Sc across, sl st in last sc of underarm, sc in end of underarm tab, sc in end of foundation ch, ch 8, sc in end of foundation ch at other end of row, sc in end of underarm tab, sl st in 1st sc of row. Fasten off. Rep for other armhole.

Sleeves: *Note:* Work in rnds along armhole edge. With right side facing, attach thread in 5th st of underarm ch-8, ch 3, sk 1 ch, make V-st in next ch, dc in 1st 2 sc, * sk 1 sc, V-st in sc, sk 1 sc, dc in next 2 sc. Rep from * around, ending V-st in 2nd underarm ch, dc in 4th underarm ch, sl st in top of ch-3.

Rnd 2: Ch 3, V-st in each V-st and dc in each st of the 2-dc grps bet; dc in last dc and join to ch-3. *Rnd 3:* As Rnd 2, but sk last dc on rnd, join to ch-3.

Rnd 4: Ch 3, * V-st in next V-st, dc in next 2 dc, V-st in next V-st, *holding back on hook last lp of each st, make dc*

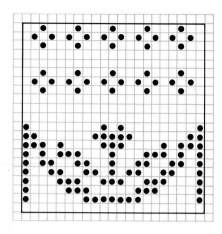

*in each of next 2 dc, thread over and draw through all lps on hook—dec made. Rep from * around, join to ch-3. Rnd 5:* Rep Rnd 4, dec in rem 2-dc grps to leave only 1 dc bet all V-sts. *Rnds 6-9:* Work even with V-st; dc around. *Rnd 10:* Ch 3, dc in each dc and each V-st around—55 dc plus beg ch; join to ch-3. *Rnd 11:* Ch 4, * sk dc, cl in dc, ch 1. Rep from * around, join in 3rd st of ch-4—27 cls.

Rnd 12: Ch 4, (dc in cl, ch 1) around, join in 3rd ch of ch-4—28 sps. *Rnd 13:* Ch 3, * dc in sp, dc in dc, (ch 1, dc in dc) 3 times. Rep from * around, join to ch-3. *Rnd 14:* Ch 4, * sk dc, (dc in dc, dc in sp, dc in dc, ch 1) twice. Rep from * around, join in 3rd ch of ch-4.

Rnd 15: Ch 3, * dc in sp, dc in dc, ch 1, sk dc, (dc in dc, ch 1) twice; sk dc, dc in dc. Rep from * around, join to ch-3. *Rnd 16:* Ch 4, * sk dc, dc in dc, (ch 1, dc in dc) 3 times; ch 1. Rep from * around, join to 3rd ch of ch-4. *Rnd 17:* Ch 3, cl in dc around; join. *Rnd 18:* Ch 1, sc in top of each cl around, sl st to 1st sc. *Rnd 19:* Ch 1, sc in sc around, join to 1st sc. Fasten off. Rep for 2nd sleeve.

Neckline: Right side facing, beg at center lower corner of left back, sc along back edge, neck, and right back edge; don't break thread.

Skirt: Sc along foundation and underarm chs, making 30 sc across each back section, 10 sc on underarm chs, 53 sc across front—133 sc; ch 3, turn.

Row 2: Make V-st in 2nd sc, (dc in next sc, V-st in next sc) 26 times—27 V-sts; 2 dc in next 2 sc, (ch 1, dc in next sc) 10 times; ch 1, V-st in sc, (ch 1, dc in next sc) 10 times; ch 1, 2 dc in next 2 sc, (V-st in next sc, dc in next sc) 27 times.

Row 3: Turn to right side, align last 2 V-sts atop V-sts of left back; sl st in following dc of left back, ch 3; make V-st through next V-st of both layers, dc through both dc, V-st in both of next V-st, dc in both dc and top of ch-3. Working in rnds, make V-st in center of next 25 V-sts with dc bet, dc in each of next 4 dc, (ch 1, dc in dc) 23 times; dc in next 3 dc, make V-st in next 25 V-sts with dc bet, sl st in top of ch-3.

Rnd 4: Ch 3, (V-st in V-st, 2 dc in next dc) 26 times; V-st in last V-st, dc in each of next 4 dc, (ch 1, dc in dc) 23 times; dc in next 3 dc, (V-st in center of next V-st, 2 dc in dc) 24 times; V-st in last V-st, sl st in top of ch-3.

Rnds 5-10: Ch 3, V-st in 27 V-sts with 2 dc bet, dc in next 4 dc, (ch 1, dc in dc) 23 times; dc in 3 dc, V-st in 25 V-st with 2 dc bet, sl st in top of ch-3.

Rnds 11-15: Continue V-st pat. Beg design in center front mesh panel, beg at top of chart. (There will be 1 additional sp on each end of rows shown.)

Rnd 16: Ch 3, (dc in dc, dc in V-st, dc in 3 dc) 26 times; V-st in V-st, dc in next 4 dc, continue with chart across panel, dc in next 4 dc, V-st in V-st, sk dc of this V-st, (dc in next 3 dc, dc in center of V-st, dc in dc) 24 times; sl st in top of ch-3. *Rnd 17:* Ch 3, cl in sl st, (ch 1, sk 1 dc, cl in dc) 65 times; V-st in V-st, dc in 4 dc, continue chart, dc in 4 dc, V-st in V-st, sk dc of this V-st, (cl in next dc, ch 1, sk next dc) 60 times; sl st in top of 1st cl made.

Rnd 18: Ch 4, dc in top of next cl, (ch 1, dc in top of next cl) 64 times; V-st in V-st, dc in 4 dc, continue chart, dc in 4 dc, V-st in V-st, (dc in top of cl, ch 1) 60 times; sl st in 3rd st of ch-4.

Rnd 19: Ch 4, dc in dc, * ch 1, dc in dc, dc in sp, dc in dc, (ch 1, dc in dc) twice. Rep from * 15 times; V-st in V-st, dc in 4 dc, continue chart, dc in 4 dc, V-st in V-st, * (dc in dc, ch 1) twice; dc in dc, dc in sp, dc in dc, ch 1. Rep from * 14 times; sl st in 3rd ch of ch-4.

Rnd 20: Ch 4, (dc in dc, dc in sp, dc in dc, sk dc, dc in dc, dc in sp, dc in dc, ch 1) 15 times; dc in dc, V-st in V-st, dc in 4 dc, follow chart across, dc in 4 dc, V-st in V-st, dc in dc, ch 1; rep ( ) 15 times, ending with dc in sp and sl st in 3rd st of ch-4.

Rnd 21: Ch 4, dc in dc, * ch 1, sk dc, dc in dc, dc in sp, dc in dc, sk dc, (ch 1, dc in dc) twice. Rep from * to front section, V-st in V-st, dc in 4 dc, follow chart, dc in 4 dc, V-st in V-st, work side and back section as 1st, end with ch-1, sl st in 3rd ch of ch-4.

Rnd 22: Ch 4, dc in dc, * ch 1, dc in

dc, sk dc, (ch 1, dc in dc) 3 times. Rep from * 15 more times; V-st in V-st, dc in 4 dc, follow chart across front, dc in 4 dc, V-st in V-st, work mesh across side and back, sl st in 3rd ch of ch-4.

Rnd 23: Ch 3, cl in sl st, (ch 1, cl in dc) 65 times; V-st in V-st, dc in 4 dc, follow chart, dc in 4 dc, V-st in V-st (cl in next dc, ch 1) 60 times; sl st in 1st cl.

Rnd 24: Ch 3, (dc in next sp, dc in top of cl) 65 times; V-st in V-st, dc in 4 dc, follow chart across front, dc in 4 dc, V-st in V-st, (dc in top of cl, dc in next sp) 60 times; sl st in top of ch-3.

Rnd 25: Ch 3, (sk dc, V-st in dc, sk dc, dc in next 2 dc) 26 times; V-st in V-st, dc in 4 dc, follow chart, dc in 4 dc, V-st in V-st, (dc in next 2 dc, sk dc, V-st in dc, sk dc) 24 times; sl st in top of ch-3. *Rnds 26-31:* Work V-st with 2 dc bet around, following chart.

Rnd 32: Work V-st pat, dc in 4 dc, dc in each dc and sp across front mesh panel, dc in 4 dc; finish rnd in V-st. *Rnd 33:* Work V-st pat, dc in 53 dc across front panel; finish rnd in V-st.

Rnd 34: V-st pat to front panel, (sk dc, dc in next 2 dc, sk dc, V-st in next dc) 10 times; sk dc, dc in last 2 dc; finish rnd in V-st pat. *Rnds 35-39:* Work V-st pat. *Rnd 40:* Ch 3, dc in dc and sp around, join in top of ch-3.

Rnd 41: Ch 3, cl in sl st, (ch 1, sk 1 dc, cl in next dc) around, sl st in 1st cl. *Rnd 42:* Ch 4, dc in cl, (ch 1, dc in cl) around, sl st in 3rd ch of ch-4.

Rnd 43: Ch 4, dc in dc, * (ch 1, dc in dc) twice; dc in sp, dc in next dc, ch 1, dc in dc. Rep from *, end with ch 1 and sl st in 3rd ch of ch-4. *Rnd 44:* Ch 3, * dc in sp, dc in dc, ch 1, sk dc, dc in dc. Rep from *; join to ch-3.

Rnd 45: Ch 4, sk dc, dc in dc, * ch 1, dc in dc, ch 1, sk dc, dc in dc, dc in sp, dc in dc, ch 1, sk dc, dc in dc. Rep from * around, end with ch 1 and sl st in 3rd st of ch-4.

Rnd 46: Ch 4, dc in dc, * (ch 1, dc in dc) twice; ch 1, sk dc, dc in dc, ch 1, dc in dc. Rep from * around, end with ch 1 and sl st in 3rd ch of ch-4. *Rnd 47:* Ch 3, cl in same place as sl st, (ch 1, cl in next dc) around, end with ch-1 and sl st in top of 1st cl.

Rnd 48: Ch 3, (dc, ch 2, 2 dc) in sl st, * sk 1 cl, in next cl work 2 dc, ch 2, 2 dc. Rep from *; join in top of ch-3.

Rnds 49-54: Sl st in dc and in ch-2 sp, ch 3 and complete shell in this sp; (shell in shell) around; join in top of ch-3. Sew on buttons; sl through dc.

Crocheted Christening Pillow

shown on page 106

Materials

Bucilla Blue Label Crochet Cotton: 1 skein; size 6 steel crochet hook; fabric scraps for lining; polyester fiberfill or cotton batting; grosgrain ribbon.

Instructions

Note: Pillow is worked in 2 pieces. Work Rnds 1-16 for the top; work Rnds 1-12 for the bottom. See finishing instructions below.

To begin doily: Ch 7, sl st to join.

Rnd 1: Ch 6, dc in ring, (ch 3, dc in ring) 6 times; ch 3, sl st to ch-3 of ch-6 at beg of rnd—8 sps.

Rnd 2: Sl st into ch-3 lp, ch 3, 5 dc in same lp, (6 dc in next ch-3 lp) 7 times; join with sl st to top of ch-3 at beg of rnd—48 dc around.

Rnd 3: Ch 3 to count as 1st dc, dc in each dc around; sl st to ch-3 at beg of rnd.

Rnd 4: Ch 4, *yo twice, draw up lp in next dc, (yo, draw through 2 lps on hook) twice—2 lps rem on hook—yo twice, draw up lp in next dc, (yo, draw through 2 lps on hook) twice; yo, draw through rem 3 lps on hook—cluster (cl) made;* ch 4, work cl over next 3 dc as follows: [* yo twice, draw up through lp in *next* dc, (yo, draw through 2 lps on hook) twice. * Rep bet *s twice more; yo, draw through rem 4 lps on hook, ch 4]. Rep pat bet [ ]s 14 times more—16 clusters around.

Rnd 5: Sl st into next ch-4 lp, ch 3, 5 dc in same lp, ch 3, 5 dc in same lp; work 6 dc in *every* ch-4 lp around; join with sl st to top of ch-3.

Rnd 6: Ch 3, in each of next 11 dc, ch 3, * dc in each of next 12 dc, ch 3. Rep from * around; join last ch 3 to top of ch-3.

Rnd 7: Sl st into next dc, ch 3, dc in next 9 dc, * ch 3, sc in next ch-3 lp, ch 3, sk next dc, dc in each of next 10 dc. Rep from * around, ending ch 3, sc in ch-3 lp, ch 3; join last ch-3 to top of ch-3.

Rnd 8: Sl st into next dc, ch 3, dc in each of 7 dc, * (ch 3, sc in ch-3 lp) twice, ch 3, sk next dc, dc in each of next 8 dc. Rep from * around, ending (ch 3, sc in ch-3 lp) twice, ch 3; join to top of ch-3.

continued

Rnds 9-10: Continue in same pat as previous 2 rnds. Rnd 9 will have 6 dc in grp and 4 ch-3 lps. Rnd 10 will have 4 dc in grp and 5 ch-3 lps.

Rnd 11: Ch 3, dc in each of next 3 dc, * (4 dc in ch-3 lp—dc grp made) 5 times; dc in each of next 4 dc. Rep from * around, ending rnd in pat; join last dc to top of ch-3.

Rnd 12: Ch 8, sk next 3 dc, tr in sp after 3rd dc, ch 4, * tr bet next 2 dc grps, ch 4. Rep from * around; join last ch-4 to 4th ch of ch-8 at beg of rnd.

Rnd 13: Sl st into ch-4 lp, ch 3, 5 dc in same lp; 6 dc in every ch-4 lp around; join to top of ch-3.

Rnd 14: Ch 3, dc in each of next 5 dc, * ch 3, sc in sp bet 3rd and 4th dc, ch 3, sk 3 dc, dc in each of next 6 dc. Rep from * around, ending rnd in pat and join last ch-3 to top of ch-3.

Rnd 15: Sl st into next dc, ch 3, dc in next 3 dc, * ch 3, sc in ch-3 lp, ch 3; dc, ch 3, dc in next sc; dc; ch 3, dc; ch 3, sc in ch-3 lp, ch 3, sk dc, dc in each of next 4 dc. Rep from * around, ending rnd in pat and join to top of ch-3.

Rnd 16: Sl st into next dc, ch 3, dc in next dc, * ch 3, sc in ch-3 lp, ch 3, dc in next ch-3 lp, ch 3; dc, ch 3, dc in next ch-3 lp; ch 3, dc in next ch-3 lp, ch 3, sc in ch-3 lp, ch 3, sk next dc, dc in each of next 2 dc. Rep from * around, ending rnd in pat; join last ch-3 to top of ch-3. Fasten off.

Finishing: Cut 2 fabric circles to the size of the smaller crocheted (bottom) piece, adding ½-inch seam allowance. Pin right sides together; stitch around, leaving an opening for stuffing. Turn, stuff, and slip-stitch closed. Sandwich pillow between crocheted pieces; align so that trs of Rnd 12 match. Weave ribbon through; tie with a bow.

Knitted Christening Gown

shown on page 107

Materials

Reynolds Parfait (1-ounce balls): 6 balls ecru; sizes 2 and 3 knitting needles, or size to obtain gauge below; 1 set size 3 double-point knitting needles; 2 stitch holders; 12 small buttons.

Gauge: On large needles, 7 sts = 1 inch over stockinette stitch.
Abbreviations: See pages 218-219.

Instructions

Bodice back: With single strand of yarn and larger needles, cast on 67 sts and work in stockinette stitch (k 1 row, p 1 row) for 6 rows. Cast off 12 sts at beg of next 2 rows. Work even over 43 rem sts for 35 rows.

Next row: Work across 16 sts; cast off next 11 sts; work across rem 16 sts. Working on right shoulder only, cast off 4 sts at armhole edge 3 times and *at the same time* dec 1 st at neck edge 2 times. Fasten off. Attach yarn at neck edge of left shoulder and work left side as for right side, reversing all shaping.

Skirt back: With right side facing, pick up 67 sts along bottom of back bodice; turn; p 3, (yo, p 2) 3 times, (yo, p 1) 46 times, p 1 (yo, p 2) 5 times—122 sts.

Row 1: K 5, * p 2, k 2, yo, k 2 tog, p 2, k 1, yo, sl 1, k 1, psso, k 1, k 2 tog, yo, k 1, p 2, k 2, yo, k 2 tog, p 2, k 7. Rep from * 3 times more, ending last rep with k 4.

Row 2: P 4, * k 2, p 2, yo, p 2 tog, k 2, p 7. Rep from * 7 times more, ending with p 5.

Row 3: K 5, p 2, k 2, yo, k 2 tog, p 2, k 2, yo, sl 1, k 2 tog, psso, yo, k 2, p 2, k 2, yo, k 2 tog, p 2, * k 7, p 2, k 2, yo, k 2 tog, p 2, k 2, yo, sl 1, k 2 tog, psso, yo, k 2, p 2, k 2, k 2 tog, p 2. Rep from * 2 times more, ending with k 4.

Row 4 and every even-number row: Rep Row 2.

Row 5: Rep Row 1.

Row 7 (cable twist row): K 5, p 2, sl 2 to a double-point needle (dpn) and hold in front of work, k 2, k 2 from dpn, p 2, k 2, yo, sl 1, k 2 tog, psso, yo, k 2, p 2, sl 2 to dpn and hold in front, k 2, k 2 from dpn, p 2, * k 7, p 2, sl 2 to dpn and hold in front, k 2, k 2 from dpn, p 2, k 2, yo, sl 1, k 2 tog, psso, yo, k 2, p 2, sl 2 to dpn, and hold in front, k 2, k 2 from dpn, p 2. Rep from * twice more; k 4.

Row 9: Rep Row 1.
Row 11: Rep Row 3.
Row 13: Rep Row 1.
Row 15: Rep Row 13.
Row 16: Rep Row 2. Rep Rows 1-16 for pat, inc 1 st at each side of the stockinette stitch panel on the 20th and every 20th row thereafter. (On the 1st and last st st inc on the inside edge only.)

Work in pat as established until beg and end stockinette stitch panel con- tains 8 sts and the inside stockinette stitch panels contain 13 sts. When the cable panels have been twisted 4 times (146 sts), end with the last right side cable twist row.

For a short gown, work 5 rows in garter st (k each row); cast off. For a longer gown, omit the garter st and continue with pat following:

Row 1: K on wrong side. *Row 2:* P.
Row 3: K. *Row 4:* K, inc 7 sts across row, evenly spaced.
Row 5: P. *Row 6:* K 1, * yo, k 2 tog. Rep from * across, ending with k 2.
Row 7: P. *Row 8:* K. *Row 9:* P.
Row 10: K 2, * yo, sl 1, k 1, psso, k 5, k 2 tog, yo, k 1, rep from * to end.
Row 11 and every other row: P to end.
Row 12: K 3, * yo, sl 1, k 1, psso, k 3, k 2 tog, yo, k 3, rep from * to last 10 sts, yo, sl 1, k 1, psso, k 3, k 2 tog, yo, k 3.
Row 14: K 4, * yo, sl 1, k 1, psso, k 1, k 2 tog, yo, k 5, rep from * to last 9 sts; yo, sl 1, k 1, psso, k 1, k 2 tog, yo, k 4.
Row 16: K 5, yo, sl 1, k 2 tog, psso, yo, k 7, rep from * to last 8 sts, yo, sl 1, k 2 tog, psso, yo, k 5.
Row 18: K 2, * yo, sl 1, k 1, psso, k 2 tog, yo, k 1. Rep from * to end; k 2.
Row 19: P.
Rows 20-27: Rep Rows 18 and 19 four times.
Row 28: K 3, yo, sl 1, k 1, psso, k 3, k 2 tog, yo, k 3, rep from * to last 10 sts, yo, sl 1, k 1, psso, k 3, k 2 tog, yo, k 3.
Row 29: P.
Row 30: K 4, * yo, sl 1, k 1, psso, k 1, k 2 tog, yo, k 5. Rep from * to last 8 sts; yo, sl 1, k 1, psso, k 1, k 2 tog, yo, k 4.
Row 31: P.
Row 32: K 5, * yo, sl 1, k 2 tog, psso, yo, k 7, rep from * to last 8 sts; yo, sl 1, k 2 tog, psso, yo, k 5.
Row 33: P. Rep Rows 18 thru 33 twice. Knit 6 rows (garter st) and loose- ly cast off in knit on wrong side.

Right bodice: Cast on 36 sts.
Row 1: K 4, * k 2, yo, sl 1, k 1, psso, p 2. Rep from * twice, ending k 13.
Row 2: P 13, k 2, * p 2, yo, p 2 tog, k 2, repeat from * twice, k 4.
Row 3: Rep Row 1.
Row 4: P 13, k 2, * p 2, yo, p 2 tog, k 2. Rep from * twice, ending (k 1, yo, k 2 tog, k 1) buttonhole just made. (Work buttonholes on the right for girls and left for boys. If desired, omit button- holes and use snaps.)
Row 5: Rep Row 1.
Row 6: Cast off 12 sts, * k 2, p 2, yo, p 2 tog. Rep from * twice; k 4.

Row 7: K 4, * k 2, yo, sl 1, k 1, psso, p 2. Rep from * twice; k 1. Rep Rows 6 and 7 for pat, placing buttonholes on Rows 12 and 22. When 24 rows have been completed, work as follows:

Row 25: Cast off 8 sts; work in pattern to end.

Rows 26, 28, 30, 32: Rep Row 6.

Rows 27, 29, 31, 33: Dec 1 st at neck edge, keeping in pattern.

Row 34: Cast off 4 sts at armhole edge.

Row 35: Work even in pat. Rep last 2 rows until no stitches remain.

Left bodice: Work as for right front, reversing all shaping.

Right front skirt: Beg at armhole edge, pick up 38 sts along bottom of right front bodice. K 5, * (yo, p 1) 28 times, p 5—66 sts. *Row 1:* K 5, * p 2, k 2, yo, k 2 tog, p 2, k 1, yo, sl 1, k 1, psso, k 2 tog, yo, k 1, p 2, k 2, yo, k 2 tog, p 2, k 7. Rep from * once more, ending with k 8.

Row 2: K 5, p 3, k 2, p 2, yo, p 2 tog, k 2, p 7, k 2, p 2, yo, p 2 tog, k 2, p 7, k 2, p 2, yo, p 2 tog, k 2, p 7, k 2, p 2, yo, p 2 tog, k 2, p 5.

If buttonholes are being made, continue to make buttonholes in band after every 4 garter st ridges.

Row 3: K 5, * p 2, k 2, yo, k 2 tog, p 2, k 2, yo, sl 1, k 2 tog, psso, yo, k 2, p 2, k 2, yo, k 2 tog, p 2, k 7. Rep from * once more, ending with k 8.

Row 4: K 5, * p 3, k 2, p 2, yo, p 2 tog, k 2, p 7, k 2, p 2, yo, p 2 tog, k 2, p 7.

Rep from * once more, ending with p 5. Pat is now established and is worked as for back *except* for the 5 band sts worked in garter st on center front edge.

Continue in pat using back as a guide until 4 cable twists have been worked and the right skirt front matches the back skirt pat. At this point, 10 buttonholes and 78 sts are on needle. Change pat and work as for back.

Next, refer to back and right front, taking care to reverse all shaping and omitting buttonholes.

Left front skirt: Pick up 38 sts along bottom of left bodice front.

Row 1: P 3, * (yo, p 1) 28 times, p 2, k 5 (66 sts).

Row 2: K 8, * p 2, k 2, yo, k 2 tog, p 2, k 1, yo, sl 1, k 1, psso, k 1, k 2 tog, yo, k 1, p 2, k 2, yo, k 2 tog, p 2, k 7. Rep from * once, end with k 5.

Row 3: P 5, * k 2, p 2, yo, p 2 tog, k 2, p 7, k 2, p 2, yo, p 2 tog, k 2, p 7. Rep from * once, end with p 3, k 5.

If buttonholes are being made, continue to make buttonhole in band after 4 garter-stitch ridges have been made.

Row 4: K 8, * p 2, k 2, yo, k 2 tog, p 2, k 2, yo, sl 1, k 2 tog, psso, yo, k 2, p 2, k 2, yo, k 2 tog, p 2, k 7. Rep from * once, ending with k 5.

Row 5: P 5, * k 2, p 2, yo, p 2 tog, k 2, p 7. Rep from * twice, ending with k 2, p 2, yo, p 2 tog, k 2, p 3, k 5.

Sleeve: Pick up and purl 77 sts and put 1st 12 sts on holder, p across to last 12 sts, put these last sts on 2nd holder. Turn, knit 33 sts, turn; sl 1, p 13, turn; sl 1, k 16, turn; sl 1, p 19, turn; sl 1, k 22, turn; sl 1, p 25, turn; sl 1, k 28, turn; sl 1, p 31, turn; sl 1, k 34, turn; sl 1, p 37, turn; sl 1, k 40, turn; sl 1, p 43, turn; sl 1, k 46, turn; sl 1, p 50, turn; sl 1, k 52, slip 12 stitches from holder to dpn.

Row 1: P 1st st tog with 1 st from dpn, p to last st, p it tog with st from dpn at this end of work.

Row 2: K 1 st on dpn tog with 1 st on main needle, k to last st, k this st tog with st from dpn. Rep these 2 rows until all sts on dpn have been worked (53 sts). P 1 row even.

Next row: K 14, (k 2 tog) 13 times, k last 13 sts.

Row 2: P. *Row 3:* K. *Row 4:* P.

Row 5: K 1, * yo, k 2 tog, rep from *, ending with k 1.

Row 6: P. Change to No. 2 needles and work 5 rows of garter st. Bind off on wrong side.

Collar: With wrong side of dress toward you and using No. 3 needles, beg at 6th cast-off stitch on left front, pick up 14 sts on left front, 1 st at shoulder seam, 25 sts across back of neck, 1 st at shoulder seam, and 14 sts on right front (leaving 6 cast-off sts not picked up).

Row 1: P. *Row 2:* K inc 1 st in every 5th st across (66 sts).

Row 3: P. *Row 4:* K. *Row 5:* P. *Row 6:* K. *Row 7:* P.

Row 8: K 2 tog, k to last 2 sts, sl 1, k 1, psso.

Row 9: Turn 1st 2 sts around on left needle to p tog through back of loop, p to last 2 sts, p 2 tog.

Row 10: Rep Row 8.

Row 11: Rep Row 9; break yarn.

Attach yarn at front edge of collar on left side, pick up 10 sts around curve of collar, k across collar sts and pick up 10 sts around right collar curve.

Row 13: P 1, yo, p 2 tog, across end with yo, p 1.

Row 14: K. *Row 15:* With No. 2 needles, k.

Row 16: K. *Row 17:* K and bind off; loosely stitch down collar to center of band at each front edge.

Finishing: Weave in ends. Sew side seams, matching patterns. Sew on 12 buttons down front. Steam lightly.

Pink and Blue Sweater and Trousers

shown on page 108

Materials

Pingouin Pingorex Baby (50-gram balls): *for sweater,* 1 ball each of No. 102 light blue (A), No. 111 rose (B), and No. 103 white (C). *For trousers,* 1 ball No. 103 white (C), scraps of No. 102 light blue (A); sizes 2 and 3 knitting needles, or size to obtain gauge below; 3 white buttons; elastic.

Gauge: With larger needles over st st, 32 sts = 4 inches; 43 rows = 4 inches.
Abbreviations: See pages 218-219.

Instructions

Directions are for size 6-9 months; changes for size 12 months follow in parentheses. Finished chest size is 19 (20) inches.

Note: Sweater is worked in 1 piece, beg at lower front edge.

Sweater: With smaller needles and A, cast on 75 (81) sts. Work in k 1, p 1 ribbing for 1 inch. Change to larger needles and work with A in st st for 4 rows.

Next row: Work 1st 7 (10) sts in A; referring to chart (page 118), complete row, working 1 st per square in color indicated. Work even until length measures 6¼ (7) inches, or until 3 rows past the 2nd (3rd) row of dot motifs have been completed.

*Neck opening and left front sleeve: Next row—*Work across 37 (40) sts; sl rem sts to holder to be worked later. Keeping center opening edge even, cast on at armhole edge for sleeve as follows: 9 (10) sts 4 times, and 12 (14) sts once—85 (94) sts.

continued

Eliminate dot motif at center of sweater front. Work even until length measures 8¾ (9½) inches.

Neck shaping: Cast off 7 (8) sts at center edge and continue casting off at neck edge every other row as follows: 3 sts once, 2 sts once, 1 st 4 times—69 (77) sts. Work even until total length measures 10¼ (11) inches, or 2 rows past the 5th row of motifs. Mark end of each row for center of work (top of shoulder). Continue working dot pattern, but reversing direction of "arrow," and inc at neck edge on every alternate row as follows: 1 st twice, 14 (15) sts once—85 (94) sts. Sl sts to a holder.

Right front and sleeve: Sl 38 (40) sts from 1st holder to needles and work same as for the left front and sleeve. Work until incs behind the neck have been completed.

Next row: Work across sts on needle; sl sts from holder to left-hand needle and complete as for other side. Keeping to pat as established, work even until total length measures 13½ (14¼) inches or after the 9th row of blue motifs on a white background has been completed, cast off for sleeves as follows 12 (14) sts once, and 9 (10) sts 4 times—75 (81) sts. Complete back of sweater as for front, reversing instructions.

□ Rose   1 Square = 1 Stitch
✕ Light Blue

Sleeve borders: With smaller needles and A, pick up and k 44 (46) sts along sleeve edge and work in k 1, p 1 ribbing for 1 inch. Cast off.

Stitch side and sleeve seams.

With smaller needles and A, pick up and k 85 (89) sts around neckline and work in k 1, p 1 ribbing for ½ inch. Cast off. With smaller needles and A, pick up and k 33 sts along the right front opening and work 4 rows in ribbing, marking for 3 buttonholes on Row 1.

Row 2: Work in ribbing to buttonhole marker, cast off 2 sts, work to next marker, cast off 2 sts, work to next marker, cast off 2 sts; complete row.

Row 3: Cast on 2 sts above each cast-off grp.

Row 4: Work in ribbing as established. Cast off. Work other side of front opening similarly, omitting buttonholes. Sew on buttons.

Trousers: *Front:* Beg at lower edge of 1 leg with C, cast on 36 (39) sts. Work in k 1, p 1 ribbing for ½ inch. Change to larger needles and st st and work even for 5 rows. Beg with Row 45 of chart (below, left), work 2-color pat with A, beg on the 8th st.

Inside leg shaping: Inc 1 st at right-hand side of work every 4th row 4 times—40 (43) sts. When total length measures 2¼ inches, and 2 rows of motifs have been worked, sl sts to a holder and set aside.

Work 2nd leg similarly, reversing position of motifs and shaping.

Joining row: Work across sts on needle, cast on 3 sts, work sts from holder—83 (89) sts. Work 1 more row of motifs in pat established. Drop A. Work even until total length measures 7½ (8) inches. Change to smaller needles and work in k 1, p 1 ribbing for 1 inch. Cast off.

Back: Work same as for front until total length measures 8¼ (8¾) inches.

Back shaping: Leave 7 (8) sts unworked at each end of every alternate row 5 times. Change to smaller needles and work in k 1, p 1 ribbing across all sts. Cast off.

Finishing: Sew side seams and inside leg seams. Thread 3 rounds of elastic through waistband sts.

Crocheted Bib

shown on page 109

Materials

J. & P. Coats Knit-Cro-Sheen mercerized cotton (250-yard ball): 1 ball each of No. 1 white and No. 46A mid rose *or* No. 25 crystal blue; size 3 steel crochet hook, or size to obtain gauge; 1½ yards ¼-inch-wide satin ribbon.

Gauge: 9 sc = 1 inch; 5 rows = 1 inch.
Abbreviations: See pages 218-219.

Instructions

Finished size is 5¾ inches across.

Beg at neck edge of center section with white, ch 29.

Row 1: Sc in 2nd ch from hook and in each ch across—28 sc. Mark Row 1 for wrong side; ch 1, turn.

Row 2: Sc in back lp of 1st 13 sc; make 2 sc in back lp of next sc—inc made; sc in back lp of each rem 14 sc; ch 1, turn.

Row 3: Sc in back lp of 1st 13 sc, inc in back lp of next sc, sc in back lp of each rem sc; ch 1, turn. *Note:* Hereafter, work in back lp of each sc throughout.

Rows 4-5: Sc in 1st 14 sc, inc in next sc, sc in each rem sc; ch 1, turn.

Rows 6-7: Sc in 1st 15 sc, inc in next sc, sc in each rem sc; ch 1, turn.

Rows 8-9: Sc in 1st 16 sc, inc in next sc, sc in each rem sc; ch 1, turn.

Rows 10-11: Sc in 1st 17 sc, inc in next sc, sc in rem sc; ch 1, turn.

Rows 12-13: Sc in 1st 18 sc, inc in next sc, sc in each rem sc—40 sc on Row 13. Fasten off.

Next section: Foundation row—With pink, ch 17; with wrong side of center section facing, sc in end st at neck edge, (sc in end st on next row) 12 times; sc in back lp of next 21 sc, place a contrasting color thread bet last 2 sc worked for marker, sc in back lp of next 19 sc, (sc in end st on next row) 13 times; ch 18, turn.

Row 1: Sc in 2nd ch from hook, sc in next 16 ch, sc in back lp of each sc to 1 sc before marker, inc in next sc, carry marker up bet last and next sc on each row; sc in back lp of each sc to next ch, sc in last 17 ch; ch 1, turn.

Row 2: Sc in back lp of each sc to 1 sc before marker, inc in back lp of next sc, sc in back lp of each rem sc.

118

Rows 3-4: Rep Row 2—104 sc on Row 4; ch 1, turn. Now work around outer and neck edge as follows:

Rnd 1: Sc in back lp of each sc to opposite corner, (sc in end st of next row) 3 times; sc in each ch to center section, now make 14 sc evenly spaced across center section; sc in each rem ch to next corner, (sc in end of next row) 3 times. Join to 1st sc.

Beading rnd: Ch 5, sk 1 st, * dc in next st, ch 2, sk 1 st. Rep from * around. Join with sl st in 3rd ch of ch-5.

Next rnd: Sl st in next sp, ch 1, * sc in next sp, ch 3, sl st in same sp, ch 2. Rep from * around. Join, fasten off.

Draw ribbon through beading rnd and secure. Cut two 18-inch lengths of ribbon. Fold tucks at 1 end of each length and sew to narrow ends of bib. Make rosettes of ribbon scraps and sew to bib fronts.

Crocheted Afghan

shown on page 109

Materials

Unger Roly Sport (1.75-ounce balls): 4 balls white, 2 balls light green, 1 ball each of light pink, light yellow, lavender, and light blue; size F aluminum crochet hook, or size to obtain gauge given below.

Gauge: Each square measures 5x5 inches.
Abbreviations: See pages 218-219.

Instructions

Granny square: With 1 color, ch 5; sl st to form ring.

Rnd 1: Ch 3 (counts as 1st dc), 2 dc in ring—beg dc-grp made; ch 1, (3 dc in ring, ch 1) 3 times; join with sl st to top of beg ch-3. Fasten off.

Rnd 2: Attach another color in any ch-1 sp, make beg dc-grp, ch 1, 3 dc in same sp, (3 dc, ch 1, 3 dc) in next sp—corner dc-grp made, ch 1 three times; sl st to top of beg ch-3. Fasten off.

Rnd 3: Attach another color in any corner sp, make beg dc-grp, ch 1, 3 dc in same sp, * 3 dc in next sp, ch 1,

corner grp in next corner sp. Rep from * around, ending with ch 1, 3 dc in next sp; sl st to top of beg ch-3. Fasten off.

Rnds 4-5: Rep Rnd 3, making 1 additional 3-dc grp along each side, and working each rnd in a separate color.

Rnd 6: With white, rep Rnd 4.

Rnd 7: With white, ch 1, sc in same place as join, sc in each of next 2 dc, (sc, ch 2, sc) in corner sp; continue around, making sc in top of each dc, sk each ch-1, and working (sc, ch 2, sc) in each corner. Fasten off.

Make 21 granny squares.

Flower square: With yellow, ch 5; sl st to form ring.

Rnd 1: (Ch 5, sc in ring) 8 times—8 lps. Fasten off.

Rnd 2: With pink, blue, or lavender, attach yarn from wrong side to ring (not to sc in ring), * ch 6, sk next ch-5 lp, sc in ring at next lp. Rep from * around, sl st to 1st sc; turn.

Rnd 3: With right side facing, and pulling lps forward to work behind them, in each ch-6 lp around, work 7 dc and sc; sl st to 1st st; turn.

Rnd 4: With wrong side facing, ch 3, * sl st to 4th dc of petal, ch 7. Rep from * around; ending with sl st in same place as 1st sl st; turn.

Rnd 5: With right side facing, work sc, hdc, 3 dc, ch 1, 3 dc, hdc and sc in each ch-7 lp around; sl st to 1st sc. Fasten off.

Rnd 6: With right side facing, attach green in any ch-1 sp (in center of any petal), ch 3, 2 dc in same sp, ch 1, 3 dc in same sp, * ch 1, 3 dc bet dc and next hdc of same petal, ch 1, 3 dc bet 1st hdc and 1st dc of next petal, ch 1 (3 dc, ch 1, 3 dc) in ch-1 sp of petal for corner. Rep from * around, ending with 3 dc bet dc and hdc, ch 1, 3 dc bet hdc and dc, ch 1; sl st to top of beg ch-3. Do not fasten off.

Rnd 7: Turn, ch 1, sl st in last ch-1 sp made; ch 3, turn. Work 2 dc in same sp as ch-3, work as for Rnd 5 of granny square. Fasten off green.

Rnds 8-9: With white, work same as for Rnds 6-7 of granny square. Make 21 flower squares, 7 each of pink, blue, and lavender squares.

Assembly: Arrange squares in pleasing pattern, alternating granny and flower squares. Crochet tog.

Border: Work 4 rnds sc around edge in white, working (sc, ch 2, sc) in each corner.

Knitted Overalls

shown on page 110

Materials

Pingouin Pingorex Baby (50-gram balls): 2 balls No. 102 blue; sizes 2 and 3 knitting needles, or size to obtain gauge below; 2 buttons; ½-inch-wide elastic.

Gauge: With larger needles over st st, 31 sts = 4 inches; 42 rows = 4 inches.
Abbreviations: See pages 218-219.

Instructions

Directions are for size 3 months; changes for sizes 6 months and 9 months follow in parentheses. Finished chest size is 16 (18, 20) inches. Overalls are worked in 1 piece, beg at leg cuff.

Pat st: Row 1 (cables will appear on wrong side): * P 4, k 4. Rep from * across.

Rows 2-3: K the k sts, p the p sts.

Row 4: * Sl 2 sts to cable needle and hold in front of work, p 2, p 2 from cable needle, k 4. Rep from * across.

Rows 5-9: K the k sts, p the p sts.

Row 10: P 4, * sl 2 sts to cable needle and hold in back of work, k 2, k 2 from the cable needle. P 4. Repeat from * across.

Row 11-15: K the k sts, p the p stitches. Rep Rows 1-15 for pat.

Beg at bottom edge of leg with larger needles, cast on 74 (80, 86) sts. Work 6 rows garter st. Change to st st and work even until total length measures 6¼ (7, 8) inches. Inc 1 st each end of every 4th row 6 times, 1 st at each end of every other row twice—90 (96, 102) sts. Sl sts to holder and set aside.

Work other leg similarly. *Joining row:* Working across sts on needle, cast off 1st 2 sts, work across sts to within last 2 sts, work 2 sts tog, join sts on holder, working 1st 2 sts tog; complete row.

Next row: Cast off 1st 2 sts—174 (186, 198) sts. Body is now established—mark the center 2 sts for front; seam is to fall along center back.

Body shaping: Continue in st st, dec 1 st at each end of every 4th row 8 times, every 6th row 3 times, *and at the continued* *same time,* dec 1 st each side of center 2 sts every 4th row 6 times—140 (152, 164) sts. Work even until total length measures 14¼ (15¼, 16½) inches. Work across center 61 (67, 73) sts. Then work 9 additional sts and turn, then work 18 sts and turn. Continue in this way, always adding 9 sts on each side until all sts worked. Change to smaller needles and work in k 1, p 1 ribbing for ½ inch.

Buttonhole row: Work across 20 sts, cast off 3 sts, work to within last 23 sts, cast off 3 sts; complete row.

Next row: Cast on 3 sts above each grp of cast-off sts. Continue in ribbing as established until total length of ribbing measures 1¼ inches.

Bib: Cast off 47 (53, 59) sts at beg of next 2 rows—46 sts rem at center for bib. Change to larger needles and work 1st 5 sts of row in k 1, p 1 ribbing; work next 36 sts in pat st; complete row in ribbing. Keeping center 36 sts in pat st, work even until bib measures 3¼ inches. Change to smaller needles and work in k 1, p 1 ribbing across for ½ inch.

Straps: Work across 1st 9 sts in ribbing as established, attach another ball of yarn and cast off center 28 sts; complete row in ribbing. Working both sides at once, work even until straps measure 11 inches. Cast off.

Stitch back and leg seams. Sew buttons to straps. Stitch elastic to ankles.

One-Piece Romper

shown on page 111

Materials

Pingouin Perle fin (50-g balls): 2 balls No. 27 blue; sizes 2 and 3 knitting needles, or size to obtain gauge given below.

Gauge: With larger needles over st st, 30 sts = 4 inches; 40 rows = 4 inches.
Abbreviations: See pages 218-219.

Instructions

Directions are for size 6 months; changes for sizes 9 months and 12 months follow in parentheses. Finished chest size is 18 (20, 22) inches.

Front: Beg at lower edge of 1 leg with smaller needles, cast on 31 (35, 39) sts and (1st row) work in k 1, p 1 or (2nd row) p 1, k 1 ribbing for ½ (¾,

¾) inch. Change to larger needles and st st, inc 1 st at left-hand side of work every other row 3 times. Work even until total length measures 1¼ (1¼, 1¼) inches. Sl sts to holder.

Work a 2nd leg, reversing shapings.

Joining row: Work across sts on needle, then work across sts on holder—68 (76, 84) sts.

Work even until total length measures 6¾ (7½, 8¼) inches.

Bib shaping: At each end, cast off 6 sts once (56 sts left on needle), 2 sts 4 times (40 sts left on needle), and 1 st 8 (10, 12) times—24 (28, 32) sts left on needle. Change to smaller needles and work in k 1, p 1 ribbing for ½ inch. Cast off.

Back: Work same as for front.

Pocket: With larger needles, cast on 30 (36, 42) sts and work even in st st until total length measures 2½ (3, 3½) inches. Change to smaller needles and work in k 1, p 1 ribbing for ½ inch. Cast off.

Straps (make 2): With larger needles, cast on 11 (13, 15) sts and (1st row) work in k 1, p 1 or (2nd row) p 1, k 1 ribbing until total length measures 12½ (15, 17¼) inches. Cast off.

Finishing: Sew side and inside leg seams. Stitch pocket in place, aligning top of pocket with armholes. Stitch the straps along the back and the front armholes, then stitch the edges along the side seam.

Cloud Trousers

shown on page 111

Materials

Pingouin Pingorex Baby (50-gram balls): 2 (3) balls No. 102 blue (A), 1 (1) ball No. 103 white (B), scraps of No. 144 red (C); sizes 2 and 3 knitting needles, or size to obtain gauge below; 2 buttons.

Gauge: With larger needles over st st, 30 sts = 4 inches; 41 rows = 4 inches.
Abbreviations: See pages 218-219.

Instructions

Directions are for size 3 months; changes for size 6 months follow in parentheses. Finished chest size is 16 (18) inches.

Front: Beg at crotch with larger needles, cast on 31 sts. Work in st st, casting on at each end of every other row

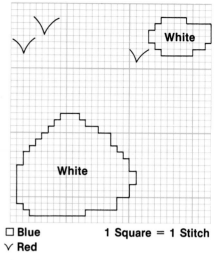

White

White

□ Blue
∨ Red

1 Square = 1 Stitch

for the legs as follows: *For size 3 months:* 6 sts 4 times, and 8 sts twice; *for size 6 months:* 6 sts 1, 7 sts 3 times, and 8 sts twice—111 (117) sts.

Work even until total length measured along edge is 1¼ (1½) inches. Dec 1 st each end of every 8th row 6 times—99 (105) sts. Work even until total length of side measures 6 (6¼) inches.

Next row: Dec 26 sts evenly spaced across—73 (79) sts. Change to smaller needles and work in k 1, p 1 ribbing for ¾ inch.

Next 2 rows: Cast off 16 (19) sts at beg of row—41 sts. Change to larger needles.

Bib: Mark center 31 sts. Keeping center sts in st st, work 5 sts along each outside edge in seed st.

Row 1: * (K 1, p 1) twice, k 1, work across in st st to last 5 sts, (k 1, p 1) twice, k 1.

Row 2: (P 1, k 1) twice, p 1, work across in st st to last 5 sts (p 1, k 1) twice, p 1. Rep Rows 1 and 2, inc 2 sts evenly spaced across 1st row—43 sts. Work even until total length measures 4 inches. Change to B and work across all 43 sts in seed st for ½ inch.

Next row: Work seed st over 1st 5 sts, cast off center 33 sts, work last 5 sts in seed st. Attach another ball of yarn at other strap and, working both sides at once, work seed st over rem 5 sts each side until total length measures 9¾ inches. Cast off.

Back: Beg at crotch, pick up and k 31 sts across cast-on edge. Work same as for front until total length measured along sides is 6 (6¼) inches.

Back shaping: Work in shortened rows as follows: Work across 10 sts; turn, slip 1st st on left-hand needle to right-hand needle, work back to beg, turn. Work across 20 sts; turn, slip 1st st on left-hand needle to right-hand needle, work back to beg, turn. Work across 30 sts, slip 1st st on left-hand needle to right-hand needle; turn, work back to beg, turn. Work across 40 sts; turn, slip 1st st on left-hand needle to right-hand needle, work back to beg, turn. Work in same way across the sts at other edge, then work 1 row across all sts, dec 26 sts evenly spaced across—73 (79) sts. Work even in ribbing for ¼ inch.

Buttonhole row: Mark center 22 sts; cast off 2 sts on outer side of markers.

Next row: Cast on 2 sts above cast-off sts. Work even until ribbing equals that of front.

Refer to chart (left), and work cloud pat across front of bib in duplicate stitch. Embroider birds with fly stitch.

Using smaller needles and A, pick up and k 73 (79) sts around each leg opening and work in k 1, p 1 ribbing for ½ inch. Cast off. Sew side seams; sew buttons to ends of straps.

Cloud Cardigan

shown on page 111

Materials

Pingouin Pingorex Baby (50-g balls): 2 (2) balls No. 102 blue (A), 1 (1) ball No. 103 white (B), scraps of No. 144 red (C); sizes 2 and 3 knitting needles, or size to obtain gauge given below; 4 buttons.

Gauge: With larger needles, over st st, 30 sts = 4 inches; 41 rows = 4 inches.
Abbreviations: See pages 218-219.

Instructions

Directions are for size 3 months; changes for size 6 months follow in parentheses. Finished chest size is 16 (18) inches.

Note: Cardigan body is worked in 1 piece.

Beg at lower edge with smaller needles and A, cast on 143 (155) sts. Work in k 1, p 1 ribbing for ¾ inch. Change to larger needles and work even in st st until total length measures 5½ (6¼) inches.

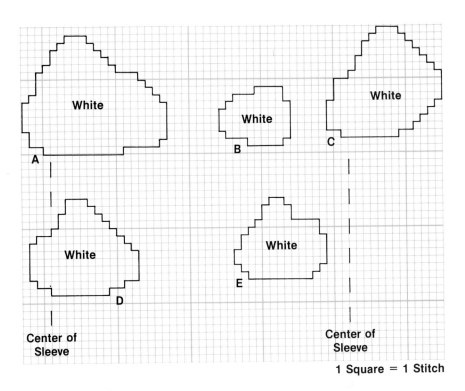

1 Square = 1 Stitch

Armhole shaping: Work across 30 (33) sts for right front, cast off 11 sts for right armhole, work across 61 (67) sts for back, cast off 11 sts for left armhole, work across rem 30 (33) sts for left front. Working over sts for left front only, cast off sts at neck edge as follows: (1 st every 2nd row; 1 st every 4th row) 7 times; then dec 1 more st after 2 rows. Work even until total length measures 9½ (10½) inches, ending at armhole edge.

Shoulder shaping: Cast off at armhole edge every other row as follows: 5 (6) sts 3 times.

Attach yarn at right front, and complete as for left front, reversing shaping. Attach yarn at back, and work even until total length measures 9½ (10½) inches.

Back shoulder shaping: Cast off 5 (6) sts at beg of next 4 rows. *Neck shaping:* Work across 5 (6) sts; cast off center 31 sts. Work across 5 (6) sts, work 1 row even each side; cast off rem sts.

Sleeves: With smaller needles and A, cast on 40 (44) sts and work in k 1, p 1 ribbing for ¾ inch. Change to larger needles and work in st st, inc 10 (12) sts evenly spaced across 1st row—50 (56)

sts. Inc 1 st at each end of every 8th row 5 times—60 (66) sts. Work even until length measures 7 (8) inches. Cast off.

Front borders: With smaller needles and B, cast on 11 sts and work in k 1, p 1 ribbing for ¼ inch.

Buttonhole row: Work 4 sts in ribbing, cast off next 3 sts; complete row.

Next row: Cast on 3 sts above cast-on sts. Work even in ribbing as established, making 3 more buttonhole spaces 1¼ (1½) inches apart. Continue in ribbing until total length of border equals measurement around front and neck opening of cardigan. Cast off.

Clouds: Using B and duplicate stitch, and referring to the chart (above), work cloud A on the right front, positioning it 1½ inches from lower edge and ¾ inch from front edge. Stitch cloud B on left front, positioning it ¾ inch from lower edge and 2¼ inches in from front edge. Stitch cloud C on left front, positioning it 4¼ inches from lower edge and ¾ inch in from front edge. Stitch cloud D on right sleeve, positioning it 1¼ inches from lower edge of sleeve and centered as shown on diagram. Stitch cloud E on left sleeve, positioning it 4¾ inches from lower edge of sleeve and centered as shown on diagram. With scraps of C, embroider 3 birds on right front and 2 on left front using fly stitches.

continued

121

To assemble the cardigan, stitch the front pieces to the back along the shoulder seams. Then stitch the side seams together. Sew each of the underarm sleeve seams and set in the sleeves. Finish by stitching the border along the front and neck opening and stitching buttons in place.

Knitted Afghan

shown on page 112

Materials

Unger Roly Sport (1.75-ounce balls): 5 balls white, 1 ball each of light yellow, light green, peach, light blue, aqua, rose, and lavender; size 8 knitting needles, or size to obtain gauge given below; size G aluminum crochet hook.

Gauge: With 2 strands of yarn tog over garter st, 4 sts = 1 inch; 8 rows = 1 inch.
Abbreviations: See pages 218-219.

Instructions

Square: With 1 strand of white and 1 strand of a color held tog, cast on 20 sts. Work even in garter st (k each row) until work measures 5 inches. Cast off.

Make 5 grps of 4 same-color squares and 4 grps of 3 same-color squares—32 squares in all. (If you use a total of 7 colors, you will have to repeat 2 colors once.)

Arrange squares diagonally, referring to photograph for placement. Sew, crochet, or weave the squares together.

Border: Attach 2 strands of white along any edge of outer square. Sc around, working inside points so that work lies flat, and working (sc, ch 2, sc) in each outer point; join to 1st sc; ch 1.

Next rnd: Continue working sc around, sk 2 sc at either side of each inside point, and working outer points as before. Work 4 rnds total in white. Fasten off.

Bow-Tie Outfit

shown on page 113

Materials

Pingouin Pingolaine (50-gram balls): *for trousers,* 2 balls No. 01 white (A). *For vest,* 1 ball No. 01 white (A). *For cardigan,* 2 balls No. 01 white (A). *For*

all garments, 1 ball No. 22 green (B). *For vest and cardigan,* scraps of No. 20 fuchsia (C), No. 23 blue (D), No. 19 yellow (E), and No. 21 lilac (F). Also, sizes 2 and 3 knitting needles, or size to obtain gauge given below; 2 buttons for trousers, 3 for vest, and 6 for cardigan.

Gauge: With larger needles over st st, 30 sts = 4 inches; 40 rows = 4 inches.
Abbreviations: See pages 218-219.

Instructions

Directions are for size 9 months; changes for size 12 months and toddler size 3 follow in parentheses. Finished chest size is 19 (20) inches.

Trousers: *Back:* Beg at 1 leg edge, with smaller needles and A, cast on 30 (32, 40) sts and work in k 1, p 1 ribbing for ¼ (¼, ¾) inch. Change to larger needles and st st, inc 18 (19, 21) sts evenly spaced across 1st row—48 (51, 61) sts. Work even until total length measures 2¾ (3¼, 4½) inches, ending on wrong side, sl sts to holder. Work a 2nd leg similarly.

Joining row: Work sts of 2nd leg; sl sts of 1st leg to left-hand needle and complete row—96 (102, 122) sts. Work even until total length measures 9½ (10¼, 13) inches.

Back shaping: Work to within last 8 (8, 10) sts; do not work rem sts, turn, sl 1st st on left-hand needle to right-hand needle. Rep last row 3 times more. Change to smaller needles and work across entire row in k 1, p 1 ribbing, dec 31 (31, 34) sts evenly spaced across—65 (71, 81) sts. Work even in ribbing for ¼ (¼, ½) inch.

Buttonhole row: Work across 1st 16 (18, 20) sts in ribbing, cast off 2 sts, work next 29 (31, 44) sts in ribbing, cast off 2 sts; complete row.

Next row: Cast on 2 sts above cast-off sts of previous row. Work even until total length of ribbing at back measures 1¼ (1¼, 2½) inches. Cast off.

Front: Work same as for back, omitting back shaping. When total length measures 9½ (10¼, 13) inches, dec 25 (24, 32) sts evenly spaced across last row—71 (78, 90) sts. Change to smaller needles and work in k 1, p 1 ribbing for 1¼ (1¼, 2½) inches, ending with a wrong-side row.

Next 2 rows: Cast off 15 (17, 19) sts at beg of rows—41 (44, 52) sts rem. Change to larger needles, and referring to chart (above), work bib with A and

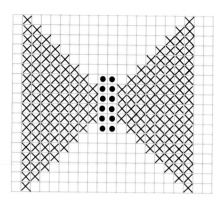

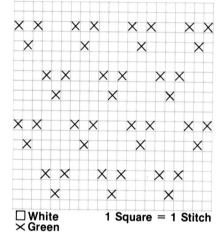

☐ **White**   **1 Square = 1 Stitch**
✕ **Green**

B. Work even with both colors until total length of bib measures 3½ (4, 6) inches. Sl sts to holder.

With smaller needles and A, pick up and k 35 (37, 44) sts along each side of the bib and work 3 (3, 6) rows in k 1, p 1 ribbing. Cast off. With smaller needles and A, rejoin yarn at top edge of bib and sl sts from holder to needle, picking up and k 3 (3, 4) sts at each end along border edges. Work 3 (3, 6) rows in ribbing, dec 1 st on the 1st row *for size 12 months only.*

Next row: Work in ribbing over 1st 10 (10, 12) sts; cast off center 27 (29, 36) sts; complete row. Attach another ball of yarn at other strap, and working both sides at once, work even until total length of straps measure 11¾ (12½, 14) inches. Cast off.

Stitch side seams. Stitch leg seams. Sew buttons to ends of straps.

Vest: *Back:* Using smaller needles and A, cast on 72 (78, 86) sts and work 6 (6, 10) rows in k 1, p 1 ribbing.

Change to larger needles and work even, dividing sts as follows: Work the 36 (39, 43) sts at right-hand side with A in st st; work the 36 (39, 43) sts on left-hand side with A and B in same pat as for bib of trousers. Work even until total length measures 5 (5½, 7) inches, or after the 9th (10th, 10th) row of pat. Now reverse the pats and work the 36 (39, 43) sts on the right-hand side with A and B in pat st, and the 36 (39, 43) sts on left-hand side with A in st st. Work even until total length measures 5½ (6, 7½) inches.

Armhole shaping: Cast off 3 (4, 5) sts at beg of next 2 rows, 2 sts at beg of next 2 rows, and 1 st at beg of next 2 rows—60 (64, 70) sts. Work even in pat as established until total length measures 9¾ (10½, 12) inches.

Shoulder shaping: Cast off 5 (6, 7) sts at beg of next 2 rows.

Next row: Cast off 6 (6, 6) sts at beg of row. Working across, next 6 sts, cast off center 26 (28, 32) sts, work across 12 sts.

Following 3 rows: Work on 12 sts of left side only and cast off 6 sts at beg of row. Attach another ball of yarn at neck edge on right side and work to correspond to left shoulder side.

Right front: With smaller needles and A, cast on 36 (39, 44) sts and work 6 (6, 10) rows of k 1, p 1 ribbing. Change to larger needles and add B; work in 2-color pat as for back, beg the 1st motif on the 4th st of the row. Continue working pat until 3 (3, 6) rows of triangle motif have been worked, ending at front edge (14, 14, 28 rows).

Next row: Work 1st 10 (10, 13) sts of row in pat; then beg bow-tie pat, referring to chart (opposite) and using C for the bows and E for the center. When motif is completed, work in 2-color pat as established. Work even with A until total length measures 4¾ (5, 7½) inches, ending at neck edge.

Neck shaping: Cast off 1 st at neck edge every other row 2 (4, 6) times; then (dec 1 st every other row, 1 st every 4th row) 5 times.

At the same time, when work measures 5 (5½, 6½) inches, drop B. Work with A in st st until total length measures 5½ (6, 7½) inches, ending at armhole edge.

Armhole shaping: Cast off 3 (4, 5) sts at beg of next row. Work 1 row even.

Next row: Cast off 2 (2, 2) sts at beg of row. Work 1 row even.

Following row: Cast off 1 (1, 2) st at beg of row. Work even 18 (18, 24) sts until total length to shoulder shaping equals that of back.

Shoulder shaping: Cast off 6 (6, 7) sts at beg of next 3 (3, 2) rows at shoulder edge. *For size 3 only:* Cast off 5 sts at beg of next 2 rows at shoulder edge.

Left front: Work as for right front, reversing all shapings. Work in A only until same number of rows to bow-tie motif. Work motif, using E for bows and F for center. Add B and beg 2-color pat when length measures 5 (5½, 7½) inches.

Front borders: With smaller needles and A, cast on 10 (10, 12) sts and work in k 1, p 1 ribbing. When total length measures ¾ inch, work buttonhole as follows:

Buttonhole row: Work 4 (4, 5) sts in ribbing, cast off 2 sts; complete row.

Next row: Cast on 2 sts above cast-off sts. Work 2 more buttonholes, spaced 1½ (1¾, 2) inches apart. When total length equals measurement of neck and front opening, cast off.

Armhole borders (make 2): With smaller needles and A, cast on 10 (10, 12) sts and work in k 1, p 1 ribbing for 9 (9¾, 11) inches. Cast off.

Assembly: Stitch shoulder seams and side seams. Stitch borders to front and armholes. Sew on buttons.

Cardigan: *Back:* With smaller needles and A, cast on 72 (78, 86) sts and work in k 1, p 1 ribbing for 1 inch. Change to larger needles and continue in st st, working the 2-color pat as for the back of the vest, but reversing the side of the pat when total length measures 5½ (6, 7½) inches. Work even in A until total length measures 6¼ (6½, 8) inches.

Armhole shaping: Dec on st at each end of every other row 20 (22, 22) times. Sl rem 32 (34, 42) sts to a holder for back of the neck.

Right front: With smaller needles and A, cast on 36 (39, 44) sts, and work in k 1, p 1 ribbing for 1 (1, 1½) inch. Change to larger needles and continue in 2-color pat. When total length measures 5½ (6, 6) inches, after the 9th (10th, 10th) row of triangles, work even in A until total length measures 6¼ (6½, 8) inches, working armhole shap-

ings as for back. At the same time, after the 3rd armhole shaping, work a bow-tie motif 5 (5, 6) sts in from front center edge, working the bows in D and the center in C. Work until 14 (15, 16) armhole shapings are completed.

Neck shaping: Sl 8 sts from neck edge to spare needle, then cast off 1 st at neck edge every other row 5 (6, 7) times—3 sts. Work these sts tog; fasten off.

Left front: Work as for right front, reversing all shapings, working in A until total length measures 5½ (6, 7½) inches, then work in 2-color pat, adding a bow-tie motif when total length measures 8¼ (9¼, 10) inches, working bows in C and the center in F.

Sleeves: With smaller needles and A, cast on 36 (42, 48) sts and work in k 1, p 1 ribbing for 1 inch. Change to larger needles and work in st st, inc 1 st at each end of every 10th row 6 times—48 (54, 60) sts. Work even until total length measures 7 (8, 9½) inches.

Armhole shaping: Work shaping as for back at each end of row; sl rem 8 (10, 16) sts to holder.

Right front border: With smaller needles and A, cast on 10 (10, 12) sts and work in k 1, p 1 ribbing. Work a buttonhole as for vest. Work 5 more buttonholes, spaced 1½ (1½, 2) inches apart. When total length measures 8¾ (9½, 12) inches, cast off. Work a 2nd border similarly, omitting buttonholes.

Assembly: Join raglan seams, stitch side and sleeve seams. With smaller needles and A, pick up and k 91 (95, 100) sts around neck, including sts left on holders. Work 4 rows in k 1, p 1 ribbing. Cast off.

Stitch the border in place. Sew on buttons.

Duplicate-Stitch Embroidery: You can give your knitted work a new look by using duplicate-stitch embroidery. This stitch (shown on the baby's bow-tie outfit) is used to duplicate the shape of each knitted stitch so that the finished design looks as though it's knitted into the fabric.

Duplicate stitches can be used in many ways. You can turn a plain knitted sweater front into an argyle design by stitching interlocking rows of diamonds across the sweater front. Or add an initial or two to a sweater piece for a monogram that looks knitted in.

continued

The most popular use for duplicate-stitch embroidery is to simulate Fair Isle knitting.

Fair Isle knitting is characterized by multicolored motifs that are repeated across sweater yokes and sleeves to form a patterned band. Traditionally (when the design is knitted in), each color of yarn is carried across the back of the work and brought to the front as it's needed. Using duplicate stitches, however, you can knit the entire piece with just the background color and add the repeat motifs after the sweater piece is completed.

Choose yarn for duplicate stitching that matches the type of yarn used for the background of the sweater (sport-weight, fingering yarn, for example) Or, use a three-ply Persian-type yarn or tapestry wool for stitching. For best results, select yarns with care requirements (washing, dry cleaning) similar to those of the background fabric.

To work duplicate stitches, thread a tapestry or yarn needle with the color of yarn needed for the design. Hold the work's right side toward you, and beginning from the wrong side, insert the needle through the designated stitch from back to front. (The tail end of the yarn should be on the back or wrong side of the piece.)

Following the shape of the stitch on the background fabric, insert the needle through and around the back of the stitch directly above, then back to the front of the work (see diagram). Then reinsert the needle through to the back of the work at the point where the stitch was begun.

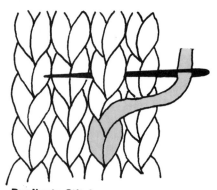

Duplicate Stitch

Crocheted Pullover and Bloomers

shown on page 101

Materials

Coats & Clark Red Heart Sport Yarn: 4 ounces No. 722 light pink, 2 ounces No. 1 white, 2 ounces No. 510 baby aqua; sizes F and G aluminum crochet hooks, or size to obtain gauge; 1 yard round elastic.

Gauge: With larger hook, 9 sts = 2 inches; 9 dc rows = 4 inches.
Abbreviations: See pages 218-219.

Instructions

Directions are for size 6 months; changes for sizes 12 and 18 months follow in parentheses. Finished chest size is 19 (20, 21) inches.

Pullover back: Beg at lower edge with aqua and larger hook, ch 46 (48, 50), with 9 ch sts equal to 2 inches.

Foundation row: Sc in 2nd ch from hook and in each ch across—45 (47, 49) sc; ch 3, turn.

Row 1: Dc in next st and in each st across—45 (47, 49) dc, counting ch-3 as 1 dc. Mark this row for wrong side of work; ch 3, turn.

Row 2: Dc in next st and in each st to turning ch; *yo and draw up a lp in top of turning ch, yo and draw through 2 lps on hook, drop aqua, with white yo and draw through 2 lps on hook to complete dc—color change made on a dc row;* ch 2, turn.

Row 3: With white hdc in next st and in each st to turning ch, *yo and draw up a lp in top of turning ch, drop white, with pink yo and draw through 3 lps on hook to complete hdc—color change made on hdc row—*45 (47, 49) hdc counting ch-2 as 1 hdc; ch 3, turn.

Rows 4-6: With pink, dc in next st and in each st across, dc in top of turning ch; ch 3, turn. At end of Row 6, change to white; ch 2, turn.

Row 7: With white, hdc in next st and in each st across, changing to aqua in last st; ch 3, turn.

Rows 8-9: With aqua, dc in each st across; ch 3, turn. At end of Row 9, change to white; ch 2, turn.

Row 10: With white, hdc in next st and in each st across, changing to pink in last st; ch 3, turn.

Rows 11-14: With pink, dc in each st across; ch 3, turn. At end of Row 14, change to white and ch 23 (25, 27) for 1 sleeve; turn.

Row 15: With white, sc in 2nd ch from hook and in next 21 (23, 25) ch, sc in each st across, drop lp from hook, join a separate strand of white to last st of previous row, ch 22 (24, 26) for other sleeve. Fasten off. Pick up dropped lp, sc in each ch across—89 (95, 101) sts; ch 1, turn.

Row 16: Sc in each st across to last st; *draw up a lp in last st, drop white, with pink yo and draw through 2 lps on hook to complete the sc—*color change made on sc row; ch 2, turn.

Row 17: With pink hdc in next st and in each st across; ch 2, turn.

Row 18: Rep Row 17, changing to white in last st; ch 1, turn.

Row 19: Sc in each st across, changing to aqua in last st; ch 1, turn.

Row 20: With aqua sc in each st across; ch 1, turn.

Row 21: Sc in 1st st; * tr in next st, sc in next st. Rep from * across; ch 1, turn.

Row 22: Sc in each st across, changing to white in last sc; ch 1, turn.

Row 23: With white, sc in each st across, changing to pink in last sc; ch 2, turn.

Rows 24-26: Hdc in next st and in each st across; ch 2, turn.

First neck shaping: Row 1: Hdc in next 32 (34, 36) sts—neck edge; do not work over rem sts; ch 2, turn.

Row 2: Hdc in next st and in each st across, hdc in top of turning ch; ch 2, turn.

Row 3: Hdc in next st and in each st to last st before turning ch; *yo and draw up a lp in next st, yo and draw up a lp in top of turning ch, yo and draw through all 5 lps on hook—hdc dec made at neck edge;* ch 2, turn.

Rows 4-5: Rep Rows 2 and 3 of neck shaping. *For sizes 12 and 18 months only:* Rep Rows 2 and 3 once more. *For all sizes:* Fasten off.

Second neck shaping: Row 1: Sk next 23 (25, 27) sts on last long row worked, join pink in next st, ch 2, hdc in each st across—33 (35, 37) sts; ch 2, turn.

Complete to correspond to the 1st neck shaping.

Front: Work as for back until 24 (26, 26) rows have been completed; ch 2, turn.

First neck shaping: Row 1: Hdc in next 33 (34, 37) sts—neck edge; do not work over rem sts; ch 2, turn. Rep Rows 2 and 3 of 1st neck shaping of back 3 (3, 4) times. Fasten off.

Second neck shaping: Row 1: Sk next 21 (25, 25) sts on last long row worked, join pink in next st, ch 2, hdc in next 33 (34, 37) sts; ch 2, turn. Complete to correspond to 1st neck shaping.

Pin pieces to measurements; dampen and leave to dry. Sew top sleeve and underarm seams; sew side seams.

Ribbing: With white and smaller hook, ch 7 (10, 13).

Row 1: Sc in 2nd ch from hook, and in each ch across—6 (9, 12) sc; ch 1, turn.

Row 2: Working in back lp of each sc, sc in each sc across; ch 1, turn.

Rep Row 2 until strip measures 20 (21, 22) inches, slightly stretched. Sew short edges tog to form a circle and sew in place on lower edge of pullover.

Edging on sleeves: Rnd 1: With wrong side of sleeve facing, and with smaller hook, attach white to under-sleeve seam at cuff; ch 1, sc in joining, sc evenly around; join with sl st in 1st sc.

Rnd 2: Attach aqua in joining, ch 1, and complete as for Rnd 1.

Rnd 3: With white, rep Rnd 2. Fasten off. Fold back lower edge of sleeves for cuffs to desired length.

Neck edging: Rnd 1: With right side facing, and with smaller hook, attach white to a shoulder seam, ch 1, sc in joining, sc evenly around entire neck edge. Join with a sl st in 1st sc. Break off white; turn.

Rnd 2: Attach aqua in joining, ch 1, sc in joining and in each st around; join to 1st sc; ch 1, turn.

Rnd 3: Sc in joining, * tr in next st, sc in next st. Rep from * across. Join to 1st st; turn.

Rnd 4: Attach white in joining, ch 1, sc in each st around. Join. Fasten off.

Bloomers: *Back:* Beg at upper edge with pink and larger hook, ch 45 (47, 51), with 9 ch equal to 2 inches.

Row 1: Dc in 4th ch from hook and in each ch across—43 (45, 49) dc, counting ch-3 as 1 dc; ch 3, turn.

Row 2: Dc in next dc and in each dc to turning ch, dc in top of ch-3; ch 3, turn.

Row 3: Make 2 dc in next st—inc made at beg of row; dc in each dc to last dc; *make 2 dc in last dc*—inc made at end of row; dc in top of turning ch; ch 3, turn. Rep last 2 rows 3 (4, 5) times more—51 (55, 61) dc, counting ch-3 as 1 dc. Then rep Row 2 until total length measures 6 (6½, 7) inches; ch 3, turn.

First leg: Row 1: Dc in next 24, (26, 29) dc; do not work over rem sts; ch 3, turn.

Row 2: Dc in next dc and in each dc across, dc in top of ch 3; ch 3, turn.

Rep last row 2 (3, 4) times more. Fasten off.

Second leg: Sk next st on last long row worked and attach pink in following st, ch 3, dc in each st across—25 (27, 30) sts. Complete as for 1st leg.

Front: Work same as for back.

Ribbing: With white and smaller hook, ch 7. Work ribbing same as for pullover until strip measures 9 (9½, 10) inches, slightly stretched.

Pin pieces to measurements, dampen and leave to dry. Sew side and crotch seams.

Sew short edges of ribbing tog to form a circle and sew in place around upper edge of bloomers.

Leg edgings: With smaller hook, attach white to a crotch seam at lower leg, ch 1, sc in joining, sc evenly around entire leg opening. Join to 1st sc.

Rnd 2: Ch 1, sc in joining, sc in each st around. Join. Fasten off.

Rnd 3: Attach aqua in joining, ch 1, sc in joining, * tr in next st, sc in next st. Rep from * around. Join. Fasten off.

Rnd 4: Attach white in joining, ch 1, sc in joining and in each st around. Join. Fasten off. Draw elastic through waist ribbing and cuff edging to fit.

Ties: With smaller hook and white, make a 24-inch-long ch for each cuff, and one 26- (27-, 29-) inch-long ch for waist. Lace ch through cuff edging and waist ribbing.

Blocking and Assembling a Garment

"Blocking" refers to the shaping of knitted or crocheted pieces to fit body measurements. Block pieces individually to smooth out wrinkles and simplify sewing pieces together.

Because yarns react differently to blocking procedures, yarn labels usually carry specific blocking instructions. For example, you should never touch acrylic yarns with a hot iron.

If the label does not give blocking directions, dampen the pieces with cool water and lay them on a folded sheet or towel. Using rust-proof pins, secure pieces to the blocking surface along outer edges. Keep tension even and smooth out any wrinkles, bumps, or twisted areas.

For flat knitting and crocheting and smooth yarns, cover pieces with a damp, lint-free cloth. Set the iron at a moderate temperature and press the pieces slowly and gently. Allow steam from the cloth to penetrate fibers. Apply light, even pressure, never pushing too hard or fast.

When you have pressed all surfaces, remove the cloth; let pieces dry for at least eight hours. Then remove pins and sew pieces together according to the directions in the pattern.

For raised stitches and textured yarns, hold a steam iron as close as possible to the pieces without actually touching them. Move the iron slowly over each piece, making sure steam penetrates yarn. Dry thoroughly before removing pieces from the board.

Make seams in knitted pieces by weaving, overcasting, backstitching, or crocheting. Use the method that is best suited to the yarn and the pattern.

To weave seams, hold the wrong sides adjacent and draw matching stitches together with yarn and needle.

To overcast seams, hold the right sides together and sew with whipstitches. Reserve this method for sewing ribbed cuffs or attaching collars.

For curved seams and tapered shoulder seams, backstitching is the best method. Just hold the right sides together and make the running stitches using a backstitch.

When assembling pieces made with nubby or tweedy yarns, these methods may cause bumpy seams. So, for these yarns, hold the right sides together and slip-stitch crochet the seams.

125

Country Comforts
to Warm the Heart

Whether your taste runs to elegant home furnishings accents or simple homespun styling, you can produce the desired effect with crochet. In this chapter you'll find imaginative crochet projects to make for your own home or to give as gifts, whichever style you prefer.

♦ For example, substituting wool yarn for fine crochet cotton magically transforms the elegant patterns of yesteryear into inviting country accessories such as these doilies (left).

The original design of the oversize, five-color doily (far left) has been updated by working with a larger hook and crocheting each round with a different color of sportweight wool yarn. The result is a multicolored doily, 23 inches in diameter, that makes the perfect centerpiece for a country table.

The heather-blue wool doily (left) is the result of a similar reworking. Its classic design features a familiar star motif. Worked in yarn instead of fine thread, it measures 32 inches in diameter when completed.

Instructions for all of the crocheted projects in this section begin on page 134.

Crocheted Comforts to Warm the Heart

Over the years, the popularity of crochet has waxed and waned, but crisp handcrafted treasures such as the tablecloth and doily shown here seem to always remain in vogue.

Whether your taste runs to sumptuous elegance or simple homespun styling, crochet work can help to achieve the desired effect.

♦ For example, the elegant pattern (left), combines several of the most popular crochet motifs to produce a cloth fit to grace the table of a queen. Lacy pineapple motifs fan out from a central spider web medallion, cascading into a stately border of scallops and diamonds. The finished tablecloth measures 72 inches in diameter and is worked with a size 10 aluminum crochet hook, using No. 30 ecru crochet cotton. It may take a bit of time to complete, but the effect is one of timeless beauty.

♦ For a smaller project with the same delicate appearance, you might try this rose pinwheel doily (above). It is worked with a size 12 crochet hook and No. 30 crochet cottons, and it features a handsome central spiral pattern with an even dozen delicate pink rose "blooms" on the outer scallops.

Crocheted Comforts
to Warm the Heart

A toasty-warm coverlet is just the thing to ward the chill off a favorite aunt or the newest little member of a family. And the two crocheted throws shown here make perfect gifts for family and friends.

♦ The sprightly colored throw (left) is a traditional ripple pattern, worked in single crochet. The textured ridges are the result of crocheting into the back loops of each row.

We stitched the afghan in a repeating pattern of maroon, gold, green, pink, and blue stripes, accented by wide bands of natural-colored yarn. But the pattern would look equally attractive worked in random, multicolored stripes, or in almost any color scheme of your choice. The finished size of this easy-to-work ripple afghan is approximately 46x68 inches—plenty large enough to wrap up in.

♦ The tri-paneled Victorian coverlet with elegantly scalloped edging (above) is conveniently cradle size (about 29x34 inches).

Although the original of this Victorian beauty is worked in a sturdy wool, you might consider using washable, easy-care yarn if the coverlet is intended as a gift for a newborn baby.

Work the three panels separately in afghan stitches. Next, using the same yarn, embroider the panels with cross-stitches in a graceful pattern of vines, leaves, and flowers. Crochet the scalloped edging separately, then join panels and edging with a lacy filet of chain stitches.

Because it is worked in small pieces, this cradle blanket is a perfect pick-up-and-go project for those who like to crochet while riding the bus to work, waiting at the doctor's office, or traveling on vacation.

131

Crocheted Comforts
to Warm the Heart

Textured pillows and snuggly afghans lend a cozy touch to any room, and the simple color schemes and country-fresh styling of crocheted accessories blend beautifully with patchwork and pine.

♦ Patterns for the charming quartet of pillows (above) are based on variations of the double crochet stitch. The pillow sham design is worked in tapestry crochet and repeats the lovely Irish chain pattern on the quilt. Each sham is approximately 20x26 inches, excluding the double-ruffled borders.

Four granny squares with two-tone adaptations of the Irish rosepoint pattern are joined for the 12-inch-square pillow top in the foreground. And the fourth pillow top features a tricolored bobble shell pattern, which can easily be enlarged or reduced to cover any size pillow.

All four pillows are worked in 4-ply knitting worsted and backed with matching or contrasting corduroy or velveteen.

♦ These homey afghans (right) are generously proportioned. Each is large enough to cuddle up in by the fire, or to cover the guest bed on a chilly winter's night.

For the textured and tasseled throw (near right), narrow bands of openwork alternate with wider bands worked in the familiar ripple pattern. The blue and white afghan (far right) is composed of thirty-five 12-inch granny squares crocheted in white and variegated blue yarns.

You can easily enlarge or reduce the size of both of these coverlets (to suit your own needs) by adding or subtracting rows or squares.

132

Five-Color Doily

shown on pages 126-127

Materials

One 2-ounce skein of sport-weight yarn in rust, blue, gray, maroon, and pink; size 1 steel crochet hook.

Abbreviations: See pages 218-219.

Instructions

Finished size is 23 inches across.

To work doily pattern in thread, substitute American Thread Puritan mercerized crochet cotton (1 ball, white) and a size 7 steel crochet hook. Delete all color changes. The finished diameter of the doily in thread will be approximately 15 inches.

Rnd 1: With rust ch 5, sl st to form ring; ch 3 (to count as 1 dc), 15 dc in ring; join to top of ch-3—16 dc.

Rnd 2: Ch 8, * sk next dc, dc in next dc, ch 5. Rep from * 6 times; join to 3rd ch of ch 8. Break off.

Rnd 3: Attach blue in any ch-5 lp; ch 3, in same sp work 1 dc, ch 3, 2 dc; * ch 3, in next ch-5 lp work 2 dc, ch 3, 2 dc. Rep from * 6 times; ch 3, join to top of ch 3.

Rnd 4: Sl st in next dc and into next lp; ch 4, work 5 trc in same sp; * ch 1, trc in next lp, ch 1, 6 trc in next lp. Rep from * 6 times; ch 1, trc in next lp, ch 1, join to top of ch-3. Break off.

Rnd 5: Attach gray in 1st trc of any 6-trc grp; ch 1, sc in same st, * (ch 3, sc in next trc) 5 times. Ch 2, 3 dc in next trc, ch 2, sc in next trc. Rep from * 7 times; join last ch-2 to 1st sc.

Rnd 6: Sl st to next lp; ch 1, sc in same lp, * (ch 4, sc in next lp) 4 times; ch 2, 3 dc in center dc of next 3-dc grp, ch 2, sk next lp, sc in next lp. Rep from * 7 times; join to 1st sc.

Rnd 7: Sl st to next lp, ch 1, sc in same lp, * (ch 4, sc in next lp) 3 times; ch 2; in center dc of next 3-dc grp work 3 dc, ch 3, 3 dc, ch 2, sk next lp, sc in next lp. Rep from * 7 times more; join to 1st sc.

Rnd 8: Sl st to next lp, * (ch 4, sc in next lp) twice; ch 2, 3 dc in center dc of next 3-dc grp, ch 2; in next lp work 2 dc, ch 3, 2 dc; ch 2, 3 dc in center dc of next 3-dc grp; ch 2, sk next lp, sc in next lp. Rep from * around; join.

Rnd 9: Sl st to next lp, * ch 4, sc in next lp, ch 2, sk next lp, 3 dc in center dc of next 3-dc grp, ch 2, sk next lp, 7 trc in next lp, ch 2, 3 dc in center of next 3-dc grp, ch 2, sk next lp, sc in next lp. Rep from * around; join. Break off.

Rnd 10: Attach maroon in next ch-4 lp, ch 4, * 3 dc in center dc of next 3-dc grp, ch 2, sc in next trc, (ch 4, sc in next trc) 6 times; ch 2, 3 dc in center dc of next 3-dc grp, sk next lp, trc in next lp. Rep from * around; join to top of ch-4.

Rnd 11: Sl st to center dc of next 3-dc grp, ch 3, 2 dc in same st, * ch 2, sk next lp, (sc in next lp, ch 4) 5 times; sc in next lp, ch 2, (3 dc in center dc of next 3-dc grp) twice. Rep from * around; join to top of ch-3.

Rnd 12: Sl st to next dc, ch 3, 2 dc in same st, * ch 2, sk next lp, (sc in next lp, ch 4) 4 times; sc in next lp, (ch 2, 3 dc in center dc of next 3-dc grp) twice. Rep from * around; join to top of ch-3.

Rnd 13: Sl st to next dc, ch 3, 2 dc in same st, * ch 2, sk next lp, (sc in next lp, ch 4) 3 times; sc in next lp, ch 2, 3 dc in center dc of next 3-dc grp, ch 2, 3 dc in next lp, ch 2, 3 dc in center dc of next 3-dc grp. Rep from * around; join. Break off.

Rnd 14: Attach blue in next dc, ch 3, 2 dc in same st, * ch 2, sk next lp, (sc in next lp, ch 4) twice; sc in next lp, ch 2, 3 dc in center dc of next 3-dc grp; ch 2, skip dc, 3 trc in each of the next 3 dc, ch 2, 3 dc in center of next 3-dc grp. Repeat from * around; join last ch 2 to top of ch 3. Break off.

Rnd 15: Attach pink in next dc, ch 3, 2 dc in same st, * ch 2, sk next lp, sc in next lp, ch 4, sc in next lp, ch 2, 3 dc in center dc of next 3-dc grp, ch 2, (3 trc in next trc, trc in each of next 3 trc) twice; 3 trc in next trc, ch 2, 3 dc in center dc of next 3-dc grp. Rep from * around; join last ch-2 to top of ch-3. Break off.

Rnd 16: Attach rust in next dc, ch 3, 2 dc in same st, * sk next lp, trc in next lp, 3 dc in center dc of next 3-dc grp, ch 2, 3 trc in next trc, trc in each of next 3 trc, 3 trc in next trc, trc in each of next 5 trc, 3 trc in next trc, trc in each of next 3 trc, 3 trc in next trc, ch 2, 3 dc in center dc of 3-dc grp. Rep from * around; join. Break off.

Rnd 17: Attach maroon in next dc, ch 3, 2 dc in same st, * 3 dc in center dc of next 3-dc grp, ch 2, 3 trc in next trc, trc in each of next 5 trc, (3 trc in next trc, trc in next 4 trc) twice; 3 trc in next trc, trc in next 5 trc, 3 trc in next trc, ch 2, 3 dc in center dc of next 3-dc grp. Rep from * around; join. Break off.

Rnd 18: Attach gray in any 1st trc of a trc-grp, ch 4, 2 trc in same st, * (trc in next 7 trc, 3 trc in next trc) 4 times; sk next two 3-dc grps, 3 trc in next trc. Rep from * around; join. Break off.

Rnd 19: Attach pink in same st as join, ch 1, sc in same st, * (ch 5, sk 2 trc, sc in next trc) 14 times; sc in next trc. Rep from * around; join to 1st sc.

Rnd 20: Sl st to next lp, ch 3, 2 dc in same lp, * (ch 3, sc in next lp, ch 3, 3 dc in next lp) 3 times; ch 1, 3 dc in next lp. Rep from * around; join last ch-1 to top of ch-3.

Rnd 21: * (Ch 4, sc in next sc, ch 4, 5 dc in center dc of next 3-dc grp) twice; ch 4, sc in next sc, ch 4, 3 dc in center dc of next 3-dc grp, 5 trc in next ch-1 sp, 3 dc in center of next dc grp, (ch 4, sc in next sc, ch 4, 5 dc in center dc of next 3-dc grp) twice; ch 4, sc in next sc, ch 4, sc in ch-1 sp bet next two 3-dc grps. Rep from * around; join to 1st ch of ch-4.

Rnd 22: Sl st to next lp, ch 1, sc in same lp, * ch 5, sk next lp, sc in next dc (ch 5, sk next dc, sc in next dc) twice; ch 5, sc in next sc. Rep from * once more; ch 5, sk next lp, sc in next dc, (ch 5, sk next st, sc in next st) 5 times, [ch 5, sc in next sc, ch 5, sc in next dc, (ch 5, sk next dc, sc in next dc) twice.] Rep bet [ ]s once more; ch 5, sk next sc, sc in next sc. Rep from 1st * around; join. Break off.

Crocheted Star Doily

shown on pages 126-127

Materials

Five 1.6-ounce skeins Unger Shetland Type Britannia No. 541 lavender; size D aluminum crochet hook.

Abbreviations: See pages 218-219.

Instructions

Finished size is 32 inches across.

Ch 6, join to form ring. *Row 1:* Work 16 sc in ring; join with sl st to 1st sc.

Row 2: Ch 1, sc in same st as sl st; * 2 sc in next sc, sc in next sc *; rep bet *s around. Join to 1st sc—24 sc.

Row 3: Ch 1, sc in same st as sl st and in next sc; * 2 sc in next sc, sc in next 2 sc *; rep bet *s around; join—32 sc.

Row 4: Ch 1, sc in same st as sl st and in next 2 sc; * 2 sc in next sc, sc in next 3 sc *; rep bet *s around; join—40 sc.

Row 5: Ch 1, sc in same st as sl st and in next 8 sc; * 2 sc in next sc, sc in next 9 sc *; rep bet *s around; join—44 sc.

Row 6: Ch 1, sc in same st as sl st and in next 9 sc; * 2 sc in next sc, sc in next 10 sc *; rep bet *s around; join—48 sc.

Row 7: Ch 1, sc in same st as sl st and in next 10 sc; * 2 sc in next sc, sc in next 11 sc *; rep bet *s around; join—52 sc.

Row 8: Ch 1, sc in same st as sl st and in next 11 sc; * 2 sc in next sc, sc in next 12 sc *; rep bet *s around; join—56 sc.

Row 9: Ch 1, sc in same st as sl st and in next 12 sc; * 2 sc in next sc, sc in next 13 sc *; rep bet *s around; join—60 sc.

Row 10: Ch 1, sc in same st as sl st and in next 4 sc; * 2 sc in next sc, sc in next 5 sc *; rep bet *s around; join—70 sc.

Row 11: Ch 1, sc in same st as sl st and in next 5 sc; * 2 sc in next sc, sc in next 6 dc *; rep bet *s around; join—80 sc.

Row 12: Ch 3, in same st as sl st work dc, ch 1, 2 dc; ch 1, * sk 3 sc, in next sc *work a shell of 2 dc, ch 1, 2 dc, ch 1 *;* rep bet *s around. Join last ch-1 to 3rd ch of ch-3 at beg of row—20 shells.

Row 13: Sl st in next dc and in ch-1 sp; ch 3, in same sp work dc, ch 1, 2 dc; * ch 2, sc in ch-1 sp bet shells, ch 2, work a shell in ch-1 sp of shell *; rep bet *s around. End row with ch 2, sc in ch-1 sp bet shells, ch 2, join to 3rd ch of ch-3 at beg of row.

Row 14: Sl st in next dc and in ch-1 sp; ch 3, in same sp work dc, ch 1, 2 dc; ch 3, * work shell in ch-1 sp of next shell. Ch 3 *; rep bet *s around. Join last ch-3 to 3rd ch of ch-3 at beg of row.

Row 15: Ch 4, * dc in ch-1 sp of shell, ch 1, sk dc, dc in next dc, ch 1, dc in 2nd ch of next ch-3 grp, ch 1, dc in next dc, ch 1 *; rep bet *s around. Join last ch-1 to 3rd ch of ch-4 at beg of row—80 ch-1 sp.

Row 16: Ch 1, sc in same st as sl st and in each st around. Join to 1st sc—160 sc.

Rows 17 and 18: Rep Row 16.

Row 19: Ch 4, * sk next sc, dc in next sc, ch 1 *; rep bet *s around. Join last ch-1 to 3rd ch of ch-4 at beg of row.

Row 20: Ch 4, * dc in next dc, ch 1 *; rep bet *s around. Join as in Row 19.

Row 21: Ch 3, in same st work dc, ch 1, 2 dc; ch 1, * sk dc; work shell in next dc, ch 1 *; rep bet *s around. Join last ch-1 to top of ch-3.

Row 22: Rep Row 13.

Row 23: Rep Row 14.

Row 24: Rep Row 15.

Row 25: Sl st in next ch-1 sp; ch 3, in same sp work 2 dc; ch 4, * sk 3 dc, sc in next dc, (2 sc in next ch-1 sp, sc in next dc) 9 times—28 sc; ch 4, sk next 3 ch-1 sps; 3 dc in next ch-1 sp, ch 4 *; rep bet *s around. Join last ch 4 to top of ch-3 at beg of row.

Row 26: Ch 3, * work 2 dc in each of next 2 dc, ch 4, sk 1st sc, sc in next 26 sc; ch 4, dc in next dc *; rep bet *s around. Join as Row 25.

Row 27: Ch 3, dc in next dc, 2 dc in next dc, dc in next 2 dc; ch 4, sk sc, sc in 24 sc, ch 4; * dc in next 2 dc, 2 dc in next dc, dc in next 2 dc, ch 4, sk sc, sc in 24 sc, ch 4 *; rep bet *s around. Join as above.

Row 28: Ch 3, dc in next 2 dc, ch 3, dc in next 3 dc, ch 4, sk sc, sc in next 22 sc, ch 4; * dc in 3 dc, ch 3, dc in 3 dc, ch 4, sk sc, sc in 22 sc, ch 4 *; rep bet *s around; join as above.

Row 29: Ch 3, dc in next 2 dc, (ch 3, dc in same lp) twice; ch 3, dc in next 3 dc; ch 4, sk sc, sc in next 20 sc, ch 4; * dc in next 3 dc, (ch 3, dc in same lp) twice; ch 3, sk sc, sc in next 20 sc, ch 4 *; rep bet *s around; join as above.

Row 30: Ch 3, dc in next 2 dc, ch 3, dc in next 3 dc; (ch 3, dc in same lp) twice; ch 3, dc in next dc; ch 3, dc in next 3 dc; ch 4, sk sc, sc in 18 sc, ch 4; * dc in next 3 dc, ch 3, dc in next dc; (ch 3, dc in same lp) twice; ch 3, dc in dc, ch 3, dc in 3 dc; ch 4, sk sc, sc in 18 sc, ch 4 *; rep bet *s around; join as above.

Row 31: Ch 3, dc in next 2 dc; (ch 3, dc in next dc) twice; (ch 3, dc in same ch-3 lp) twice; (ch 3, dc in next dc) twice; ch 3, dc in next dc; ch 4, sk sc, sc in 16 sc, ch 4; * dc in 3 dc; (ch 3, dc in next dc) twice; (ch 3, dc in same ch-3) twice; (ch 3, dc in next dc) twice; ch 3, dc in next dc; ch 4, sk sc, sc in 16 sc, ch 4 *; rep bet *s around. Join as above—7 ch-3 lps in point.

Row 32: Continue as established; there will be 14 sc in grp and 9 ch-3 lps.

Row 33: 12 sc in grp and 11 ch-3 lps.

Row 34: 10 sc in grp and 13 ch-3 lps.

Row 35: 8 sc in grp and 15 ch-3 lps.

Row 36: 6 sc in grp and 17 ch-3 lps.

Row 37: 4 sc in grp and 19 ch-3 lps.

Row 38: 2 sc in grp and 21 ch-3 lps.

Row 39: Sl st in next dc, overlap the next dc over the 3rd dc at the end of the previous point and sl st the 2 dc too. [Sl st in next ch-3 lp. * Ch 3, in next ch-3 lp *work dc, ch 3, sl st in 3rd ch from hook—picot,* and dc; ch 3, sc in next ch-3 lp. * Rep bet *s 3 times more. (Ch 3, in next ch-3 lp work dc, a picot, dc) 3 times; ch 3, sc in next ch-3 lp. Rep bet *s 4 times. Sl st in next 2 dc. Overlap the 1st dc of the *next* point (place on top) with the next dc and sl st the 2 dc too. Sl st in next 2 dc.] Rep bet [ ]s 9 times more. End rnd with sl st in last 2 dc and in same st where 1st sl st made at beg of row. Fasten off. Block.

Crocheted Pineapple Tablecloth

shown on pages 128-129

Materials
J & P Coats size 20 6-cord mercerized thread, 19 (300 yard) balls ecru; size 7 steel crochet hook.

Abbreviations: See pages 218-219.

Instructions
Finished diameter is 68 inches.

Ch 5, join with sl st to form a ring.

Rnd 1: Ch 11, trc in ring, * ch 7, trc in ring. Rep from * 3 times more, ch 7, sl st in 4th st of ch-11 at beg of rnd—6 ch lps.

Rnd 2: Sl st in each of next 3 sts of ch, ch 11, trc in same ch lp as sl sts, * ch 7 (trc, ch 7, trc) all in next ch-7 lp. Rep from * around, ending with ch 7, sl st in 4th st of 1st ch-11—12 lps.

Rnd 3: Sl st in each of 5 sts of ch, ch 4, 3 trc in same ch lp as sl sts, * ch 2 (4 trc, ch 7, 4 trc) in next ch-7 lp. Rep from * around, ending with ch 2, 4 trc in same ch lp as 1st 3 trc of rnd, ch 7, sl st in top st of 1st ch-4.

Rnd 4: St st in each of 3 trc, ch 4, * (3 trc, ch 2, 3 trc) in ch-2 sp, trc in next

continued

trc, ch 3, sk 3 trc, sc in ch lp, ch 3, sk 3 trc, trc in next trc. Rep from * around, ending last rep with ch 3, sl st in top st of 1st ch-4.

Rnd 5: Sl st in each of 3 trc, ch 4, * 2 trc in ch-2 sp, trc in next trc, ch 6, sk 3 trc, sc over end of next ch lp, sc in sc, sc in next ch lp, ch 6, sk 3 trc, trc in next trc. Rep from * around, ending with ch 6, sl st in top of 1st ch-4.

Rnd 6: Sl st in each of 3 trc, ch 4, * 3 trc in ch-6 lp, ch 6, sc in center st of sc grp, ch 6, 3 trc over end of ch lp, trc in next trc, ch 7, sk 2 trc, trc in next trc. Rep from * around, ending with ch 7, sl st in top st of 1st ch-4.

Rnd 7: Sl st in each of 3 trc, ch 4, * 3 trc in ch lp, ch 2, 3 trc over end of next ch lp, trc in next trc, ch 6, sk 3 trc, sc in ch lp, ch 6, sk 3 trc, trc in next trc. Rep from * around, ending as for Rnd 5.

Rnds 8-10: Rep Rnds 5-7 once.

Rnd 11: Rep Rnd 5 once more; end with ch-9 instead of ch-6 in last rep.

Rnd 12: Sl st across 3 trc, * 3 trc in next lp, ch 7, sc in center sc, ch 7, 3 trc in next lp, trc in next trc, ch 4, sk 2 trc, trc in next trc. Rep from * around, ending with 3 trc in next lp, ch 7, sc in center sc, ch 7, 3 trc in next lp, trc in next trc, ch 4, join in top of ch-4.

Rnd 13: Sl st in each of 3 trc, ch 4, ch 4, * 3 trc in next ch lp, ch 4, 3 trc over end of next ch lp, trc in next trc, ch 6, sk 2 trc, trc in next trc, 2 trc in sp, trc in next trc, ch 6, sk 2 trc, trc in next trc. Rep from * around, ending to correspond, sl st in top of 1st ch-4.

Rnd 14: Sl st in each of 3 trc, ch 4, * 2 trc in sp, trc in trc, ch 10, sk 3 trc, trc in each of 4 trc, ch 10, sk 3 trc, trc in next trc. Rep from * around, ending with ch 10, sl st in top st of 1st ch-4.

Rnd 15: Ch 4, trc in each of rem trc on same grp, * ch 12, sk ch lp, trc in each trc on next grp. Rep from * around, ending with ch 12, sl st in top st of ch-4.

Rnd 16: Ch 4, trc in same st as sl st, * trc in each of rem trc on same grp, trc in same st as last trc made, ch 12, sk ch lp, 2 trc in next trc. Rep from * around, ending as before.

Rnds 17, 18: Rep Rnds 15 and 16.

Rnd 19: Ch 4, trc in 3 trc, * ch 7, trc in each of 4 trc, ch 10, trc in each of next 4 trc. Rep from * around, ending as for Rnd 14.

Rnd 20: Ch 4, trc in 3 trc, * ch 4, 4 trc in center st of ch-7 lp, ch 4, trc in each of 4 trc, ch 8, trc in each of 4 trc. Rep from * around, ending with ch 8, sl st in top st of ch-4.

Rnd 21: Ch 4, trc in 3 trc, * ch 4, 2 trc in each of 4 trc, ch 4, trc in each of 4 trc, ch 6, trc in each of 4 trc. Rep from * around, ending as for Rnd 5.

Rnd 22: Ch 4, trc in each of 3 trc. * ch 4, sk ch lp (2 trc in next trc, trc in next trc) 4 times; ch 4, sk ch lp, trc in each of 4 trc, ch 3, trc in each of 4 trc. Rep from * around, ending with ch 3, sl st in top st of ch-4.

Rnd 23: Ch 4, trc in each of 3 trc, * ch 6, sk ch lp, trc in next trc, (ch 4, trc) in each of 11 trc, ch 6, sk ch lp, trc in each of 4 trc, sk ch lp, trc in each of 4 trc. Rep from * around; end with sl st in top st of 1st ch-4.

Rnd 24: Ch 3, trc in next trc; *work a joined trc over next 2 trc as follows: (thread twice around hook, draw up a lp in next st, thread over and through 2 lps, over and through 2 lps)* twice, over and through all 3 lps on hook; * ch 6, sk ch-6 lp, sc in next ch lp, (ch 4, sc) in each ch-4 lp, ch 6, sk ch-6 lp, work 2 joined trc over next 2 trc 4 times. Rep from * around, ending with ch 6, joined trc over 2 trc twice, sl st in top of 1st trc of rnd.

Rnd 25: Ch 4, trc in next st, * ch 6, sk ch-6 lp, sc in next ch lp; in each ch-4 lp of pineapple work ch 4 and sc; ch 6, sk ch-6 lp, trc in each of next 4 sts. Rep from * around, ending with ch 6, trc in each of 2 sts, sl st in top of ch-4.

Rnds 26, 27: Rep Rnd 25.

Rnd 28: Ch 4, trc in same st as sl st, 2 trc in next trc, * ch 8, sk ch-6 lp, sc in next ch lp (ch 4, sc) in 6 ch lps, ch 8, 2 trc in each of 4 trc. Rep from * around, ending with ch 8, 2 trc in each of 2 trc, sl st in top st of 1st ch-4.

Rnd 29: Ch 4, trc in each of 3 trc, * ch 8, sk ch lp, sc in next ch lp (ch 4, sc) in 5 ch lps, ch 8, trc in each of 4 trc, ch 7, trc in each of 4 trc. Rep from * around, ending as for Rnd 6.

Rnd 30: Ch 4, trc in each of 3 trc, * ch 8, sk ch lp, sc in next ch lp (ch 4, sc) in 4 ch lps, ch 8, trc in each of 4 trc, ch 4, 4 trc in center st of ch-7 lp, ch 4, trc in each of 4 trc. Rep from * around, ending with ch 4, sl st in top st of ch-4.

Rnd 31: Ch 4, trc in each of 3 trc, * ch 8, sk ch lp, sc in next ch lp (ch 4, sc) in each of 3 ch lps, ch 8, trc in each of 4 trc, ch 4, 2 trc in each of 4 trc, ch 4, trc in each of 4 trc. Rep from * around, ending as before.

Rnd 32: Ch 4, trc in 3 trc, * ch 8, sk ch lp, sc in next ch lp (ch 4, sc) in 2 ch lps, ch 8, trc in each of 4 trc, ch 4, 2 trc in each of 2 trc, trc in all except final 2 trc of same grp, 2 trc in each of 2 trc, ch 4, trc in each of 4 trc. Rep from * around, ending as before.

Rnd 33: Ch 4, trc in 3 trc, * ch 8, sk ch lp, sc in next ch lp, ch 4, sc in next ch lp, ch 8, trc in each of 4 trc, sk next ch lp (ch 4, trc) in each trc of next trc-grp, ch 4, trc in each of next 4 trc. Rep from * around, ending as before.

Rnd 34: Ch 4, trc in 3 trc, * ch 8, sk ch lp, sc in next ch lp, ch 8, trc in each of 4 trc, ch 6, sk ch lp, sc in next ch lp (ch 4, sc) in 10 ch lps, ch 6, trc in each of 4 trc. Rep from * around, ending as for Rnd 5.

Rnd 35: Ch 4, trc in each of 3 trc, * sk 2 ch lps, trc in each of 4 trc, ch 6, sk ch lp, sc in next ch lp (ch 4, sc) in 9 ch lps, ch 6, trc in each of 4 trc. Rep from * around, ending as before.

Rnd 36: Sl st in each of 4 trc; rep as for Rnd 24.

Rnd 37: Rep Rnd 25.

Rnds 38-42: Rep Rnds 28-32.

Rnd 43: Rep Rnd 32, having one ch-4 lp only in each pineapple.

Rnd 44: Work as for Rnd 33, omitting the ch-4 lp.

Rnd 45: Rep Rnd 35—14 ch-4 lps.

Rnd 46: Sl st in next 4 trc. Rep Rnd 24—13 ch-4 lps.

Rnd 47: Rep Rnd 25—12 ch-4 lps.

Rnd 48: Rep Rnd 28—11 ch-4 lps.

Rnd 49: Rep Rnd 29—10 ch-4 lps.

Rnd 50: Rep Rnd 30—9 ch-4 lps.

Rnd 51: Rep Rnd 31—8 ch-4 lps.

Rnd 52: Rep Rnd 32—7 ch-4 lps and 12 trc.

Rnd 53: Rep Rnd 32—6 ch-4 lps and 16 trc.

Rnd 54: Rep Rnd 33—5 ch-4 lps and 15 ch-4 lps.

Rnd 55: Ch 4, trc in 3 trc, * ch 8, sk ch lp, sc in next ch lp, (ch 4, sc) in 4 ch lps, ch 8, trc in 4 trc, ch 6, sk ch lp, sc in next lp, (ch 4, sc) in 14 ch lps. Ch 6, trc in each of 4 trc. Rep from * around, end as Rnd 5.

Rnd 56: Rep Rnd 55—3 ch-4 lps and 13 ch-4 lps.

Rnd 57: Rep Rnd 55—2 ch-4 lps and 12 ch-4 lps.

Rnd 58: Rep Row 55—1 ch-4 lp and 11 ch-4 lps.

Rnd 59: Ch 4, trc in 3 trc, * ch 8, sk ch lp, sc in ch-4 lp, ch 8, sk ch lp, trc in 4 trc, ch 8, sk ch lp, sc in next lp, (ch 4, sc) in 10 ch lps, ch 8, sk ch lp, trc in 4 trc. Rep bet *s around.

Rnd 60: Rep Rnd 35.

Rnd 61: Sl st in the next 4 trc. Rep Rnd 24.

Rnd 62: Rep Rnd 25.

Rnd 63: Rep Rnd 28.

Rnd 64: Rep Rnd 29.

Rnd 65: Rep Rnd 30.

Rnd 66: Rep Rnd 31.

Rnd 67: Rep Rnd 32.

Rnd 68: Rep Rnd 32—1 ch-4 lp and 16 trc.

Rnd 69: Ch 4, trc in 3 trc, * ch 8, sk ch lp, sc in next ch lp, ch 8, trc in 4 trc, sk ch lp, (ch 4, trc) in each trc of next trc grp, ch 4, trc in next 4 trc. Rep from * around, ending with ch 4, join to top of ch-4—15 ch-4 lps.

Rnd 70: Ch 4, trc in 3 trc, * ch 7, sk 2 ch lps, trc in each of 4 trc, ch 6, sk ch lp, sc in next lp (ch 4, sc) in 14 ch lps, ch 6, trc in 4 trc. Rep from * around, ending as before.

Rnd 71: Ch 4, trc in 3 trc, * sc in (ch-7) lp, sk trc, trc in each of 3 trc, ch 6, sk ch lp, sc in next ch lp, (ch 4, sc) in 13 lps, ch 6, sk ch lp, trc in each of 4 trc. Rep from * around, end as last rnd.

Rnd 72: Sl st in each of next 4 sts; rep Rnd 24.

Rnds 73-74: Rep Rnd 25.

Rnd 75: Sl st in next trc, ch 4, * 3 trc in next ch lp, ch 8, sc in next ch lp, (ch 4, sc) in 9 ch lps, ch 8, 3 trc over end of next ch lp, trc in next trc, ch 7, sk 2 trc, trc in next trc. Rep from * around, end with ch 7, sl st in top of 1st ch-4.

Rnd 76: Sl st in each of 3 trc, ch 4, * 3 trc in ch lp, ch 8, sc in next ch lp, (ch 4, sc) in 8 ch lps, ch 8, 3 trc over end of next ch lp, trc in next trc, ch 6, sk 3 trc, sc in (ch-7) lp, ch 6, sk 3 trc, trc in next trc; rep from * around, end with ch 6, sl st in top of 1st ch-4.

Rnd 77: Sl st in each of 3 trc, ch 4, * 3 trc in next ch lp, ch 8, sc in next ch lp, (ch 4, sc) in each ch-4 lp, ch 8, 3 trc over end of ch-8 lp, trc in next ch lp, ch 6, sc over end of next ch lp, sc in sc, sc in ch lp, ch 6, sk 3 trc, trc in next trc. Rep from * around; end as last rnd.

Rnd 78: Sl st in 3 trc, ch 4, * 3 trc in next ch lp, ch 8, sc in next ch lp, (ch 4, sc) in 6 ch lps, ch 8, 3 trc over end ch-8 lp, trc in next trc, ch 6, sc over end of next ch lp, sc in next 3 sc, sc in next ch lp, ch 6, sk 3 trc, trc in next trc. Rep from * around; end as last rnd.

Rnd 79: Sl st in each of 3 trc, ch 4, * 3 trc in ch lp, ch 8, sc in next ch lp, (ch 4, sc) in 5 ch lps, ch 8, 3 trc over end of ch lp, trc in trc, ch 7, sk 2 trc, trc in next trc, 3 trc in ch lp, ch 6, sk sc, sc in each of 3 sc, ch 6, 3 trc over end of ch lp, trc in next trc, ch 7, sk 2 trc, trc in next trc. Rep from * around, end with ch 7, sl st in top of 1st ch-4.

Rnd 80: Sl st in each of 3 trc, ch 4, * 3 trc in ch lp, ch 8, sc in next ch lp, (ch 4, sc) in 4 ch lps, ch 8, 3 trc over end of ch lp, trc in next trc, ch 6, sk 3 trc, sc in ch lp, ch 6, sk 3 trc, trc in next trc, 3 trc in ch lp, ch 6, sk next sc, sc in next sc, ch 6, 3 trc over end of ch lp, trc in next trc, ch 6, sc in ch-7 lp, ch 6, sk 3 trc, trc in next trc. Rep from * around; end as before.

Rnd 81: Sl st in each of next 3 trc, ch 4, 3 trc in ch lp, * ch 8, sc in next ch lp (ch 4, sc) in 3 ch lps, ch 8, (3 trc over end of next ch lp, trc in trc, ch 6, sc over end of next ch lp, sc in sc, sc in ch lp, ch 6, sk 3 trc, trc in next trc, 3 trc in ch lp), ch 2; rep sts in parentheses once. Rep from * around, ending as before.

Rnd 82: Sl st in each of next 3 trc, ch 4, * 3 trc in ch lp, ch 8, sc in next ch lp, (ch 4, sc) in 2 ch lps, ch 8, 3 trc over end of ch lp, trc in next trc, ch 6, sc over end of ch lp, sc in each of 3 sc, sc in ch lp, ch 6, sk 3 trc, trc in next trc, 2 trc in ch-2 space, trc in next trc, ch 6, sc over end of ch lp, sc in each of 3 sc, sc in ch lp, ch 6, sk 3 trc, trc in next trc. Rep from * around, ending as before.

Rnd 83: Sl st in each of 3 trc, ch 4, * 3 trc in ch lp, ch 8, sc in next ch lp, ch 4, sc in next ch lp, ch 8, 3 trc over end of ch lp, trc in next trc, (ch 7, sk 2 trc, trc in next trc, 3 trc in ch lp, ch 6, sk sc, sc in each of 3 sc, ch 6, 3 trc over end of ch lp, trc in trc); rep sts in parentheses once, ch 7, sk 2 trc, trc in next trc. Rep from * around, ending as before.

Rnd 84: Sl st in each of 3 trc. Ch 4, * 3 trc in ch lp, ch 8, sc in ch-4 lp, ch 8, 3 trc over end of ch lp, trc in trc, (ch 6, sc in ch lp, ch 6, sk 3 trc, trc in next trc, 3 trc in ch lp, ch 6, sc in center sc of sc grp, ch 6, 3 trc over end of ch lp, trc in next trc); rep sts in parentheses once, ch

Rnd 85: Sl st in each of 3 trc, ch 4, * 3 trc in ch lp, ch 2, 3 trc over end of next ch lp, trc in next trc, ch 6, sc over end of ch lp, sc in sc, sc in ch lp, ch 6, sk 3 trc, trc in next trc. Rep from * around, ending as before.

Rnd 86: Sl st in 2 trc, ch 4, trc in same st as sl st, 2 trc in next trc, * 3 trc in space, 2 trc in each of 2 trc, ch 6, sc over end of ch lp, sc in each of 3 sc, sc in ch lp, (ch 8, sk 3 trc, trc in next trc, 2 trc in space, trc in trc, ch 8, sc over end of ch lp, sc in each of 3 sc, sc in ch lp); rep parentheses once, ch 6, sk 2 trc, 2 trc in each of 2 trc. Rep from * around, ending as before.

Rnd 87: Sl st in each of 10 trc, ch 4, * 3 trc in ch lp, ch 6, sc in each of center 3 sc, ch 6, 3 trc over end of ch lp, trc in trc, (ch 7, sk 2 trc, trc in next trc, 3 trc in ch lp, ch 6, sc in each of center 3 trc, ch 6, 3 trc over end of ch lp, trc in trc); rep sts in last parentheses once, *(sk one trc, make trc, ch 2, trc in next trc—V-st made).* Rep sts in last parentheses 3 times more, sk one trc, trc in next trc. Rep from * around, ending with sl st in top st of 1st ch-4.

Rnd 88: Sl st in each of 3 trc, ch 4, * 3 trc in ch lp, sc in center sc of sc grp, ch 6, 3 trc over end of ch lp, trc in next trc, (ch 6, sc in ch lp, ch 6, sk 3 trc, trc in next trc, 3 trc in ch lp, ch 6, sc in center sc, ch 6, 3 trc over end of ch lp, trc in next trc). Rep sts in parentheses once, skip 3 trc (ch 1, V-st) in ch-2 sp of each of 4 V-sts, ch 1, sk 4 trc, trc in next trc. Rep from * around, ending with ch 1, sl st in top st of 1st ch-4.

Rnd 89: Sl st in each of 3 trc, ch 4, * 3 trc in ch lp, ch 2, 3 trc over end of next ch lp, trc in trc, (ch 6, sc over end of ch lp, sc in sc, sc in ch lp, ch 6, sk 3 trc, trc in trc, 3 trc in ch lp, ch 2, 3 trc over end of next lp, trc in trc). Rep sts in parentheses once, skip 3 trc (ch 4, V-st) in each of 4 V-sts, ch 4, sk 1st 3 trc on next grp, trc in next trc. Rep from * around, ending with ch 4, sl st in top st of 1st ch-4.

Rnd 90: Sl st in each of 3 trc, ch 4, * 2 trc in sp, trc in next trc (ch 8, sc over end of ch lp, sc in each of 3 sc, sc in ch lp, ch 8, sk 3 trc, trc in next trc, 2 trc in
continued

137

sp, trc in next trc). Rep sts in parentheses once, (ch 4, V-st) in each of 4 V-sts, ch 4, sk 3 trc; trc in next trc. Rep from * around, ending as for last rnd.

Rnd 91: Sl st in each of 3 trc, ch 4, * 3 trc in ch lp, ch 6, sc in each of center 3 sc, ch 6, 3 trc over end of ch lp, trc in trc, ch 7, sk 2 trc, trc in next trc, 3 trc in ch lp, ch 6, sc in center 3 sc, ch 6, 3 trc over end of ch lp, trc in trc (ch 6, V-st) in each of 4 V-sts, ch 6, sk 3 trc on next trc-grp, trc in next trc. Rep from * around, ending with ch 6, sl st in top of 1st ch-4.

Rnd 92: Sl st in each of 3 trc, ch 4, * 3 trc in ch lp, ch 6, sc in center sc, ch 6, 3 trc over end of ch lp, trc in trc, ch 6, sc in ch lp, ch 6, sk 3 trc, trc in next trc, 3 trc in ch lp, ch 6, sc in center sc, ch 6, 3 trc over end of ch lp, trc in trc (ch 7, V-st) in 4 V-sts, ch 7, sk 3 trc on next grp, trc in next trc. Rep from * around; end with ch 7, sl st in top of 1st ch-4.

Rnd 93-94: Work as for Rnds 89-90 without rep sts in parentheses and with ch 10 instead of ch 4 before and after V-sts.

Rnd 95: Sl st in 3 trc, ch 4, * 3 trc in ch lp, ch 6, sc in each of center 3 sc, ch 6, 3 trc over end of ch lp, trc in trc (ch 8 and trc, ch 2, ch 2, trc) in each of 4 V-sts, ch 8, sk 3 trc on next grp, trc in next trc. Rep from * around; end as before.

Rnd 96: Sl st in each of 3 trc, ch 4, * 3 trc in ch lp, ch 6, sc in center sc, ch 6, 3 trc over end of ch lp, trc in trc (ch 8, sk one ch lp, V-st in ch-2 lp, ch 2, V-st in ch-2 lp); rep sts in parentheses 3 times more, ch 8, trc in last trc on next grp. Rep from * around, end as before.

Rnd 97: Sl st in 3 trc, ch 4, * 3 trc in ch lp, ch 7, trc in 5th st from hook, trc in each of next 2 ch sts, 3 trc over next ch lp, trc in trc (ch 5, sc in ch lp, ch 5, V-st in V-st, ch 7, trc in 5th st from hook, trc in each of next 2 sts, V-st in next V-st); rep sts in parentheses 3 times more, ch 5, sc in ch lp, ch 5, trc in last trc of next grp. Rep from * around, ending as before. Fasten off.

To block the finished cloth, stretch it into a circular shape and pin it to size and shape on a padded surface (such as a floor). Cover it with a damp cloth and press carefully using a warm iron. Remove when dry.

Rose Pinwheel Doily

shown on page 129

Materials

Size 12 crochet hook, one 350-yard ball of Coats & Clark "Big Ball" crochet thread No. 30 size in white and a 2nd color of your choice (we used pink).

Gauge: 8 sc = ½ inch.
Abbreviations: See pages 218-219.

Instructions

Finished diameter is approximately 9½ inches.

With white, ch 8, join with sl st to form ring, ch 1.

Rnd 1: Work 16 sc in ring. Do not join.

Rnd 2: * Ch 6, sk 1 sc, sc in next sc, rep from * around. Join with sl st to base of 1st loop—8 loops made.

Rnd 3: Sl st in 1st 2 ch st, 2 sc in lp, * ch 4, 2 sc next lp, rep from * around. End with 2 sc in 8th lp.

Mark beg of rnds.

Rnd 4: Work in back lps of sc until end of pinwheels: Ch 4, sk sl sts and 1st sc, * sc in next sc, 2 sc next lp, ch 4, sk rem chs and next sc, rep from * around. End with 2 sc in the last lp.

Rnd 5: * Ch 4, sk rem chs, sc in next 3 sc, 2 sc next lp, rep from * around.

Rnd 6: * Ch 4, sk rem chs, sk 1st sc, sc next 4 sc, 2 sc in lp, rep from * around.

Rnds 7-13: Work same as Rnd 6, always sk 1st sc, work sc in each sc of grp, (the number of sts increases 1 st in each row), 2 sc in lp, ch 4.

Rnd 14: * Ch 5, sk rem chs, sk 1st sc, sc next 12 sc, 2 sc in lp, rep from * around.

Rnd 15: * Ch 5, sk rem chs, sk 1st sc, sc next 12 sc (sk last sc), ch 5, sc in ch-5 lp, rep from * around.

Rnd 16: * Ch 5, sk rem chs, sk 1st sc, sc next 10 sc (sk last sc), (ch 5, sc in ch-5 lp) 2 times, rep from * around.

Rnd 17: * Ch 5, sk rem chs, sk 1st sc, sc next 8 sc (sk last sc), (ch 5, sc in ch-5 lp) 3 times, rep from *.

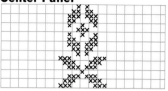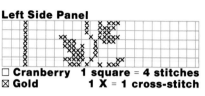
Rnd 18: Same as Rnd 17 exc sc next 6 sc, and rep sts in parentheses 4 times.

Rnd 19: Same as Rnd 17 exc sc next 4 sc and rep sts in parentheses 5 times.

Rnd 20: Same as Rnd 17 exc sc next 3 sc (don't sk last sc) and rep sts in parentheses 6 times.

Rnd 21: Same as Rnd 20 exc sc next 2 sc and rep sts in parentheses 7 times.

Rnd 22: * Ch 5, sc 1st sc, sk next sc (ch 5, sc next ch-5 lp) 8 times, rep from * around.

Rnd 23: * Ch 3, sc next lp—(1st ch-5 lp to left of sc at point of pinwheel), (ch 5, sc next lp) 8 times, rep from *. *Note:* On last rep, work parentheses only 7 times.

Rnd 24: * Ch 6, sk ch-3 lp, sc next ch-5 lp, (ch 5, sc next lp) 7 times, rep from * around. On last rep, work parentheses only 6 times.

Rnd 25: * Ch 5, sc in ch-6 lp, (ch 5, sc next lp) 7 times, rep from * around.

Rnd 26: * Ch 5, 6 dc next lp, (ch 5, sc next lp) 5 times, rep from * 7 more times; ** ch 5, 6 dc next lp, (ch 5, sc next lp) 4 times, rep from ** 2 more times, ch 5, sc next lp.

Rnd 27: * Ch 5, sc in 4th dc of 6 dc grp, (ch 5, sc next lp) 6 times, rep from * 7 more times; ** ch 5, sc in 4th dc of grp (ch 5, sc next lp) 5 times. Rep from ** 2 more times.

Rnd 28: * Ch 5, sc in next lp, rep from * around. Fasten off.

Flower motif: (Make 12) With 2nd color, ch 7, sl st to form ring, ch 1.

Rnd 1: Work 18 sc in ring, join with sl st to 1st sc.

Rnd 2: * Ch 4, sk 2 sc, sc next sc, rep from * 4 more times, ch 4, join with sl st to 1st sc—6 lps.

Rnd 3: * Ch 2, 6 dc in lp, sc in sc, rep from * around, sl st to 1st sc, ch 1, turn.

Rnd 4: Sc in 1st unworked sc of Rnd 1. * Ch 5, sk next 2 sc, sc next sc, rep from * around, join with sl st to 1st sc, turn.

Rnd 5: Rep Rnd 3 except do not work ch-1, do not turn.

Rnd 6: * Ch 7, sk petal of dcs, sc next sc, rep from * around, join with sl st to sl st at beg of rnd.

Rnd 7: In next lp work (sc, ch 1, 10 dc), sl st in next sc, rep for each lp. Fasten off.

Rnd 8: Attach white in 1st dc (not sc or ch-1) of any outer petal, * ch 4, (sk 2 dc, sc next dc, ch 4) 2 times, sk 1 dc, sc next dc, ch 4, sk last dc, (sk sl st, sk sc and sk ch 1), sc in 1st dc of next petal. Rep from * around, then join with sl st to 1st ch.

Rnd 9: Sl st in next 2 ch, * ch 5, sc next lp, rep from * around. Join with sl st to 2nd sl st at beg of rnd.

Rnd 10: Sl st to middle of ch-5 lp, * *ch 6, sl st in 4th ch from hook, ch 2, sc next lp—picot lp made,* rep from * until 11 picot lps have been made.

Attaching flower motif to doily: Flower motifs attach to Rnd 28 in 7-lp section located between 2 grps of 6 dc (made in Rnd 26) as follows: Ch 3, sc in 1st of 7 lps of doily, ** ch 3, sc next lp on flower motif, ch 3, sc next lp on doily. Rep from ** 5 more times, ch 3, sc next lp on flower. Finish rnd in picot lps; join with sl st to beg of rnd.

To attach rest of flower motifs, work each as for 1st flower thru Rnd 10 until 11 picot lps are made.

Attach next 3 lps to 3 picot lps of motif already attached to doily as follows (1st 3 picot lps made after attaching last motif to doily): (ch 3, sc in corresponding picot, ch 3, sc in next lp on motif) 3 times, attach to doily as before and complete rnd.

Note: Use sc in 7th lp where last motif was joined to doily as 1st lp for joining new motif to doily.

Continue adding roses until all 12 have been worked into the main doily; the 12th motif should be attached to 8 lps on the doily and joined in pattern to 3 picot lps of the very 1st motif. Fasten off after the last motif is added. Press and starch if desired.

Ripple Afghan

shown on page 130

Materials

Unger Roly Poly (3.5-ounce balls): 8 balls of No. 8841 natural, 1 ball each of No. 7090 blue, No. 9381 pink, No. 2765 green, No. 8825 gold, No. 8468 maroon; size G aluminum crochet hook, or size to obtain gauge.

Gauge: 9 sc = 2 inches.
Abbreviations: See pages 218-219.

Instructions

Finished size is about 46x68 inches. With natural, ch 311.

*Pat row: Sc in 2nd st from hook and in each of next 10 sts, * 3 sc in next st, sc in each of next 11 sts, sk 2 sts, sc in each of next 11 sts. Rep from * across, ending with 3 sc in next st, sc in each of next 10 sts, sk 1 st, sc in front of last st, ch 1, turn.*

Working in back lp only, work 9 more pat rows with natural. Then work stripe pat as follows: 3 rows of blue, 2 rows of natural, 3 rows of pink, 2 rows of natural, 3 rows of green, 2 rows of natural, 3 rows of gold, 2 rows of natural, 3 rows of maroon, 10 rows of natural. Rep the stripe pat 5 times more. Fasten off.

Baby Afghan

shown on page 131

Materials

Sport yarn (or type of yarn suitable for gauge given below): 10 ounces of cranberry, 6 ounces of dark gold; size H afghan hook, or size to obtain gauge given below; size F aluminum crochet hook; tapestry needle.

Gauge: 5 afghan sts = 1 inch; 10 rows = 2 inches.
Abbreviations: See pages 218-219.

Instructions

Finished size is 29x34 inches.
Center panel (make 1): With gold and afghan hook, ch 37.

Row 1: Working from right to left, sk 1st ch, insert hook into 2nd ch from hook, yo, and draw through a lp, * insert hook into next ch, yo, and draw through a lp. Rep from * across; keep all lps on hook.

Row 2: Working from left to right, yo, and draw through 1st 2 lps on hook, * yo, and draw through next 2 lps on hook.

Row 3: Working from right to left, sk 1st vertical bar on the front of the fabric, * insert hook from right to left into next vertical bar, yo, and draw through a lp. Rep from * to end; keep all lps on hook.

Row 4: Rep Row 2.

Rep Rows 3 and 4 until 133 rows have been completed. Fasten off.

Side panels (make 2): With cranberry and afghan hook, ch 45. Work same as for center panel.

Joining panels: With right sides up, lay 1 side panel next to the center panel. Working along the sides of the panels, join gold in end st of 1 side panel, ch 3, sc in corresponding st of center panel, ch 3, sc in end st 2 rows below where yarn was joined, * ch 3, sc in end st 3 rows below last sc on opposite panel.

Rep from * along vertical edges of panel until entire length is worked, ending with sc in end of 1st row of 1 panel, ch 3, sc in end of 1st row of the other panel. Fasten off. Rep with the other side panel.

Edging: With standard crochet hook and cranberry, ch 4.

Row 1: In 4th ch from hook *work dc, ch 2, 2 dc—shell made;* ch 4, turn.

Row 2: In ch-2 sp of shell work 2 dc, ch 2, 2 dc—shell over shell made;* ch 4, turn.

Row 3: Work shell over shell, in ch-4 turning lp 2 rows below work 8 dc; ch 1, turn.

Row 4: Sc in 1st dc, *(ch 3, sc in next dc) 7 times—scallop made;* ch 1, shell over shell; ch 4, turn.

Rows 5-6: Shell over shell; ch 4, turn.

Row 7: Shell over shell, in ch-4 turning lp 2 rows below work 8 dc, sl st in ch-1 sp at end of previous scallop.

Rep Rows 4-7 until 64 scallops have been completed. Fasten off, leaving an 8-inch-long tail; sew edges tog.

Next rnd: With gold, join thread in any turning ch-4 lp along straight edge of edging, ch 3, in same sp work dc, ch 2, dc, * ch 1, shell in next ch-4 lp. Rep from * around. Fasten off.

continued

Assembly: Position the crocheted edging around the panel assembly so that 16 scallops fall along each edge. Pin in place. With gold, join yarn in ch-2 sp of any shell of edging, sl st in st on afghan opposite the joining, sl st in next st, * dc in ch-1 sp bet 2 shells of edging, sl st in next 2 sts on afghan, sc in ch-2 sp of shell of edging, sl st in next 2 sts of afghan. Rep from * around. Fasten off.

Embroidery: Begin the embroidery with the center panel, referring to the chart (page 138). Thread a large-eye tapestry needle with cranberry yarn, and noting those squares marked with an X, make a cross-stitch for each X indicated. Begin working at the bottom of the panel and repeat the motif until you reach the top edge.

For the left side panel, thread the needle with gold yarn, and referring to chart on page 138, work cross-stitches from the bottom to the top as before.

For the right side panel, reverse the chart so that the vertical cross-stitches run along the outer, right-hand edge of the afghan panel. Complete the cross-stitches as indicated on the chart.

Chevron-and-Lace Afghan

shown on page 133

Materials
2-ply sport-weight yarn: 28 ounces off-white; size H crochet hook.

Abbreviations: See pages 218-219.

Instructions
Finished size is 48x70 inches.

With crochet hook, make a ch about 1½ yards long.

Row 1: Dc in 4th ch from hook and in each of next 6 ch, make dec over next 3 ch.

To make a dec: Holding back on hook last lp of both dc, make dc in 1st st, sk 2nd st, dc in 3rd st; thread over and draw through all lps on hook.

Dc in each of next 6 ch, 2 dc in next ch, * sk 3 ch, (dc, ch 3, dc) in next ch, sk 3 ch, 5 dc in next ch, sk 3 ch, 2 dc in next ch, dc in each of next 6 ch, dec in next 3 ch, dc in each of next 6 ch, 2 dc in next ch. Work from * 7 times across; ch 3, turn.

Cut off rem ch about ½ inch beyond end of row, unravel back to last dc, and weave end into work.

Row 2: (*Note:* Always work in back lp of dc of previous row when making solid dc panels.) Dc in 1st dc, dc in each of next 6 dc, dec over next 3 sts, dc in each of next 6 dc, 2 dc in next dc, * (dc, ch 3, dc) in center st of 5-dc grp, 5 dc in ch-3 sp, 2 dc in 1st st of solid panel, dc in each of next 6 dc, dec over next 3 sts, dc in each of next 6 dc, 2 dc in next dc. Rep from * across; ch 3, turn. Rep Row 2 for desired length.

Fringe: Cut four 9-inch lengths of yarn. Fold in half, pull lp through edge of afghan. Draw ends through lp and pull tight to form knot. Make a fringe knot at center and each side of solid dc panels on both ends of afghan.

Crocheted Medallion Afghan

shown on page 133

Materials
Coats & Clark Red Heart Preference 4-ply handknitting yarn (or a suitable substitute): 28 ounces of No. 4 cream, 21 ounces of No. 353 taupe, and 17½ ounces of No. 977 variegated blue (or colors of your choice); size G aluminum crochet hook; large-eye needle.

Abbreviations: See pages 218-219.

Instructions
Finished afghan measures approximately 54x75 inches. Each square measures 10½x10½ inches.

Square (make 35): Beg at center with cream, ch 2. *Rnd 1:* Make 8 sc in 2nd ch from hook; join with sl st to 1st sc.

Rnd 2: Ch 2, *holding back on hook last lp of each dc, make 2 dc in joining, yo and draw through all 3 lps on hook—beg 3-dc cluster made; (ch 3, holding back on hook last lp of each dc, make 3 dc in next sc, yo and draw through all 4 lps on hook—3-dc cluster (cl) made)* 7 times; ch 3. Join to the tip of 1st cl. Fasten off.

Rnd 3: Join taupe in any ch-3 lp, ch 1, 5 sc in same ch-3 lp; (5 sc in next ch-3 lp) 7 times; join to 1st sc. Fasten off.

Rnd 4: Join variegated blue to center sc on any 5-sc grp; in same sc make 3-dc beg cl, ch 3, and 3-dc cl; ch 2, (in

center sc on next 5-sc grp make 3-dc cl, ch 3, and 3-dc cl, ch 2) 7 times. Join to 1st cl. Fasten off.

Rnd 5: Join taupe to any ch-3 lp, ch 1, *make 5 sc in same lp, make dc, ch 3, and dc in next ch-2 sp—shell made;* (5 sc in next ch-3 lp, shell in next ch-2 sp) 7 times; join to 1st sc. Fasten off.

Rnd 6: Join cream to center sc on any 5-sc grp, ch 1, sc in same place where yarn was joined, ch 1, * in ch-3 lp of next shell make (dc, ch 1) 4 times; *in center sc on next 5-sc grp make sc, ch 3, and sc—corner made;* ch 1, in ch-3 lp on next shell make (dc, ch 1) 4 times; sc in center sc on next 5-sc grp, ch 1. Rep from * around, join to 1st sc.

Rnd 7: Sl st in next ch-1 sp, ch 3, * (sc in next ch-1 sp, ch 1) twice; in corner ch-3 lp make trc, ch 1, trc, ch 5, trc, ch 1, and trc; ch 1, sk next 2 dc, (sc in next ch-1 sp, ch 1) twice; (hdc in next ch-1 sp, ch 1) twice. Rep from * around; end last rep with hdc in next ch-1 sp, ch 1; join to 2nd ch of ch-3.

Rnd 8: Ch 1, sc in joining, (ch 1, sc in next sc) twice; * (ch 1, hdc in next trc) twice; ch 1, in ch-5 corner lp make hdc, ch 3, and hdc; (ch 1, hdc in next trc) twice; (ch 1, sk next ch, sc in next st) 6 times. Rep from * around; end last rep with (ch 1, sk next ch, sc in next st) 3 times; ch 1; join to 1st sc. Fasten off.

Rnd 9: Join taupe in any ch-3 corner lp, ch 1, in same lp make sc, ch 3, and sc; * ch 1, sc in next st, (ch 1, sk next ch, sc in next st) 11 times; ch 1, in corner lp make sc, ch 3, and sc. Rep from * around; end with ch-1; join.

Rnd 10: Sl st in ch-3 corner lp, * ch 1, in corner lp make sc, ch 3, and sc, (ch 1, sc in next ch-1 sp) 13 times. Rep from * around; end with ch 1; join. Fasten off.

Rnd 11: Join variegated blue in any ch-3 corner lp, ch 4, *holding back on hook last lp of each dc, make 2 dc in same corner lp, yo, and draw through all 3 lps on hook—2-dc cl made;* * (ch 1, 2-dc cl in next ch-1 sp) 14 times; ch 1, in corner lp make 2-dc cl, ch 1, dc, ch 1, and 2-dc cl. Rep from * around; end with 2-dc cl in 1st corner lp, ch 1; join to 3rd ch of ch-4. Fasten off.

Rnd 12: Join taupe to next ch-1 sp following the dc on any corner, ch 1, sc in same sp, * (ch 1, sc in next sp) 16 times; ch 3, sc in sp bet next dc and cl on corner. Rep from * around; end with ch 3; join to 1st sc.

140

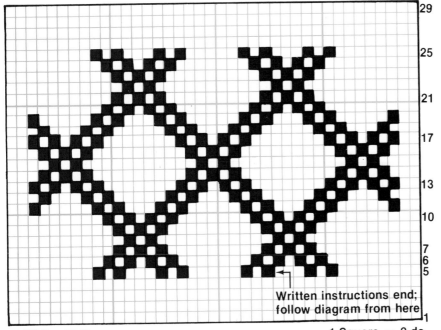

☐ White ■ Rose

1 Square = 2 dc

Rnd 13: Ch 1, sc in joining, * (ch 1, sc in next sc) 16 times; ch 1, in corner ch-3 lp make sc, ch 3, and sc; ch 1, sc in next sc. Rep from * around; end with ch 1; join. Fasten off.

Rnd 14: Join cream in ch-3 lp on any corner, ch 3, in same lp make dc, ch 3, and 2 dc; * (ch 1, dc in next ch-1 sp) 18 times; ch 1, in the next corner lp make 2 dc, ch 3, and 2 dc. Rep from * around; end with ch 1; join to the top of ch-3. Fasten off.

On a padded surface, pin squares to measurements (10½ inches square); dampen and leave to dry.

Assembling the afghan: With right sides of squares facing, and using cream-colored yarn, sew the squares into 5 rows of 7 squares each.

Border: With the right side of the afghan facing, attach cream-colored yarn in any ch-3 corner lp on afghan.

Rnd 1: Ch 1, in same corner lp make sc, ch 3, and sc, * ch 1, sk next dc, sc in next dc, (ch 1, sc in next dc) 19 times; ch 1, sk next dc, ** hdc in next sp, ch 1. sk seam, hdc in next sp, ch 1, sk next dc, sc in next dc, (ch 1, sc in next dc) 19 times; ch 1, sk next dc. Rep from ** to next ch-3 corner lp; in corner lp make sc, ch 3, and sc. Rep from * around, ending with ch 1, sk next dc; join to the 1st sc.

Rnd 2: Sl st in corner lp, * ch 1, in corner lp make sc, ch 3, and sc; ** ch 1, sc in next ch-1 sp. Rep from ** to next corner. Rep from * around, ending with ch-1; join to 1st sc.

Rnd 3: Ch 1, sc in joining, * ch 1, sc in corner lp, ** ch 1, sc in next sc. Rep from ** to next corner. Rep from * around, ending with ch 1; join to 1st sc. Fasten off.

Irish Chain Pillow Shams

shown on page 132

Materials
Bernat Sesame 4-ply knitting worsted (3.5-ounce balls): 6 balls of white, 4 balls of rosewood (or substitute a yarn of comparable weight in the colors of your choice); size H aluminum crochet hook, or size to obtain gauge given below; backing fabric.

Gauge: 4 dc = 1 inch; 3 rows = 1¾ inches.

Abbreviations: See pages 218-219.

Instructions
The finished size of each pillow is 20x26 inches, excluding the ruffle.

Note: To change yarn colors, drop the 1st color and pick up the 2nd just before working the last step of the 1st color stitch. The new color is then in position to work.

This pattern in most cases allows you to work over the color not in use to avoid fastening off after each color change in a row. Exceptions to this are the three rows in the center of each diamond shape where the space between color changes is greater.

After working the final stitch of the 2nd color in each row, drop that color and pick it up again in the next row where it is needed. Do not carry it across and back.

With white yarn, ch 80.

Row 1: Dc in 4th ch from hook and in each ch across; ch 3, turn—78 dc.

Row 2: Dc in each dc across row; ch 3, turn.

Rows 3-4: Rep Row 2.

Row 5: (Ch counts as 1st dc), dc in 2nd dc and in next 14 dc, attach rosewood, dc in each of next 2 dc, change to white, dc in each of next 2 dc, with rosewood, dc in next 2 dc, with white dc in each of next 6 dc. Using the diagram, above, begin work as indicated with arrow, and work 2 dc for each square in the grid. Dc in each dc for 29 rows total. Fasten off.

Border: *Rnd 1:* With right side facing, attach rosewood in beg of last row worked, ch 3, dc in each dc across row to corner, in corner st work (2 dc, ch 2, 2 dc); 2 dc in end of each row worked, work corner as before and continue around, ending with 2 dc, ch 2, dc in beg st; join with sl st to top of beg ch-3.

Rnd 2: Rep Rnd 1, ending with 2 dc, ch 2, 2 dc in corner sp; join with sl st to top of beg ch-3.

Rnds 3-4: With white, rep Rnd 1.

Carefully block the pillow front to measure 20x26 inches.

From the fabric of your choice, cut a backing piece that is the same size as the blocked pillow front. (Add seam allowances.) Press the seam allowance under and pin the backing piece to the back of the crocheted pillow front, wrong sides facing.

Hand-sew three sides together, leaving one short end open for inserting the pillow. Do not sew through the last row of crochet stitches—the ruffle will be worked into these stitches.

continued

141

Large ruffle: *Rnd 1:* (*Note:* Work in back lps only for this rnd.) Attach rosewood in any center corner ch (just to the right of 1st dc in row you choose), ch 3, dc in same st, * 2 dc in next dc, dc in next dc. Rep from * to corner ch-2, work 2 dc in 1st ch of corner, ch 2, 2 dc in rem ch of corner. Continue around making incs and corners as established, ending with 2 dc in corner ch, ch 2, join to top of beg ch-3.

Rnd 2: (*Note:* Work this and rem rnds through both lps.) Ch 3, * dc in each dc to corner, in corner sp work 2 dc, ch 2, 2 dc. Rep from * around, ending with 2 dc, ch 2, 2 dc in corner sp, join with sl st to top of ch-3.

Rnds 3-4: Rep Rnd 2, ending with corner as before, join to top of ch-3.

Rnd 5: Ch 5, sk 2 dc, sc in next dc, * ch 4, sk 2 dc, sc in next dc. Rep from * around; join to ch-1 with sl st. Fasten off.

Small ruffle: *Rnd 1:* (*Note:* Work this rnd in front lps only.) Attach white in front lp of same st where large ruffle was started (ch in corner sp), ch 3, dc in same st, * dc in next lp, 2 dc in following lp. Rep from * to corner, in corner ch-2 work 2 dc in 1st ch, ch 2, 2 dc in rem ch. Continue around, making incs and corners as established. End with 2 dc in corner ch, ch 2, sl st to top of beg ch-3.

Rnd 2: Work same as for Rnd 2 of large ruffle.

Rnd 3: Work same as for Rnd 5 of large ruffle. Fasten off.

Granny-Square Rose Pillow

shown on page 132

Materials

Bernat Sesame 4 four-ply knitting worsted (3.5-ounce skeins) or a suitable substitute: 1 skein each of the following: blue, olive green, white, rosewood, and ocher (or substitute a comparable yarn in the colors of your choice); size G aluminum crochet hook; backing fabric; 12-inch-square pillow form.

Abbreviations: See pages 218-219.

Instructions

Rose motif (make 2): With ocher, ch 5, join with sl st to form ring. *Rnd 1:* * Ch 5, sc in ring. Rep from * 7 times more; join with sl st to 1st sc—8 lps made. Fasten off.

Rnd 2: With wrong side facing, attach rosewood yarn by putting the hook through the center ring and draw through lp, securing st on base ring (not on lp itself). * Ch 6, sk next lp, in next lp (in same way as before) work sl st through. Rep from * around; join with sl st to beg st; ch 1, turn.

Rnd 3: * Sc in ch-6 lp, in same lp work (7 dc, sc). Rep from * around—4 petals made; join with sl st to turning ch-1. Fasten off.

Rnd 4: With wrong side facing, attach ocher in bar (horizontal yarns at base of dc) of 4th dc of 1st petal, * ch 7, sl st in bar of 4th dc of next petal. Rep from * around; join with sl st to beg bar; ch 1, turn.

Rnd 5: In 1st ch-7 lp work (sc, hdc, 4 dc, hdc, sc). Rep in each lp around; join with sl st to 1st sc; do not turn.

Rnd 6: * Ch 6, sk hdc, sl st in 1st dc, ch 6, sk 2 dc, sl st in next dc, ch 6, sk next 2 sts, sl st in next sc. Rep from * around; join with sl st in beg sc. Fasten off.

Rnd 7: (*Note:* This rnd will leave lps made in Rnd 6 unworked. Work only in sts of Rnd 5. Bend lps forward for ease in working.) With right side facing, olive, and in hdc directly left to where last rnd was fastened off, work (ch 4, 2 trc, ch 2), * sk dc where sl st was made, in next dc work 2 dc, in next dc work dc, ch 2, in next hdc work 2 trc, in next sc work trc, ch 3 (makes corner ch), in next hdc work 3 trc, ch 2. Rep from * around; end with ch 3, sl st to top of beg ch-4. Fasten off.

Rnd 8: Attach white in any ch-3 corner sp, work (ch 3, 2 dc, ch 1), * in next ch-2 sp work (3 dc, ch 3, 3 dc, ch 1), in next corner sp work (3 dc, ch 3, 3 dc, ch 1). Rep from * around; join with sl st to top of beg ch-3. Fasten off.

Rnd 9: Attach blue in any corner ch-3 sp, work ch 3, 2 dc, ch 1. * In each of next 3 ch-1 sps, work 3 dc, ch 1. In next corner sp work 3 dc, ch 3, 3 dc, ch 1. Rep from * around. Join with sl st to top of beg ch-3. Fasten off.

Granny motif (make 2): With rosewood, ch 4, sl st to form ring. *Rnd 1:* Ch 3, 2 dc in ring, ch 3, * 3 dc in ring, ch 3. Rep from * 2 times more, ending with sl st in top of beg ch-3. Fasten off.

Rnd 2: Attach ocher in any corner sp, ch 3, 2 dc in same sp, * ch 2, in next sp work 3 dc, ch 3, 3 dc. Rep from * around, ending with ch 3, sl st to top of beg ch-3. Fasten off.

Rnd 3: Attach light olive in any corner sp, ch 3, 2 dc in same sp, * ch 2, in next sp work 3 dc, ch 2 in corner sp, work 3 dc, ch 3, 3 dc. Rep from * around; end with 3 dc in beg corner, ch 3, sl st to top of beg ch-3. Fasten off.

Rnd 4: Attach white in any corner, ch 3, 2 dc in same sp, * ch 1, in each of next ch-2 sp work 3 dc, ch 1; in corner work 3 dc, ch 3, 3 dc. Rep from * around; end with 3 dc in beg corner, ch 3, sl st to top of beg ch-3. Fasten off.

Rnd 5: Attach blue and work same as for Rnd 4. Fasten off.

Pillow: Block squares to 5¾ inches. Arrange with roses and granny squares in opposite corners. With blue yarn and wrong sides facing, sl st together in back lps only inside edges of squares.

Border: Work in back lps with blue, attach in ch-2 of any ch-3 corner, ch 3, dc in same ch, * dc in each st across row to corner. In ch-2 of ch-3 corner work 2 dc, ch 2, 2 dc. Rep from * around, ending with 2 dc in beg st (ch 3 and dc already worked in this st), ch 2, sl st to top of ch-3.

Press and block finished front to 12½-inch square. Attach the fabric back on three sides, insert pillow form, and sew remaining side closed.

Bobble Shell Pillow

shown on page 132

Materials

Bernat Sesame 4 four-ply knitting worsted (3.5-ounce balls) or a suitable substitute: 1 ball each of white, blue, and ocher, *or* leftover yarn from Granny-Square Rose Pillow, above; size G aluminum crochet hook, or size to obtain gauge given below; backing fabric; 12-inch-square pillow form.

Gauge: 1 colored bobble from sc to sc = 1½ inch; 1 row = 1 inch.

Abbreviations: See pages 218-219.

Instructions

The pillow is 12½ inches square.

With white, ch 51. *Row 1:* Sc in 4th ch from hook, sc in each ch across, change to ocher; ch 4, turn. (*Note:* When changing colors, drop 1st color and pick up 2nd color just before working last step of st before change will be made.)

Row 2: With ocher, work 2 dc in 1st sc, * sk 2 sc, sc in next sc, sk 2 sc, in next sc work 2 dc, ch 1, trc, ch 1, 2 dc. Rep from * across, ending with 2 dc, trc in top of ch; drop ocher, attach white; ch 1, turn.

Row 3: Sc in trc, * in next sc, work 2 dc, ch 1, trc, ch 1, 2 dc; sc in next trc. Rep from * across, ending with sc in top of ch-4; change to blue; ch 4, turn.

Row 4: 2 dc in 1st sc, * sc in trc, in next sc work 2 dc, ch 1, trc, ch 1, 2 dc. Rep from * across, ending with 2 dc, trc in last sc, change to white; ch 1, turn.

Rep Rows 3 and 4, always working Row 3 in white and Row 4 alternately in blue and ocher, until there is a total of 13 blue and ocher rows, ending with ocher and changing to white. Ch 1, turn.

Last row: Sc in each st across row, omitting ch. Fasten off.

Border: With right side facing (white rows are indented), attach blue in corner ch at beg of last row worked. Work dc in each sc and dc evenly along ends of rows, working in each corner.

Assemble according to directions for Granny-Square Rose Pillow (opposite).

Pipe Dolls

shown on page 8

Materials

Adult doll: White clay pipe; four cotton balls; two 12-inch-long white pipe cleaners; ¾x1½x2-inch wood block.

Child doll: Scrap of shiny fabric; one 6-inch-long white pipe cleaner; small empty thread spool; satin ribbon; three wooden skewers; stiff florist's wire; 1-inch-diameter plastic foam ball.

For both dolls: ¼ yard of dress fabric; fabric scraps for apron and slip; lace trims; scrap of white knit fabric; yarn for hair; quilt batting; acrylic paint; black fine-tip permanent marker; clear acrylic spray; glue; tracing paper.

Instructions

For adult doll: The pipe stem should measure 9 inches; break off any excess. Drill a hole in wood block to match diameter of stem. Push stem into wood.

The bottom of the pipe bowl will become doll's face. Enlarge face pattern

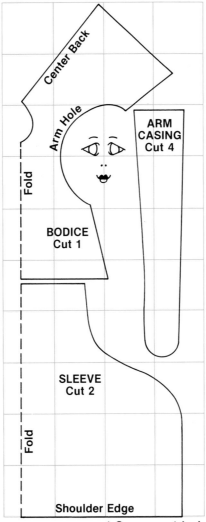

1 Square = 1 Inch

(above) and transfer to bowl. Outline eyes, brows, and nose with a felt pen. Paint pupils and lips. Add cheek color, then spray head with clear acrylic.

To make arms: Twist two pipe cleaners together; make a loop on each end for hands. Together, pipe cleaners should be 9 inches long. Center and tape them to back of stem 1 inch below head. Wrap ½-inch-wide strips of batting around the top 4 inches of stem, crossing over and around arms.

To shape body: Place three cotton balls on chest; wrap with batting strips. Add a cotton ball to back side; wrap. Whipstitch batting in place. To cover batting, cut two 2½x4½-inch rectangles from knit fabric. Using a ¼-inch seam, sew pieces together on long sides. Leave ends open, and leave openings in seams near one end for arms. Turn, then gather ends, folding under seam margins. Gather the waistline.

Slip the covering onto body from the bottom up, pulling arms through openings. Gather snugly; secure. Lightly glue neck, bottom edges to pipe stem.

Run a bit of glue along pipe cleaners, then wrap arms with narrow batting strips, making upper arms thicker than lower arms. On a double thickness of knit fabric, trace the enlarged arm casing pattern. Stitch along this line, leaving end open. Cut out close to stitching; turn right side out, pull casing onto arm. Turn under raw edge; blindstitch to body. Repeat for other arm.

For the clothes: Enlarge patterns (left). Cut bodice and sleeves from fabric. Gather shoulder edge of sleeves to fit into armhole openings in bodice; stitch, using ¼-inch seam. Hem sleeves; finish edges of bodice center back. Stitch arm seam and bodice side seam. Trim sleeves with lace.

To make skirt, cut a 9½x16-inch fabric rectangle. Matching short ends, stitch center back seam, stopping 1 inch from top edge. Gather top edge, stitch to bodice; hem. Make a slip from a rectangle cut the same size as skirt. Slip dress onto doll. Stitch center back opening closed. Add tiny beads for buttons. If desired, fashion other clothes from fabric rectangles and squares.

Glue wool yarn to doll's head; style as desired. Add a hat or dried flowers.

Glue pipe stem into wooden stand.

For child doll: Pipe stem should measure 4¾ inches. Break off excess.

Enlarge face using a scale of 1 square equals ½ inch. Transfer and paint face as for adult doll. Follow same procedures for making arms and body, except make loops for hands so pipe cleaner is 4½ inches long after hands are bent. Also, wrap batting strips only 1¾ inches down pipe stem; do not use cotton balls. Make body covering from two 1¼x1¾-inch rectangles; wrap arms with one layer of batting strips.

Make clothes as for adult doll, enlarging patterns on a scale of 1 square equals ½ inch, and making skirt from 4½x9-inch rectangle. For hair, wind yarn tightly around skewers. Bake in 350° oven for 10 minutes. Cool; unwind. Cut into ringlets; glue to head.

For balloon, cover plastic foam ball with shiny fabric. Insert wire into ball and glue to one of doll's hands.

Glue cardboard circle to bottom of spool; add peas for weight. Glue pipe stem into spool.

143

Country Toys to Craft by Hand

Youngsters will love this collection of country-style dolls and toys—and so will adults who have an eye for fine workmanship and folk-art styling.

♦ The graceful chest and four-poster bed (right) are scaled-down replicas of authentic 19th-century furniture designs. Lovingly crafted of fir and mahogany, these pieces are designed to be played with, not just displayed. The dresser drawers actually open and close and have plenty of storage space for doll-size treasures.

♦ When the winsome knitted grandma (right) comes to call, she's sure to charm children and adults alike. Knit her of sportweight yarn on No. 3 needles, then gently stuff her to a grandmotherly plumpness with polyester fiberfill.

Embroider her features with leftover knitting yarn, and complete her wardrobe by making the detachable knitted bonnet, old-fashioned pantaloons, pinafore, and shawl.

Instructions for making all country-style toys begin on page 150.

144

Country Toys
to Craft by Hand

Put your sewing and stitchery skills to good use crafting these imaginative stuffed animals for the youngsters on your gift list.

♦ The gingham goose (left) is a gift that is a delight to make and give. With her polka dot wings, flowered felt bonnet, and appliqués of doilies, lacy handkerchief, and antique lace edgings and ribbons,

she's sure to entertain a favorite little girl.

♦ The embroidered cat (right) is patterned after an antique doorstop. Transformed into fabric, she makes a perfect pillow toy for small children—and an adorable accent pillow for grown-up cat-lovers. Work the design in simple embroidery stitches that enhance the traditional folk-art motifs.

♦ Make a herd of mascots like these (left) for your favorite young range-riders. Stitch them in soft woolens or corduroys, then trim them with manes and tails of handspun yarn or string. They'll have just the sort of rough-and-tumble character that appeals to children.

Use purchased wool or old suiting to make the hand-stitched donkey (far right) and piece together velvety corduroy scraps for the pair of patchwork ponies. Or, stitch them of wonderful handwoven fabrics for a special treat.

147

Country Toys
to Craft by Hand

Handcrafted toys in bright, shiny colors always seem to capture the attention of toddlers. Their simple designs allow plenty of room for a child's active imagination, in addition to being easy to craft and stitch.

♦ The sprightly horse and cart (above) are sized for toddlers: The horse measures less than a foot long; the cart is just over 9 inches. If you have access to a basic woodworking shop and a few tools, you can craft this simple toy easily—and in far less time than you might expect.

You need no whittling talent to complete the details of the horse. Just cut pieces from 1-inch-thick pine using an elec-

tric jigsaw. Then smooth and shape the horse's body with a rasp and a belt sander.

Treat the completed horse and cart to a splash of bright red paint (or a color of your choice). Protect it with several coats of polyure-thane or clear acrylic spray for a kid-proof fin-ish that will stand up to years and years of play-time hauling and carting.

♦ The cuddly little moppet (right) is a rag doll with a slightly dif-ferent twist. Machine-stitch the doll from ordinary unbleached muslin, then stitch over the seams with gray em-broidery floss in a ran-dom crisscross pattern to enhance her homespun personality.

Use handspun yarn to give her hairdo a casual, ragamuffin look and

stitch her primly patched clothing from traditional calico fabrics.

Embroider the doll's wide eyes with satin stitches, and use narrow stem stitches for the mouth and eyebrows. Fi-nally, bring a subtle blush of color to her muslin cheeks with an artful scribble of pink permanent marker.

To make the portable doll bassinet, stain a pur-chased wicker basket with red liquid fabric dye (protect the colored stain with several coats of polyurethane). Then pad the basket with a fi-berfill mattress, and add a fabric sheet, a pillow, and a quilt to complete the cozy doll bed.

Doll Chest

shown on page 144

Materials

10x20 inches of ⅛-inch-thick hardboard; ½x12x60 inches of mahogany; brads; wood glue; six ½-inch-diameter drawer knobs; stain; varnish.

Instructions

The finished size of the chest is 9½x10¼x4¾ inches.

Referring to the exploded diagram (below, right) for sizes, cut drawer bottoms and chest back from hardboard. (*Note:* The top drawer is slightly shallower than the lower drawers.)

To make legs on chest end panels and lower front panel, cut shallow rectangles as shown in the diagram.

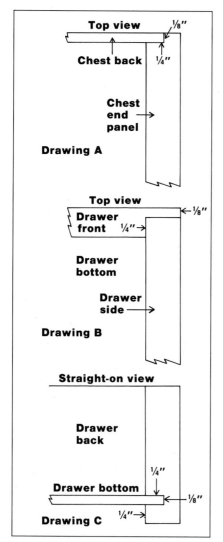

Next, cut rabbets along the back edges of the chest sides (see Drawing A). Also cut rabbets on drawer fronts (see Drawing B). To make the grooves for the drawer bottoms, cut dados along the lower edges on the insides of the drawer fronts and sides (see Drawing C).

To assemble the chest, glue and nail the shelves between the end panels, positioning the rabbeted edges toward the rear of the chest. Nail the chest back between the end panels, fitting it between rabbets.

Glue the decorative front panel under the bottom shelf, setting it back ⅛ inch. Glue and nail the top to the chest.

To assemble the dresser drawers, glue and nail the sides to the fronts. Then glue and nail the drawer backs between the sides, making the bottom edges of the backs flush with the tops of the dados. Slide the drawer bottoms into the dados and nail into the drawer backs. Attach knobs to drawer fronts.

Carefully sand all surfaces until they are glass smooth. Then stain or paint the dresser the desired shade or color.

Finally, protect the surface of the finished chest with several coats of varnish, sanding lightly between coats to ensure a smooth finish.

Doll Bed

shown on page 145

Materials

Four 9-inch-tall and four 4-inch-tall spindles (available at building supply stores); two ⅞x⅞x14⅜-inch mahogany pieces (side rails); two ⅞x⅞x9½-inch mahogany pieces (end rails); ½x5½x10 inches of mahogany (headboard); 18 inches of ¼-inch doweling (pegging); 15 feet of seine twine (mattress support); sandpaper; white glue; wood glue; cardboard; stain; varnish.

Instructions

The finished bed is 13x18x13 inches.

Enlarge the headboard pattern (opposite), and transfer it to cardboard. (This pattern fits the spindles illustrated in the diagram. Adjust circular cuts in your headboard pattern to accommodate spindles of a different variety.)

Cut out the cardboard pattern and trace around it onto mahogany. Cut out the headboard with a jigsaw.

Cut doweling into twelve 1½-inch lengths for pegs.

To make four 13-inch-tall bedposts, combine one short and one long spindle, end to end, for each post. Drill a ¼-inch-diameter hole ¾ inch deep

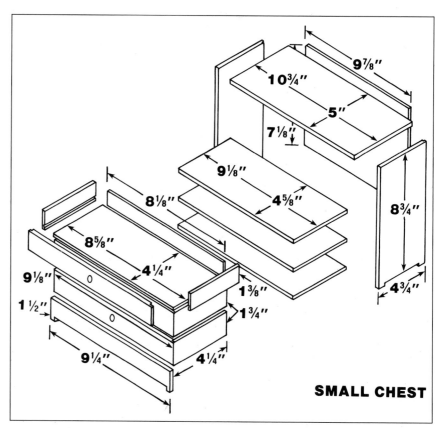

SMALL CHEST

into the center end of each spindle. Join the ends by gluing and pegging each pair with a 1½-inch length of dowel.

Drill holes the diameter of the doweling ¾ inch deep into each end of the end and side rails (see the exploded drawing, below). Drill matching holes ¾ inch deep into the thickest parts of the posts, where they will be joined to the side and end rails. Drill ³⁄₁₆-inch-diameter holes through the sides of the end and side rails for lacing. Refer to the pattern (below) for the spacing of the holes.

To assemble the bed, apply wood glue to all joining ends and into the holes drilled for the pegs. Carefully assemble the bed, inserting pegs into holes as you join the end and side rails to the spindles.

Tie strips of soft dish towels or other fabric around the bed to support the joining until the glue dries.

With an 80-inch length of twine, lace the bottom of the bed from end to end, gluing the ends of the twine into the beginning and ending holes. Then repeat the lacing process from side to side with a 90-inch length of twine.

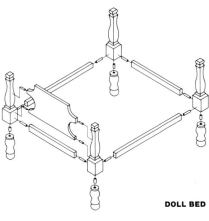

DOLL BED

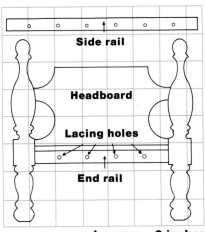

Side rail

Headboard

Lacing holes

End rail

1 square = 2 inches

Sand wood surfaces; stain and protect bed with several coats of varnish.

To dress the bed, make a mattress by cutting two rectangles of muslin. Stitch pieces together, leaving an opening. Stuff the mattress lightly with fiberfill.

Use lace or eyelet for a dust ruffle. Make sheets and pillowcases from fabric scraps; trim with lace if desired. To make a doll-size quilt, piece together 4-inch squares of calico, then line with contrasting fabric.

Knitted Doll

shown on page 145

Materials

Coats & Clark Red Heart Sport Yarn: 2 ounces cranberry, 1 ounce each of eggshell, camel, black, gray, and blue; size 3 knitting needles, or size to obtain gauge given below; fiberfill.

Gauge: 13 sts = 2 inches; 9 rows = 1 inch.
Abbreviations: See pages 218-219.

Instructions

Finished size is 18 inches high.

Body and head: Beg at lower edge with eggshell, cast on 54 sts. Work even in st st (k 1 row; p 1 row) until total length is 4½ inches; drop eggshell and attach cranberry. Work even in cranberry until total length measures 9 inches; drop cranberry and attach eggshell. Work even until total length measures 12 inches. Cast off. Fold work in half lengthwise and sew back seam; sew lower edge. Stuff firmly, leaving top open. Draw a strand of eggshell through sts of 1st row of eggshell; pull tightly to form neck and secure.

Hair section: Beg at back of neck and with black, cast on 8 sts. *Row 1* (wrong side): K in front and back of 1st st, k to last st, k in front and back of last st—2 incs made.

Row 2: P in front and back of 1st st, p to last st, p in front and back of last st. Rep Rows 1 and 2 alternately until there are 68 sts on needle. Work even in st st for 1 inch more. Break off, leaving a 20-inch tail.

Thread this end into a needle and draw through sts on needle. With another strand of black, sew edges of last 1 inch tog. With seam at center front and cast-on sts ½ inch above neck, pin hair section in place as shown in the

photograph on page 145 and sew. Add more fiberfill as necessary to fill in hair section. Draw sts on yarn tightly tog and secure. Wind a 1-inch-diameter black ball for bun; tack in place.

Embroider eyes with black; embroider mouth and cheeks with cranberry.

Leg (make 2): Beg at upper edge with black, cast on 26 sts. Work in st st for 5 inches, ending with a p row. Now work in pat as follows:
Rows 1-2: P across.
Row 3: K across.
Rows 4-8: P each row.
Row 9: * P 2 tog. Rep from * across. Break off, leaving a 20-inch tail. Thread this end into a needle and draw through rem sts. Draw tog tightly and secure; then sew seam, leaving top open. Stuff firmly. Sew top seam tog and sew to body.

Arm (make 2): Beg at top edge with cranberry, cast on 4 sts. Working in st st, cast on 3 sts at end of next 6 rows—22 sts. Work even until total length measures 5 inches. Fasten off cranberry, attach eggshell, and continue in st st for 1¼ inches more. Break off, leaving a 20-inch tail. Thread this end into a needle and draw through sts on needle. Draw tog tightly, secure. Sew seam, leaving top open. Stuff firmly. With cast-on sts on top, sew arm opening to body 1 inch below neck.

Bloomers: *Front*—1st leg section: Beg at lower edge with camel, cast on 16 sts. *Row 1:* K across.
Row 2: P across.
Rows 3-4: Rep Rows 1 and 2.
Row 5 (1st eyelet row): K 1, * k 2 tog, yo. Rep from * across, ending k 1.
Row 6: P across.
Rows 7-10: Rep Rows 1 and 2 alternately.
Row 11: (2nd eyelet row): K 2, (k 2 tog, yo, k 3) twice; k 2 tog, yo, k 2.
Row 12: P across. Work even in st st until total length measures 3½ inches, ending with a p row. Break off, sl sts onto a holder to be used later. Make another leg section in the same way; do not break off.

Joining row: K across sts on needle, cast on 4 sts, then k across sts on holder—36 sts. Work even in st st for 3 inches; cast off.

Back: Work same as for front. Sew side seams and crotch seam. Fold 1st 4 rows to wrong side on 1st eyelet row; sew in place. Pull on bloomers; add
continued

more fiberfill to round out body. Sew top edge to body. Thread needle with 15-inch double strand of eggshell. Draw through sts of each leg section ¼ inch above 2nd eyelet row; tie them at the side.

Petticoat: Beg at lower edge with camel, cast on 116 sts.

Rows 1-10: Work as for Rows 1-10 of leg section of bloomers.

Row 11: K 2, * k 2 tog, yo, k 3. Rep from * to last 4 sts; k 2 tog, yo, k 2. Beg with a p row, work in st st until total length measures 5½ inches. Fasten off, leaving a 20-inch tail. Thread this end into a needle and draw through sts on needle. Fold 1st 4 rows to wrong side on 1st eyelet row and sew in place. Pull on petticoat, draw sts on yarn end tog to fit around body, and sew in place ½ inch above bloomers.

Skirt: Beg at lower edge with cranberry, cast on 124 sts.

Rows 1-4: Rep Row 1-4 of leg section of bloomers.

Next row: P across for turning ridge. Beg with a p row, work even in st st until total length measures 6 inches. Break off, leaving a 20-inch tail. Draw yarn end through sts on needle. Turn 1st 4 rows to wrong side on turning ridge and sew in place. Draw sts on yarn end tog.

Apron: *Lower part:* Beg at lower edge with gray, cast on 46 sts. K 6 rows, then work in pat as follows: *Row 1* (right side): K 4, p to last 4 sts, k 4.

Row 2: K across. Rep Rows 1 and 2 alternately until total length measures 5 inches. Break off, leaving a 20-inch tail; draw ends through sts on needle.

Upper part: Beg at lower edge with gray, cast on 20 sts. K 4 rows, then work in pat as follows: *Row 1* (right side): K 3, p to last 3 sts, k 3.

Row 2: K across. Rep Row 1 and 2 alternately until total length measures 2 inches.

Next 4 rows: K across. Cast off. Draw sts on yarn end of lower part to width of upper part; secure and sew tog. For tie, cast on 90 sts; k 6 rows and cast off. Place center of tie at center of apron on seam; tack in place.

Shawl: With blue, cast on 3 sts.

Row 1: K 2; with yarn in front of needle, sl 1 as to p. Always sl last st in this way.

Row 2: K 1; k in front and back of next st—inc made; sl 1.

Row 3: K 3, sl 1.

Row 4: K 2, inc in next st, sl 1.

Row 5: K 4, sl 1.

Row 6: K 3, inc in next st, sl 1.

Row 7: K 5, sl 1.

Row 8: K to last 2 sts, inc in next st, sl 1.

Row 9: K to last st, sl 1. Rep Rows 8 and 9 alternately until there are 40 sts on needle, ending with Row 8. Work 3 rows even.

Next row: K to last 3 sts, k 2 tog, sl 1.

Following row: K to last st, sl 1. Rep last 2 rows until 3 sts rem. Cast off. Drape shawl over shoulders, crossing points at front. Tack each point to waist at side. Tie apron at back. Tack each corner of upper apron part to shawl.

Bonnet: Beg at center back with eggshell, cast on 18 sts.

Row 1: K across.

Row 2: P across.

Row 3: Inc 1 st in each st across—36 sts.

Row 4: P across.

Rows 5-6: Rep Rows 1 and 2.

Row 7: * K 1, inc on st in next st. Rep from * across—54 sts.

Row 8: P across.

Rows 9-12: Rep Rows 1 and 2 alternately. With a different color yarn, make each end of last row.

Rows 13-18: Work as for Rows 7-12—81 sts.

Row 19: Inc 1 st in 1st st, * k 1, inc on st in next st. Rep from * across—122 sts. Beg with a p row, work even in st st until total length measures 3½ inches. Break off, leaving 20-inch tail. Draw yarn through sts on needle.

Brim: With eggshell, cast on 66 sts. Work even in st st for 1¼ inches, ending with a p row.

Next row: P across for turning ridge. Beg with a p row, continue in st st for 1¼ inches; cast off. Draw cast-on sts at center back tightly tog and secure. Sew seam to marker. Draw sts on yarn end to length of brim and secure. Fold brim on turning ridge, place gathered end of bonnet bet the two layers of brim, and sew in place.

Cord: Cut two 72-inch strands. Twist these strands tightly in 1 direction, then fold twisted strands in half and twist in opposite direction. Cut in half and knot each end. Tack 1 cord to each side of bonnet; tie.

Gingham Goose

shown on page 146

Materials

(*Note:* All fabrics are 45 inches wide.) ⅞ yard of yellow prequilted gingham; ½ yard of yellow dotted fabric; ¼ yard of orange fabric; five 9x12-inch pieces of orange felt and two of white felt; 3¼ yards of ⅛-inch-wide orange satin ribbon; 2¼ yards of ⅛-inch-wide and 1½ yards of 1-inch-wide gold satin ribbon; 1¼ yards of ⅜-inch-wide white satin ribbon; 10-inch-square white handkerchief with gold embroidery in corners; 8-inch-diameter white doily; ⅔ yard of 1¾-inch-wide and 1¼ yards of ½-inch-wide white crocheted lace; orange and white silk flowers and leaf stems; 1 yard of 22-inch-wide heavy fusible interfacing; ½ yard of 45-inch-wide fleece interfacing; black, white, and blue acrylic paints; bird grit or marbles for weight; polyester fiberfill; graph paper; dressmaker's carbon paper.

Instructions

Enlarge pattern pieces (opposite). (*Note:* Pattern pieces include necessary seam allowances. Unless otherwise indicated, use a ½-inch seam allowance. When cutting the pieces, lay the arrows on the patterns along the straight grain of the fabric.)

Body: From quilted gingham, cut two body pieces, one underbody, and one head gusset. Also, cut *on the bias,* a 2¾ x22¼-inch front gusset.

Transfer the eyes to the body with dressmaker's carbon paper. Mix black, blue, and white paint to make a dark gray-blue. Then paint the eyebrows, eyelashes, outline, and pupils. Add more blue and white to lighten the color; paint the inside of the eyes. Paint the dot in the pupils white.

Trace the cheek shown on the body pattern and, *without adding seam allowances,* cut two cheeks from orange felt. Whipstitch the cheeks to the body, or apply with glue stick.

Shape the front gusset by trimming one end to 2 inches wide, beginning the tapering 4 inches from that end.

With right sides facing and the narrow end of the gusset at the head, pin one long edge of the front gusset to the body. Begin and end at the Xs indicated on the pattern. Stitch, clip curves; repeat for other side.

With right sides facing and matching the dots on the patterns, pin the head gusset to one body. Stitch, clip curves, and then repeat for the other side.

Staystitch along the opening line marked on the body pieces. This will reinforce the opening when you turn and stuff the goose.

With right sides facing, pin and sew body pieces together along the center back. Leave the seam open as indicated. Clip curves.

With right sides facing, pin the underbody to the body. Stitch, clip curves, and turn the body right side out.

Working through the opening in the back, stuff the bottom of the goose generously with fiberfill. Place bird grit or marbles (secured in a plastic bag) in the back half of the bottom and surround it with fiberfill. Then stuff the neck area firmly and pin the back opening closed.

To stuff the neck and head, turn the squared-off extension at the front of the head to the inside. Stuff the neck until it is solid. Pull the extension to the outside and stuff.

Turn the seam allowance of the extension to the inside. Bring the edges of the extension together, forming a vertical ridge, and whipstitch edges together. If necessary, add more stuffing through the back opening, then blindstitch it closed.

Feet: (*Note:* Use ¼-inch seam allowances throughout.) Cut four foot pieces from orange felt and four from interfacing. Fuse one piece of interfacing to each felt piece. With right sides together, pin feet together in pairs. Stitch, leaving straight ends open. Trim seam allowances close to the seam. Clip curves. Turn to the right side and press.

Moderately stuff the wide part of the feet and topstitch the foot detail shown on the pattern. Continue stuffing until feet have a rounded look. Whipstitch open ends closed and stitch feet to underbody as indicated.

Beak: (*Note:* Use ¼-inch seam allowances throughout.) Cut two lower and four upper beaks from orange felt, and cut two lower and four upper beaks from fusible interfacing. Fuse one interfacing piece to each beak piece.

With right sides facing, pin the lower beaks together. Stitch, leaving a 2-inch opening along one side. Trim the seam allowance close to the seam. Clip curves and turn to the right side. Press, and blindstitch the opening closed.

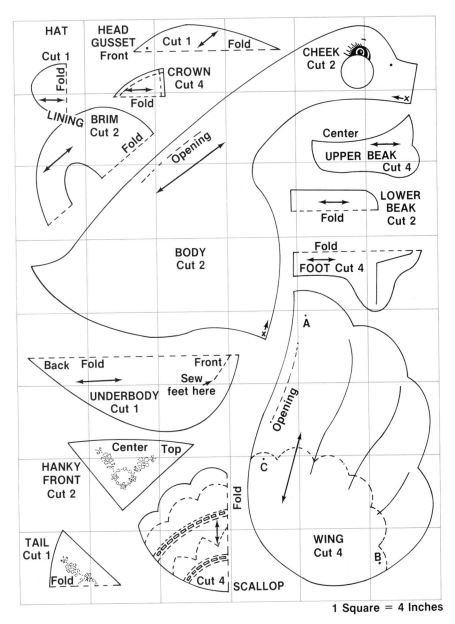

1 Square = 4 Inches

With right sides facing, pin the upper beaks together in pairs along the center seams. Stitch, leaving a 2-inch opening in the middle of the seam on one pair. Trim the seam allowance close to the stitching and clip curves.

Pin the two pairs together, right sides facing and matching the center seams. Stitch, then turn right side out through the opening in the center seam. Press; blindstitch the opening closed.

Blindstitch the lower beak to the head 1 inch in from the front of the head. Then blindstitch the upper beak to the head so that it overlaps the lower beak at the sides.

Handkerchief front and tail: Cut two hanky fronts and one tail from the corners of the handkerchief.

Pull gold ribbon through the ½-inch-wide crocheted lace. Press under ¼ inch on the raw edge of the tail. Pin lace along the outer edges of the tail, mitering corners and turning lace ends under. Topstitch along the inner edge of the lace, then pin the tail to the body and blindstitch it in place.

With right sides facing, pin hanky front pieces together along the center. Stitch, using a ¼-inch seam. Clip curves and press the seam open.

Pin lace with ribbon along the edges, mitering the corners and turning the ends under. Topstitch along the inner edge of the lace. Pin the hanky front to the body front; blindstitch in place.

continued

Wings: Cut four wing pieces from yellow dotted fabric, four scallops from orange fabric, two wings from fleece interfacing, and two wings from heavy interfacing.

With right sides facing, pin the scallops together in pairs. Stitch together along the scalloped edge using a ¼-inch seam allowance. Trim the seam; clip curves. Turn to the right side and press. Baste the raw edges together.

Pull orange ribbon through the wide crocheted lace and pin the lace to the upper half of the scallop. Topstitch along the bottom of the lace. Cut two 10-inch pieces of orange ribbon, tie them into bows, and tack them to the center of the lace.

Cut the doily in half. Pull gold ribbon through it and pin the doily to the bottom of the scallop. Topstitch close to the ribbon. Cut gold ribbon into two 10-inch pieces and tie them into bows; tack the bows to the center of the ribbon insertion.

Following the dotted scallop placement line on the wing pattern, pin the scallops to the right sides of wing fronts. Baste along the seam line, leaving scalloped edge open.

Fuse interfacing to the wrong side of the wing backs. With right sides facing, pin wings together in pairs, placing fleece interfacing against the wrong side of the front. Stitch, leaving an opening as indicated. Grade seams and clip curves. Turn to the right side and press. From points A to B, topstitch ¼ inch from the edge.

Lightly stuff the wings above the scallops; blindstitch the opening closed. Topstitch ¼ inch from the edge from A to C, then along the solid lines indicated on the pattern, beginning at the tip edge and ending under the scallop.

Lightly stuff fiberfill between the scallop and wing, ending the stuffing at the bottom of the lace. Pin the scalloped edge to the wing and topstitch along the bottom of the lace.

Blindstitch the wings to the body along the lower edge of the scallops.

Hat: (*Note:* Use ¼-inch seams throughout.)

Cut four crowns, two brims, and one lining from white felt. Cut two brims from fusible interfacing and fuse one interfacing to each brim.

With *wrong* sides facing, pin brims together. Stitch ¼ inch from the outer edge, ¼ inch from the first stitching,

and ¼ inch from the center opening. Clip the curves along the center.

Pin and stitch the crown pieces together along the curved edges. Finger-press the seams open.

With right sides facing, stitch the crown to the center opening of the brim. Clip curves. Lightly stuff the crown with fiberfill, then lay the lining over the stuffing and pin the edges to the brim. Arrange flowers and leaves on one side of the hat. Tack in place.

For the strap, tack one end of wide gold ribbon to the hat lining. Put the hat on the goose's head and wrap the ribbon under its chin. Tack the ribbon to the lining on the other side.

Tie remaining ribbons into bows and tack them to the brim opposite the flowers.

Embroidered Cat

shown on page 147

Materials

½ yard white linen or cotton fabric; pearl cotton embroidery floss in pale blue, lavender, purple, gold, burgundy, light green, dark green, red, and black; dressmaker's carbon paper; two 10x18-inch pieces of quilt batting; polyester fiberfill; embroidery hoop; graph paper.

Instructions

Enlarge the patterns (above, right), including all design lines, onto graph paper, creating a master pattern.

Lay the white fabric over the master pattern and lightly trace around the outline of the cat, two ears, and tail, leaving at least 1 inch between pieces. Transfer the embroidery lines from the master pattern onto the fabric with dressmaker's carbon paper.

Following the stitch key (above, right) and referring to the photograph for colors, embroider the cat front, ears, and tail. Press the embroidered fabric lightly on the wrong side.

To assemble the cat, cut out the embroidered pieces, leaving ½ inch all around for seam allowances. Then cut the body, ear, and tail backs the same size as the fronts.

Cut two pieces of batting the same size as the cat body; baste one to the wrong side of the embroidered cat

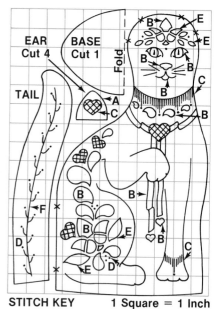

STITCH KEY   1 Square = 1 Inch
A = Outline stitch
B = Laid stitch
C = Straight stitch
D = French knots
E = Close herringbone
F = Feather stitch

front. Then lay the cat front flat, right side up. On top, lay the cat back, right side down, and place the other piece of batting on top. Pin and stitch through all four layers, leaving the bottom and the middle of one side open. Trim seams and clip curves.

Adding ½-inch seam allowances, cut one base piece from white fabric. With right sides together, fit and pin the base around the bottom of the cat. Stitch. Turn the cat right side out through the side opening.

Stuff the cat with fiberfill and slip-stitch the opening closed.

To finish the ears, pair each embroidered ear with an unembroidered one. With right sides together, stitch ears along curved edges, leaving the straight edge open. Trim the seams, clip curves, and turn right side out.

Stuff the ears lightly with fiberfill and turn the bottom raw edges to the inside. Stitch the ears in place on top of the head where indicated by the Xs on the cat body pattern.

For the tail, stitch front to back, right sides together, leaving the straight end open. Trim the seams and turn right side out. Stuff the tail firmly, turn the raw edges to the inside of the tail, and slip-stitch closed. Tack the tail to the bottom and side of the cat.

154

Homespun Donkey

Shown on page 147

Materials

½ yard of 45-inch-wide brown wool; 8 yards tan coarsely handspun linen cord; 3 yards loosely handspun gray yarn; scrap of muslin; 8 ounces polyester fiberfill; thread; graph paper.

Instructions

Enlarge the pattern pieces (right) onto graph paper. *Note:* The pieces include ¼-inch seam allowances.

From wool, cut two bodies and two ears. Cut two gussets (the part of the body below the line from X to X) from wool. Cut two ear facings from muslin.

With right sides facing, sew the upper donkey body pieces together from X to X. Do not stitch the legs. Turn the body right side out.

With right sides facing, pin a gusset to each side of the body, matching Xs and raw edges of the legs. Stitch, leaving the straight edges between Xs open.

Trim the seams, clip curves, and turn the legs right side out. Stuff the body and legs firmly with fiberfill; whipstitch closed the long straight edge on the stomach.

With right sides together, sew one facing to each ear, leaving the straight ends open. Turn the ears right side out and press them flat. Slip-stitch the openings closed.

To give the donkey its hand-stitched look, use the stitch marks on the pattern as a guide for decorating the body with large running and cross-stitches made with linen cord. Decorate the edges of the donkey's ears as well.

To attach the ears to the donkey, gather them along the straight end, then blindstitch them to the sides of the head where indicated on the pattern. Add linen-cord hand stitches, puckering the ears at the top as desired to make them floppy.

To make the tail, braid 12-inch lengths of handspun gray yarn, leaving the ends loose. Tack the end of the braid to the back of the donkey; tack the loose end to the side of the donkey where desired.

For the mane, loosely wrap 4- to 8-inch lengths of gray yarn with thread. Tack the centers of the yarn in a tousle atop the donkey's head.

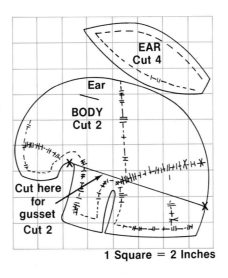

1 Square = 2 Inches

Patchwork Ponies

shown on page 147

Materials

For one pony: Scraps of brown, purple, gray, and ecru corduroy; scrap of unbleached muslin; ecru handspun yarn or cotton string; polyester fiberfill; graph paper.

Instructions

Both ponies are made from the same pattern, but the scale is different depending on the size you wish to make. The pattern (above, right) is for the smaller pony. To make the larger size, use a scale of 1 square = 1¼ inch. Determine your scale, then enlarge the pattern onto graph paper.

Cut corduroy into squares and rectangles of different sizes and piece them together until you have a 15x24-inch length of fabric for the small pony, or a 21x32-inch length for the large pony.

Adding ½-inch seam allowances, cut two body pieces from the pieced fabric. From scraps of corduroy, cut two ears and two gussets (the part of the body below the line from X to X). From muslin, cut two ear facings.

From the yarn or string, cut sixty-five 6-inch lengths for the mane and twenty 8-inch lengths for the tail. On the right side of one body piece, baste the mane and tail in place as indicated on the pattern so that the ends of the yarn are even with the raw edge of the fabric piece.

With right sides together, checking to see that the yarn lies flat while you stitch, sew the upper halves of the horse together between the Xs, leaving the

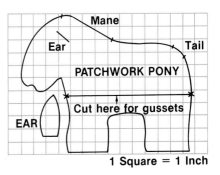

1 Square = 1 Inch

legs and straight edge from X to X open. Turn the horse right side out.

With right sides facing, pin a gusset to each side of the body, matching the Xs and the raw edges of the legs. Stitch, leaving the straight edges between the Xs open. Trim seams, clip curves, and turn legs right side out. Stuff firmly with fiberfill; whipstitch closed the long straight edge on the stomach.

With right sides together, sew one facing to each ear, leaving the straight ends open. Turn the ears right side out and press them flat. Slip-stitch the openings closed and tack the ears to the pony's head.

Wooden Horse and Wagon

shown on page 148

Materials

Scraps of 1-inch-thick and 5⁄16-inch-thick pine lumber; ¼-inch-diameter and 3⁄8-inch-diameter dowels; wood glue; four 1-inch screws and one 1½-inch screw; washer; four screw eyes.

Instructions

Enlarge the patterns on page 156. Trace two body pieces onto 1-inch-thick pine and two of each leg pattern onto 5⁄16-inch-thick pine. Cut out each shape with a jigsaw. Sand edges of each leg lightly to round corners.

Glue the two body pieces together, clamp, and let dry. Sand to round off sharp edges along curves of body.

Position legs on the body as shown on the pattern and drill ¼-inch holes through Xs. Use ¼-inch dowel pegs and a touch of glue to join legs to body.

Next, drill 5⁄16-inch-diameter holes through lower portion of each leg (as shown by Xs); drill a ¼-inch-diameter hole in center of each wheel.

continued

155

Cut two 3-inch-long pieces of dowel for axles. Insert axles through wheels and legs, gluing ends into each wheel.

For the wagon, use a jigsaw to cut axle block pieces from 1-inch pine. Then cut a 3x7½-inch piece of pine for the wagon bottom and two 2½x3-inch pieces for the ends. Cut two 2¼x9-inch pieces of ⁵⁄₁₆-inch pine for the sides, a 1x3-inch piece for the seat back, and a 1½x3-inch piece for the seat. Cut two 7¾-inch pieces of ³⁄₈-inch-diameter dowels for the tongues and two 4¾-inch pieces of ¼-inch-diameter dowel for the wheel axles.

For the cart, cut two 1¾-inch-diameter front wheels and two 2¼-inch-diameter back wheels. Add decorative carvings or incised spokes with a whittling knife, if desired.

To assemble the wagon box and seat, first glue the pieces together and let dry. Drill ⁵⁄₁₆-inch holes through the axle blocks (see dotted lines on pattern). Screw the back axle block to the wagon bottom (see arrows) with 1-inch screws. Insert the axle dowel and glue the wheels at either end.

Next, screw the front axle block to the wagon front (see arrow) with a 1½-inch screw and insert a washer between the wagon bottom and the front axle, to allow wheels to swivel. Install the axle and wheels as for the back. With 1-inch screws, attach wagon tongues to the axle front as shown on the patterns.

To hitch wagon to horse, screw two open screw eyes to the ends of the tongues and two closed screw eyes to the sides of the horse behind the front legs. Hook the wagon screw eyes through the closed eyes.

Country Doll

shown on page 149

Materials

½ yard muslin; ½ yard white printed fabric; ½ yard red paisley fabric; white handspun yarn; two 2-inch fabric squares; 4 inches of ⅛-inch-wide elastic; thread; gray, white embroidery floss; pink marker; 9 inches of ecru piping; polyester fiberfill; graph paper; dressmaker's carbon paper.

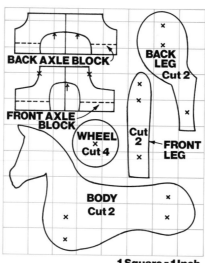

1 Square = 1 Inch

Instructions

Enlarge the patterns (opposite) onto graph paper. (*Note:* Patterns include ¼-inch seam allowances.)

Referring to the patterns for the number of each piece needed, cut the pieces as follows: from muslin, the body parts; from white printed fabric, dress bodice and sleeves and a 12x45-inch skirt; from red paisley, a 10x16-inch apron front, two 1½x5-inch apron straps, and a 1½x12-inch waistband.

To construct the doll: First stitch the two face pieces, right sides together, along the center seam. Matching the center seams, transfer the embroidery lines to the face with dressmaker's carbon paper.

Embroider the eyes, mouth, and stitches along the center seam with two strands of gray floss. Color the cheeks with pink marker.

On the body front, stitch the dart as indicated. With right sides together, match the neck edges of the chin and body front; stitch. Pin the curved edge of the chin to the face, right sides facing, matching the chin fold line to the center seam of the face. Stitch.

With right sides together, pin the two head and body back pieces together along the center back seam; stitch. Sew the body and head back to the front, right sides facing, easing curves and leaving the bottom open. Clip curves and trim seams.

Turn the body right side out and stuff it firmly. Slip- or zigzag-stitch the bottom closed.

Sew the arm and leg backs to the fronts, right sides together, and stitch, leaving the top of each open. Trim

seams, clip curves, and turn inside out. Stuff and slip-stitch closed. Sew the arms and legs to the body where indicated on the pattern.

To make the hair, cut the yarn in 5-inch lengths. Separate the lengths into several bunches. Then wrap thread around the center of each bunch and tack to the head.

To make the dress: Sew the bodice and sleeve pieces together along the shoulders and underarms, right sides facing. Slash the back along the length of the fold line.

Fold under ¼ inch on the raw edges of the bottoms of the sleeves and tuck a 2-inch length of elastic under the seam allowance on each. Pulling the elastic taut while you sew, stitch through the seam allowance and elastic. This will gather the bottom of the sleeves.

Sew the short sides of the skirt together, right sides facing, leaving the seam open 2 inches at one end. This seam will be the center back, and the opening will be at the top.

Hem the skirt bottom and gather the top edge to fit the bodice waist. With right sides facing, sew the skirt to the bodice, matching the back openings. Trim the bodice neck with ecru piping.

Put the dress on the doll and sew the back openings closed, tucking raw edges inside and catching the back of the doll in the stitches.

For the apron: Finish the short sides of the apron front with rolled hems and stitch a 1-inch hem along one long edge. Using white floss and long, straight stitches, sew the fabric-square "patches" to the apron front. Gather the upper edge of the apron front until it is 5 inches long.

Center the waistband strip over the apron front, right sides together. Stitch. Fold under the raw edges of the waistband; press. Wrap the waistband around the doll and tack in place, catching the doll in the stitches.

Fold the raw edges of the shoulder straps to the inside along the long edges; press. Topstitch close to the edges of the straps. Then position the straps over the doll's shoulders, tucking the ends under the waistband in the front and back. Stitch in place.

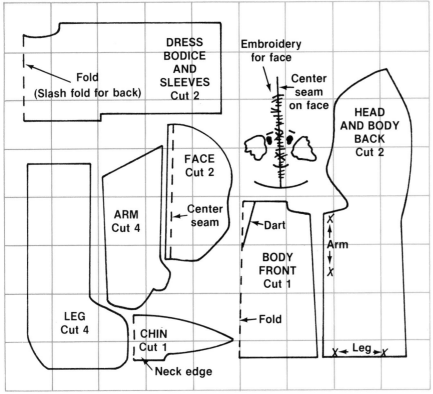

DRESS BODICE AND SLEEVES Cut 2

Fold (Slash fold for back)

Embroidery for face

Center seam on face

HEAD AND BODY BACK Cut 2

FACE Cut 2

Center seam

ARM Cut 4

Dart

BODY FRONT Cut 1

Arm

LEG Cut 4

CHIN Cut 1

Fold

Neck edge

Leg

1 Square = 2 Inches

Doll Basket and Linens

shown on page 149

Materials

14x22-inch oval wicker basket; red fabric dye; ⅔ yard ecru fabric; 2 yards red-and-white, 2-inch-wide gathered ruffling; 1¾ yards red wide bias tape; 1½x13-inch strip red paisley fabric; two 2-inch fabric squares; red, green embroidery floss; two pounds polyester fiberfill; thread.

Instructions

Mix the fabric dye according to the manufacturer's instructions and apply it to the basket by brushing it on or immersing the basket in a dyebath. Let dry, then fill the basket with fiberfill.

For the pillow, cut an 8½x13-inch rectangle from ecru fabric. Trim one long edge with gathered ruffling, then sew the red paisley strip over the seam. Add fabric "patches" at random to the right side with straight stitches in red or green floss. Fold in half, right sides together and, using a ½-inch seam allowance, stitch along the two straight edges. Turn the pillow right side out and stuff with fiberfill.

From ecru fabric, cut an oval that is 1 inch larger than the perimeter of the basket. Trim the raw edges of the oval with the remaining ruffling and stitch red bias tape over the seam. Lay the sheet over the fiberfill in the basket and tack it to the basket edges.

Doll Quilt

shown on page 149

Materials

One 17-inch square each of red paisley, green printed fabric, and thin quilt batting; thread.

Instructions

With right sides facing, place the red and green squares together and lay the batting on top; pin. Sew around all four edges, using a ½-inch seam allowance and leaving an opening for turning. Trim the seams and corners, and turn the quilt right side out.

Topstitch ½ inch from the edges and sew five rows of topstitching 3 inches apart across the quilt.

Baby Bunting

shown on page 7

Materials

Five 6x36-inch strips of colored fabrics; 30x36 inches each of quilt batting and lining fabric; 1½ yards of ¼-inch-wide grosgrain ribbon; four 1¼-inch-long wooden toggles.

Instructions

With right sides facing, sew the five colored strips together along the long edges, using ½-inch seam allowances. Press the seams open.

Lay the lining out flat, right side down. On top, lay the batting, then the pieced top, faceup. Trim the edges of the batting and lining even with the pieced top.

Pin all three layers together along the seam lines in the top, and 2 inches in from the raw edges on all sides. Along the two long sides and one short side, fold the lining up over the edge of the batting, then fold under the edge of the pieced top. Pin, keeping corners sharp. The one short side left open will be the bottom of the bunting, and will be finished with a drawstring casing.

Cut four 3½-inch pieces of ribbon for toggle tabs. Fold the pieces in half; pin. Position the ribbons on the left side of the bunting front, centering each on one of the four lower colored strips. Tuck the ends of each ribbon between the edges of the top and lining so that about 1 inch of the ribbon loop extends past the edge; pin in place.

Topstitch ¼ inch from the edge along the three folded sides, catching the ribbon ends in the stitching, and ending the stitching 2 inches above the bottom of the bunting. Topstitch 2 inches from the bottom edge, and along the seams joining the colored strips.

To make the drawstring casing along the bottom, trim the batting between the fabric layers along the open bottom edge, and fold the bottom raw edges inside as for the top and sides. Topstitch ¼ inch from the bottom edge, up the sides of the bunting 1 inch, and back across the bunting 1¼ inches from the bottom edge.

Thread the remaining length of ribbon through the casing created by the rows of stitching along the bottom of the bunting.

Sew toggles on the right side of the bunting front 2½ inches from the edge.

157

Handsome Accessories for the Country Look

Calico prints and homespun fabrics, roughhewn textures, and natural materials are all staples of the country look. In this chapter you'll find lovely gifts to make from these ingredients of country style.

It's an enticing collection of home accessories with classic country styling. There are decoys to carve, a grapevine wreath and twig basket to craft, a cross-stitch sampler design, Early American comb-painted boxes, plus patterns for patchwork and quilting.
♦ Begin with a gaily garlanded tablecloth, pillow, and guest book (left)—delightful examples of the appliquérs' art. And each variation of the floral pattern shown here lends itself easily to many other projects as well.

For example, graceful arcs of vines, leaves, and calico blossoms are stitched around the border of this 54-inch-square tablecloth. By adjusting the number and placement of the appliqué pieces, you could easily extend the same basic pattern to fit a larger square or angle it to suit a round or rectangular tablecloth.

Similarly, the small circle of flowers shown here on an 11-inch pillow would look equally pretty on a square pillow top or stitched into a quilt block.

For a perfect housewarming present, make an appliquéd and embroidered guest book like the one displayed on the table. Or use the same techniques to personalize a purchased scrapbook or photo album.

The instructions for these and all of the charming country accessories that follow begin on page 166.

159

Handsome Accessories for the Country Look

A set of rustic goose decoys (right) makes a splendid gift for your favorite outdoorsman. The strong, simple lines and stark coloring of this stately pair lend a welcome touch of drama to any room's decor, whether it be country or contemporary.

Carve a pair of these 15-inch-long Canada goose decoys from a single log of softwood, such as pine or poplar.

Roughly shape the bodies with a hatchet, then carve the feathers and features using a chisel, gouge, and jackknife. Whittle the head and neck from a block of pine (or the crook of a small tree) and fit each one with glass eyes.

Finally, enhance the texture and grain of the wood by painting the birds with thinned-down artist's acrylics. Subtle shades of black, gray, brown, and white lend a realistic mottled coloration to these striking folk-art birds.

♦ The patterned boxes (left) have an antique, combed finish. Early American craftsmen used this ingenious technique to lend surface interest to painted wooden objects of all kinds.

Re-create the country feeling of this old-fashioned, combed finish on anything from furniture to trinket boxes for unusual hand-painted gifts or home accessories.

Scrape the painted surface with a cardboard comb to reveal an undercolor and create enhancing rippled, waved, or fanned patterns that can disguise even the largest flaws in the surface of the painted object.

You might wish to experiment with this technique on a small project such as the simple band

160

boxes (left). Then try your hand at transforming secondhand or unfinished furniture into unique accessories.

♦ A grapevine wreath is a country classic of which true country enthusiasts never tire. Embellish a simple wreath of twisted grapevines with wooden hearts and ribbon streamers (above) for a contemporary approach, or just leave it *au naturel* for a down-home wall decoration with year-round appeal.

♦ Cross-stitched samplers are often the focal point of a country decorating scheme, and the cheerful stitchery (above) is sure to be the center of attention wherever it hangs. It is a successful blending of old-fashioned sentiment and traditional, quilt-pattern motifs with a new-fashioned sense of color and design—easy to stitch and a pleasure to give.

161

Handsome Accessories
for the Country Look

Here are two more ways to turn natural materials into country accessories.

♦ Flexible grapevines, stripped of loose bark but with their curly tendrils intact, make this graceful basket (near left). Add narrow satin ribbons and dried ferns and flowers for a woodsy centerpiece. Or use the basket simply as a decorative accent—filled with a small pot of flowers or a green plant, a dozen handcrafted wooden eggs, or an assortment of unshelled nuts.

♦ The delicate corn husk maiden in the foreground (left) is a welcome addition to any country collection. She's a lovely display piece, sure to delight young and old alike. Although more sophisticated than the crude corn husk dolls that pioneer children often played with, she's crafted from the same simple materials.

Tint the doll's dress, bonnet, and shawl with liquid fabric dyes. And fashion her hair from slender strips of dampened corn husk that have been curled around a pencil or a small dowel and allowed to dry.

Use morning glory vines, woven together and trimmed with tiny dried flowers, for the miniature wreath.

♦ The three lampshades (above) bring the pleasures of a country garden indoors to enjoy year round.

Graceful blossoms and clusters of berries adorn the undersides of the paper shades. Delicate cuts, pierced paper patterns, and gentle furls along the edges of the flowers and leaves accent the designs, making them especially lovely when the lamps are lit.

Paint the designs with watercolors on purchased or made-to-size paper shades. Line the shades with parchment-weight tracing paper to provide a softly diffused light behind the patterns.

Edge the completed shades with braid, ribbon, or velvet trim—whatever is most appropriate for your own country decor.

Floral Tablecloth

shown on page 158

Materials

1½ yards of 54-inch-wide linen; ¼ yard each of 5 calico prints (flowers); ¼ yard of gold calico print (flower centers); 1 yard of green fabric (leaves and stems); matching threads.

Instructions

Enlarge the flower, flower center, leaf, and stem patterns (right). Add ¼ inch to all pieces for seam allowance. Cut out a total of 32 flowers from various colors of calico, 32 centers from gold calico, plus 96 leaves and curved stems.

Clip the curves of pieces and fold selvage under; press. Baste all raw edges under. Slip-stitch the flower centers to flowers.

The chart (right) represents a quarter of the total design. Mark the position of the pattern pieces on the linen cloth. Slip-stitch the vines, leaves, and flowers to the linen square using the marked guidelines on the cloth and the chart as a guide. To finish, hem the tablecloth with a ½-inch double-folded hem; press.

Floral Pillow

shown on page 159

Materials

⅓ yard of white linen; ½ yard of blue calico (backing and ruffle); scraps of calico (flowers); scraps of green fabric (leaves); ¼ yard of gold calico (flower centers and cording); 1 yard of narrow cording; polyester fiberfill.

Instructions

Enlarge the pattern pieces (above, right) onto tissue paper. Draw an 11-inch-diameter circle on brown paper for the outside edge of the pillow top. Center and draw a 6¾-inch-diameter circle inside the larger one.

Referring to the photograph for placement, position the flower design along the inner circle. Trace and repeat the design until the entire wreath is formed to create the master pattern.

Cut the flower pieces from calico fabric, the flower centers from gold calico fabric, and the leaves from green fabric. Clip all curves and baste under the raw edges; press. Slip-stitch the flower centers to the flowers. Pin the wreath pieces to the linen, using the master pattern as a guide. Slip-stitch the pieces to linen cloth.

Cut and piece enough strips of bias-cut gold calico to cover 1 yard of cording. Baste the covered cording around the outside edge of the pillow.

Piece a 3x72-inch strip of blue calico for the pillow ruffle. Fold the fabric in half lengthwise, gather, and pin to the pillow front. Stitch in place, securing cording in the stitching.

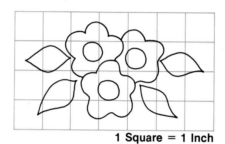

1 Square = 1 Inch

Cut a blue calico circle the same size as the linen pillow front. Place the right sides together; pin and stitch around the circumference, leaving an opening for stuffing. Clip curves to ensure smooth seams. Turn right side out, stuff with polyester fiberfill, and slip-stitch closed.

Guest Book

shown on page 158

Materials

Purchased guest book; 6x8 inches of 24-count aida cloth or even-weave linen; ¼ yard of print fabric to cover book; scraps of calico; scraps of green fabric; size 8 gold pearl cotton; small piece of quilt batting; spray adhesive; scraps of wrapping paper.

1 Square = 1 Inch

Instructions

Following the chart (below), cross-stitch "Guests" on lower third of even-weave cloth (center design), working each cross-stitch over 3 sets of threads.

Enlarge the flower and leaf pattern (below) and cut the pieces from the appropriate fabrics, adding ¼-inch seam allowances to all pieces.

Baste the seam allowances under and position the flowers and leaves on the fabric; slip-stitch in place.

Frame the appliqué and embroidery with a strip of gold bias-cut fabric; baste in place. Cut a "window" in backing fabric to frame gold strip. Roll edges under to form a narrow hem; slip-stitch to linen.

Pad the top of the book with a layer of quilt batting. Press the fabric book cover and place it facedown on a newspaper-covered surface. Spray lightly with adhesive. Carefully wrap cover around guest book, pressing fabric into indentations along the book spine. Trim the fabric to 1 inch larger than the book cover. Fold over and glue the raw edges in place, clipping and trimming as necessary. When the glue is dry, cover the raw edges with gift wrap.

Goose Decoys

shown on page 160

Materials

15-inch-long, 25-inch-diameter log of softwood (such as pine, willow, or poplar); ax; hatchet; jackknife; handsaw; coping saw; large saw; rasp and files; rotary grinder; chisel; gouges; drill; 2x5x7-inch scrap of pine; glass eyes; acrylic paint in black, white, gray, light and dark brown, and beige; ½-inch-diameter dowel; sandpaper; felt; glue; graph paper; graphite paper.

Instructions

Using an ax, split the log in half lengthwise. If the halves aren't exactly the same size, use the larger one for the male and the smaller one for the female. Follow the same pattern and instructions for both decoys, but for the female, shape the neck into a more graceful arch.

Shape the half-log, with a hatchet, following the diagram (above, right). The split edge of the wood will be the flat underside of the decoy as shown in the top- and side-view diagrams (right).

Enlarge the pattern (below) onto graph paper. This will be your full-size master pattern. Using a chisel and gouges, carve the outline of the feathers, first referring to the top and side views for the general shape, then to the master pattern for more detail.

Drill a ½-inch-diameter hole in the top of the decoy, approximately 1 inch deep, between the Xs indicated on the pattern to hold a dowel that will connect the body to the head.

To make the head, enlarge the head and neck portions of the pattern (below) onto graph paper. Position the enlarged pattern onto the block of pine so that the arrow parallels the grain of the wood. This is extremely important, because proper alignment with the wood grain will prevent the head and beak from splitting or chipping. Trace the outline onto the block of pine.

With a coping saw and a small, fine handsaw, rough out the shape of the head from the pine block. Then whittle the details, using a jackknife and following the traced lines on the wood. Round the head and cheeks with the grinder. If you whittle away too much, build up the beak or head with wood putty. Then sand the head smooth.

If you wish, you can use the crotch of a tree branch (inverted) for the head. Shape the head as described above, following the natural grain of the branch.

Drill the holes for the eyes where indicated on the pattern. Then drill a hole up into the neck of the decoy between the Xs indicated on pattern for the connecting dowel.

continued

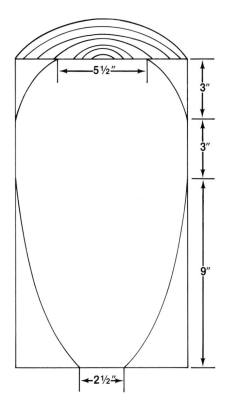

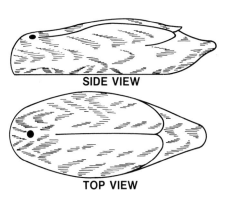

SIDE VIEW

TOP VIEW

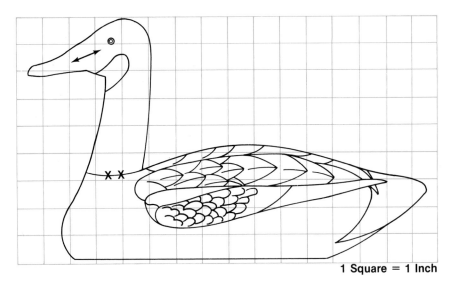

1 Square = 1 Inch

165

Insert the dowel and, with glue, join the dowel to the head. Sand the body parts thoroughly to remove any rough edges and to prepare the decoy for finishing. Attach the head to the decoy body by inserting the neck dowel into the hole drilled into the body. Glue in place and allow to dry.

To paint the decoy, first use graphite paper to transfer the feather details from the master pattern to the decoy. Refer to the photograph on page 162 as a guide for color placement. Paint the head and tail feathers black and the marking on the upper neck indicated in the diagram on page 167, white. Paint the upper feathers dark brown and the side feathers light brown, adding details in black.

Paint the decoy's breast gray toward the front, gradually fading into shades of beige and white as you move toward the back. Let the paint dry thoroughly.

Glue the glass eyes to the head. Then cut a piece of felt to fit the bottom of the decoy and glue it in place so the base of the decoy will be smooth.

Comb-Painted Boxes

shown on page 160

Materials

Wooden box; enamel and latex paints in contrasting colors; cardboard; scissors; paintbrush.

Instructions

Create the pattern on the box from two shades of paint—an undercoat and an overcoat that is "combed" to reveal the layer of paint underneath.

To begin, undercoat the box with the desired shade of enamel. While the paint is drying, make your "combs" as follows: Cut several 2x2-inch squares from cardboard. At about ¼-inch intervals, cut out narrow V-shape slits from one edge of each square.

When the enamel is dry, apply a coat of latex paint to the box. Immediately run the slit edge of the cardboard across the box in straight lines, swirls, zigzags, spirals, or whatever design you wish. When your comb becomes coated with paint, change to a dry one.

Let the paint dry thoroughly, then apply polyurethane for protection.

Grapevine Wreath

shown on page 161

Materials

Several 12- to 20-foot lengths of mature grapevine no more than ½ inch in diameter; garden clippers; wire; scraps of ¼-inch-thick pine lattice; jigsaw; red acrylic paint or fabric dye; grosgrain ribbon.

Instructions

To find wild grapevines, look along fencerows and around the outskirts of hardwood forests. The vines should be brown, not green, and are most easily pulled from spring through fall.

With garden clippers, trim the branches from the grapevines, leaving intact as many small tendrils as possible. Remove any loose bark.

Working with one vine at a time, bend each length into a wreath shape. Entwine the vines, one atop another, until the wreath is 3 to 4 inches thick.

Weaving the vines together will usually hold them, but secure them by wrapping with thin wire or monofilament, if desired.

Make a paper pattern of a heart that will fit onto the pine lattice scraps. Cut the desired number of hearts, and sand lightly. Color by painting the hearts with watered-down red acrylic paint or immersing them in red fabric dye. After they dry, decorate the wreath with the hearts and ribbon.

If you wish, decorate the wreath with ribbons, flowers, or other trims for a different effect.

East-West Cross-Stitch Sampler

shown on page 161

Materials

18-inch square of hardanger fabric in ecru or white; blue, red, and green embroidery floss; embroidery hoop or frame; small tapestry needle; graph paper; colored pencils.

Instructions

The finished stitchery measures approximately 15x15 inches.

Use graph paper to make a master pattern of the design. With blue, red, and green felt pens or colored pencils, transfer the diagram (above, right) to the graph paper. To transfer the design, begin in the lower left corner and work toward the center, copying the design from the chart. (Work the cross-stitch design directly from the chart [above], if desired.)

Complete the right side of the design by repeating the column of houses and hearts from the left side, except stitch a heart instead of a house in the top square and alternate down the column. If you wish, you can rechart the 1983 in the middle of the design, making it whatever date you desire.

Before you begin to stitch, preshrink and press the fabric, then mount it in a hoop or frame.

Use three strands of floss for the embroidery and work each stitch over two threads of fabric. Always work the cross-stitches in the same direction.

To begin, use a waste knot to anchor the thread end in the fabric. Following your master pattern, or the chart and the color key (above), make the first stitch 1½ inches from the edge and in the middle of one side of the fabric.

Work the blue border all the way around. When you finish a length of floss, clip off the beginning knot and weave the loose ends under the stitches.

Continue working the motif from the outer edges in, counting threads carefully as you go.

Stretch and frame the completed design as desired.

Corn Husk Doll with Wreath

shown on page 162

Materials

Corn husks; glycerin; two cotton balls; two 1-inch foam balls; rust and gold fabric dye; lightweight poster board; modeling clay; wire; straight pins; white glue; cheesecloth; morning glory vines; small dried flowers.

Instructions

To prepare the corn husks, soak them in warm water for a few minutes until they become pliable. (Add a drop or two of glycerin if the husks are thick and brittle.) Work while the husks are still damp.

Following the manufacturer's instructions on the fabric dye packages,

166

□ Blue   ⧄ Red   ◉ Green   1 Square = 1 Stitch

dye 4 husks rust for the shawl and bonnet, and about 8 husks gold for the sleeves, bodice, and top skirt.

Head: Place a foam ball in the center of a 3-inch-wide husk. Wrap the ball completely with the husk, then tie thread around the bottom of the ball to form the neck. Slide a 6-inch wire through the neck and head.

Arms: Cut an 11-inch wire and bend the ends inward ¾ inch to form loops for the hands. Thread a ¾-inch-wide strip of husk through each hand and wrap it around the loop and to the middle of the wire, adding strips as necessary. Wrap thread around the hands and arms to secure the husks.

Sleeves: Gather a 6-inch-wide gold husk around each wrist, extending the husks out over the hands. Wrap the husks tightly with thread, then pull them back over the arms, shaping puffed sleeves. With thread, secure each husk to the center of the 11-inch arm wire. Push the wire attached to the head through the center of the arms; wrap with thread to secure.

Bust and waist: Place 2 cotton balls side by side in the center of a vertically positioned husk. Then fold the long sides toward the center and fold the husk in half across the width over the cotton balls. Wrap thread around the husk under the cotton balls to form the waist. Position this section on the front of the neck wire ½ inch below the neck. Wrap thread over the shoulders and around the waist to secure.

Dress bodice: Center a 3-inch-wide gold husk over each shoulder and cross the husks over the bust in the front and back, gathering them at the waist. Secure with thread, tying husks tightly to the wire. Repeat with two more husks, pleating them across the shoulders. Wrap a narrow strip of husk around the waist for a waistband.

Skirt: From poster board, cut a 15-inch-diameter circle; cut circle in half. Wrap the edges of one half-circle into a cone so that it measures approximately 5 inches in diameter across the bottom and 1 inch across the top.

For the bottom skirt layer, cover half of the cone with natural-color husks, overlapping each strip slightly and pinning only at the base of the cone. Trim the husks toward the top so they lie flat against the cone and wrap them with thread to prevent buckling as they dry. Repeat for the other half of the skirt.

For the top skirt, repeat the process, using gold husks and gathering them around the cone top so that they lay in pleats. Pin them to the base of the cone and wrap with thread until dry.

Insert the bodice through the opening in the cone top. Secure the bodice to the skirt with a long needle, pushing it through the skirt, bodice, and on through to the other side of the skirt. Glue the waist area from the inside of the cone and remove needle when dry.

Hair: Cut a corn husk into long ¼-inch-wide strips. Wrap the strips around a narrow pencil and let dry. Slide the loops off the pencil and arrange them around the doll's face, securing them with pins and glue.

Bonnet: Work modeling clay around a 1-inch plastic foam ball into a bonnet shape for a mold on which to shape the husks. Cover with cheesecloth to keep the wet husks from sticking to it.

Work a wet, rust-colored husk into the desired shape on the mold; secure it with thread. Let the husk dry overnight. Remove thread and gently pull the bonnet away from the clay. Attach bonnet to head with glue.

Shawl: Pin a rust-colored husk around the doll's shoulders, pleating it as you go. Trim the ends just above the doll's elbows. Repeat, trimming the next layer of the shawl about ½ inch shorter than the first. To form the ties at the neck of the shawl, fold a narrow rust husk over the raw edge of the collar and overlap the ends in front. Pin in place until dry.

Wreath: Soak the morning glory vines in water until they are pliable. Bend them into 2½-inch-diameter circles and lay them one atop another to form a wreath. Join the circles *on the back* with dabs of white glue or wire. Pin the wreath to a flat surface, dip the dried flowers in glue, and lay them on the wreath to dry. Then glue or pin the wreath to the doll's hand.

When the doll is completely dry, remove all pins and threads that were used to secure husks in position.

continued

Grapevine Basket

shown on page 162

Materials

Several lengths of mature grapevine; garden clippers; wire; dried flowers; ribbon.

Instructions

With garden clippers, trim the large branches from the grapevines, leaving as many small tendrils intact as possible. Remove any loose bark.

Bend several vines into circles that are the desired diameter of your basket. Layer the circles one atop another until you have a stack about 4-5 inches high. These will form the sides of the basket.

With garden clippers, cut two pieces of vine that, when laid in a cross, will fit into the bottom of the basket. Wire these two pieces together, then weave other grapevines around them to form a sturdy base for the basket.

Wire the bottom to the sides of the basket and add a curved vine handle.

Decorate the basket with dried flowers, ribbon bows, and streamers.

Cut-Paper Lampshades

shown on page 163

Materials

Individual lampshade rings (*for flower with butterfly shade,* one 8-inch- and one 15-inch-diameter ring; *for lilac shade,* one 7-inch- and one 11-inch-diameter ring); *for strawberry shade,* an assembled hexagonal shade—ours is 6½ inches high and approximately 8 inches in diameter (available at hobby and craft stores); watercolor paper to cover the shade; tracing paper to line shade; dressmaker's carbon; darning needle; craft knife; two dozen spring-clip clothespins; white glue; ribbon, braid, or velvet trim; several yards of brown paper to make pattern.

Instructions

To ensure the correct amount of paper, make your pattern before purchasing any watercolor and tracing paper.

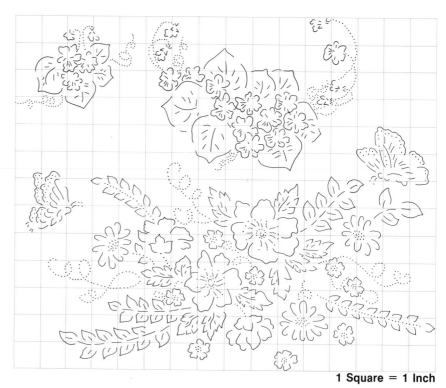

1 Square = 1 Inch

To make pattern for circular shades: Using the diagram (below, right) as a guide, on a sheet of brown paper at least 1 yard wide and 2 yards long (piece if necessary), draw a straight line 6 inches from the long edge of the paper (line A). Draw a second line parallel to the first so the distance between the lines equals the height of the shade (13 inches for the *flower with butterfly shade,* 8½ inches for the *lilac shade*). This is line B.

Fold your brown paper pattern in half widthwise. Open paper, and draw line along the fold. This is line C. Extend line C at least 3 feet.

Measure the diameter of the top ring; make two dots on line B the distance of the diameter, with line C centered between the two dots. Mark the dots D and E.

Measure diameter of bottom ring and mark on line A in same manner as directed above. Mark dots F and G.

Extend a line through dots F and D until the line crosses C. Repeat for dots G and E. *The lines should cross line C at the same point.* Mark this point H.

Place a compass point on H and pencil point on D. Draw curved line through dots D and E. Repeat for dots F and G with compass point on H.

Measure the circumference of your bottom ring, using a string. Place the string on the bottom curved line of the

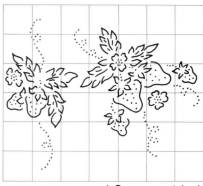

1 Square = 1 Inch

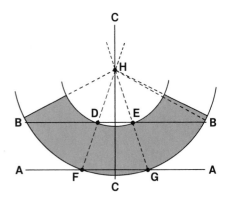

pattern, centering string on line C. Mark dots at the ends of the string on bottom line. Extend a line from each of these dots to H. Add ½ inch for seam allowance at one end. This is your complete pattern. Cut out along curved lines, disregarding A, B, and C.

To check fit, clip pattern to rings using clothespins.

To make pattern for strawberry shade: Lay the hexagonal shade onto brown paper and trace around the shape of each side. (The size of each side may vary.) Trim the edges slightly so the shapes will fit the wire frame.

Cut patterns from watercolor paper.

To craft the shades: Enlarge the patterns (left) for the desired shade onto brown paper. Transfer the patterns onto watercolor paper using dressmaker's carbon. This is the inside of lampshade. Paint the designs with watercolors; allow to dry.

Place the watercolor paper over a thick padding, such as a folded towel. Then pierce all the dots, using the compass point.

Next, cut the shapes with a craft knife. Place paper shade on heavy cardboard surface. Cut around the shapes, being careful to leave at least ⅛ inch of paper uncut so petals, fruit, leaves, and wings are still attached to shade. Cut along straight lines for stems, veins, butterfly, and flower details.

Working from the painted side, sculpture the petals, leaves, and wings by rolling them around a pencil. Trace a lining onto heavy tracing paper using the paper pattern. Run a thin line of glue around the outside edges on painted side of shade. Place liner *over* the painted surfaces.

To assemble flower with butterfly and lilac shades: With the painted side on the inside, wrap the paper over the rings, securing with clothespins set close together. The rings should be inside and even with the top and bottom edges of the shade.

Remove the pins along the overlapped portion of the paper. Run a thin line of glue along the edge and press the seam. Replace clothespins. Allow glue to dry; then remove all clothespins.

Run glue along the inside edge of the shade bottom to secure the ring and reclip with clothespins. Repeat the process for the top ring. Allow rings to dry thoroughly. Glue trim along top and bottom edges to finish.

To assemble strawberry lampshade: Run glue around the outside edges of one section of the frame. Clip paper to frame. Add sections, one at a time, allowing to dry completely before adding next section. Clip sections to frame when possible. Press unclippable edges to frame with fingers for a few minutes.

Trim top and bottom with grosgrain ribbon. Glue velvet ribbon over ribs of frame and along top and bottom of ribs.

Pewter Accessories

shown on pages 10-11

Materials

16-gauge pewter sheets or circles; ball peen hammer; leather-face mallet; fine sandpaper; files; 0000 steel wool; tin shears; sandbag; jeweler's saw; ruler; soldering torch; starting blocks (see instructions, below); flux (7 to 8 drops hydrochloric acid and 1 ounce glycerin, available at pharmacies).

Instructions

For starting blocks: Collect maple or cherry blocks that measure approximately 1½x5x5 inches. Have a wood turner scoop out bowl shapes that are about 2 inches in diameter and ½ inch deep in the center of each block. Or, hand-scoop hollows with a pocket knife and sand them smooth.

For napkin ring: Draw a 1½x5¼-inch strip on a pewter sheet. Cut out the strip with tin shears, then trim and round the ends with a file. Sand the edges smooth. Place the metal on a flat surface (the back of a starting block, an anvil, or a piece of hardwood). With the ball peen hammer, use light, random strokes to hammer the metal to the desired texture.

To shape the ring, bend the metal around a 1½-inch-diameter chair leg. With a leather-face mallet, hammer the ends snugly around the chair leg. Slip the napkin ring from the leg. File the edges and polish with steel wool.

For berry spoon: Enlarge the template pattern (above, right) onto cardboard; cut out. Place the template on a pewter sheet; draw the spoon outline onto the sheet and cut it out with a jeweler's saw. File and sand the edges.

To form the bowl of the spoon, place the edge in the starting block and, with a leather-face mallet, hammer concentric, overlapping strokes around the

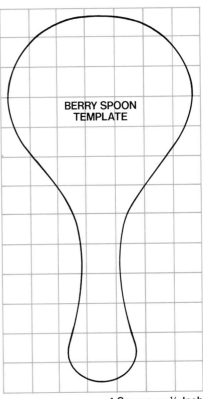

BERRY SPOON TEMPLATE

1 Square = ½ Inch

edge of the metal along the edge of the starting block. Apply light, concentric strokes around the handle to form the desired shape. Drill ⅛-inch-diameter holes randomly in the spoon bottom, and drill a ¼-inch hole in the handle for hanging. Clean with steel wool.

For porringer: File off the burr along the outer edge of a 6-inch pewter disk and place the edge of the disk in the starting block. Rotating to the left, hammer light, overlapping, concentric strokes to mold the metal into a bowl shape. Continue rotating, moving in over the edge of the starting block until the bowl reaches a depth of 1½ inches. Smooth with sandpaper and steel wool.

Saw a handle from a piece of sheet pewter to fit the radius of the porringer bowl. Sand the handle smooth and clean it with steel wool.

To solder the handle to the bowl, first prepare scrap pewter by hammering it thin, cleaning it with sandpaper, and cutting it into thin sniplets. Turn the clean bowl upside down and fit the handle snugly against the radius of the bowl. With an artist's brush, apply flux to the part to be soldered. Solder the pewter sniplets over the joint, using a soldering torch. *Pewter melts at 450 degrees, so use a very light flame.*

169

To Have & To Hold

Keepsakes for the Perfect Wedding

Instead of buying a conventional gift, delight your favorite bride-to-be with a hand-crafted heirloom. Here and on the following pages we've collected charming, useful, and wonderfully original gifts for you to create for the bride of your choice.

For a uniquely personal contribution to the ceremony itself, choose from an elegant assortment of tatted, quilted, knitted, and crocheted accessories to make for the bride and her wedding party.

Or you might create an extravagantly romantic frame for the couple's favorite photograph, or embroider a special memento to commemorate the occasion.
♦ As a case in point, a pretty pair of cross-stitched albums would make an especially

thoughtful gift. Friends and family can fill the guest book with good wishes at the reception. And the large photograph album has ample space to document the wedding celebration—from the rehearsal right through the honeymoon.
♦ Sporting ribbons and lace and rounds of ruffles, the gracefully garlanded frame (far right) would be the perfect setting for a sentimental photograph—whether it's a formal portrait of the bridal couple or a candid snapshot of their firstborn.

For a description of the tatted flowers and crocheted gloves, please turn the page.

Instructions for all of the projects shown in this section begin on page 176.

170

Keepsakes for the Perfect Wedding

These enchanting bridal accessories are designed to complement any wedding scheme, from down-home country to classic Victorian.
♦ A scattering of white and whimsical tatted flowers (above) mixes beautifully with almost any combination of fresh flowers for an elegant

and original arrangement. Why not work up a baker's dozen as a wedding gift—twelve for the bridal bouquet and one extra for the bridegroom's boutonniere.
♦ Crochet a pair of lacy, three-button gloves like this pair (below, left) to beguile a young bride with an old-fashioned bent. They're the perfect finishing touch for a softly feminine wedding ensemble, but they'll do wonders for a crisply tailored silk wedding suit as well.
♦ For a richly traditional, yet highly personal gift that's sure to please both bride and groom, cross-stitch particulars of their wedding on a charmingly nostalgic sampler (right). Stitched in vibrant colors on hardanger cloth, the pattern features all the symbols of love and fidelity —from hearts and flowers to rings and doves. Whether the couple's new home is country or contemporary, they're sure to hang this handsome 13x15-inch sampler in a place of honor.

Keepsakes for the Perfect Wedding

One hallmark of a memorable wedding is a beautifully turned out bridal party. For a wedding procession straight out of your favorite fairy tale, give attendants a touch of medieval elegance with flower-strewn and softly quilted caps and weskits. If understated sophistication is more to your liking, dress the attendants in chic little sweaters knitted in pastel shades of velvety chenille.

♦ The sculptured, satin-trimmed vests (left) slip over the head and are worn over lace-collared, long-sleeved gowns made from a purchased pattern. The stylized leaves and flowers are machine embroidered, then appliquéd or simply tacked to the vests and caps for an elegant and gracefully sculptured effect.

♦ For a more contemporary approach, knit a set of sleek, short-sleeved sweaters for the bridesmaids, in flattering shades of plush chenille yarn (right). Pair each sweater with a purchased skirt of flared wool crepe and belt with a length of lovely ribbon for a pretty and practical outfit that's guaranteed to see the bridesmaid through many an occasion long after the wedding is over.

Guest Book and Wedding Album

shown on pages 170-171

Materials

For the photograph album: 12½-inch-square album; 13½x27 inches of ecru hardanger cloth; one 13½x27-inch piece and two 13½x10-inch pieces of lining fabric; 12½x26 inches of batting; 42 inches of ecru lace.

For the guest book: 7x9-inch guest book; 8x21 inches of ecru hardanger cloth; one 8x21-inch piece and two 5½x8-inch pieces of lining fabric; 7x20 inches of batting; 29 inches of ecru lace.

For both: embroidery floss in colors noted in the color key (right and opposite); embroidery hoop, needle; graph paper; colored pencils.

Instructions

To create master patterns, use colored pencils to transfer the diagrams (right and opposite) to graph paper. To complete the patterns, flop the designs.

The burgundy border on the finished photograph album will be 10 inches square; on the guest book, 5¾x7¾ inches. Mark these boundaries on the fabric as follows: Lay the hardanger cloth for the album out flat, right side up. Measure in 2 inches from the right and top edges of the fabric and mark lightly with a pencil. Follow the same procedure for the guest book, measuring in 1½ inches from the right and 1¼ inches from the top.

For the embroidery: Use three strands of floss; work each stitch over two threads of fabric. Work the cross-stitches in the same direction, so the top (crossing) thread always falls in the same direction on the fabric.

To begin stitching, use a waste knot to anchor the thread end in the fabric. (When you finish a length of floss, clip off the beginning knot and weave the loose ends under the stitches.)

Following the master patterns, color key, and penciled guide marks on your fabric, work the first stitch in the top right-hand corner of the border. Embroider the border completely around the design.

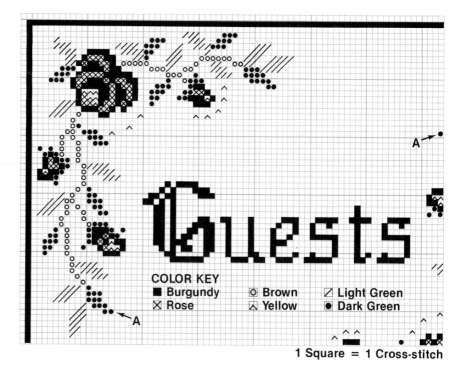

COLOR KEY
- ■ Burgundy
- ☒ Rose
- ◉ Brown
- ◣ Yellow
- ⧄ Light Green
- ● Dark Green

1 Square = 1 Cross-stitch

Next, cross-stitch the interior motifs following the charts and counting the threads carefully.

To assemble the book cover: Hem one long side on each of the small lining-fabric rectangles. With the right sides together and raw edges matching, baste one hemmed rectangle to one end of the large lining rectangle. Repeat this step on the other end. This creates the pocket flaps that will slip over the ends of the book.

Lay out the batting on a flat surface. On top of the batting, lay the lining rectangle so that the small rectangles are faceup. Then lay the embroidered fabric on top, wrong side up.

Using ½-inch seams, machine-stitch the three layers together around three sides. Leave one short side open. Clip the corners, turn to the right side, and press. Slip-stitch the opening closed.

Insert the album into the pocket flaps. Tack lace around the embroidered border, overlapping the ends and stitching them together.

Bridal Picture Frame

shown on page 171

Materials

1⅛ yards of 1½-inch-wide pregathered ecru lace ruffle; ¾ yard of tan suede-type knit fabric; 1⅝ yards of burgundy piping; ⅝ yard of ecru Venetian lace; 2½-millimeter-diameter pearls; three 8x10-inch pieces *each* of mat board and quilt batting; assorted pink and burgundy silk flowers; ¼-inch-wide pink velvet ribbon; nylon filament tape (clear, reinforced package tape, available in drugstores); double-face tape; white and silicone glues.

Instructions

The size of the finished frame, including the ruffle, is about 12x14 inches, suitable for a 5x7-inch picture.

To begin, cut the following from the knit fabric: three 10x12-inch pieces, enough strips to equal one 5x75-inch length when pieced together, and one 1x36-inch strip.

Cut a 4¼x6-inch oval in the center of one piece of the mat board. Cut a matching oval from one piece of the quilt batting. With double-face tape, secure the batting (minus the oval cutout) to the back of the board.

Lay one 10x12-inch piece of fabric flat, wrong side up. Center the mat board over the fabric and trace the oval onto the wrong side of the fabric. Stay-stitch the fabric along the oval outline.

Cut out the oval from the fabric, *leaving a 1-inch seam allowance beyond the stay-stitching.* Clip through the seam allowance to the stitching.

To form the front of the frame, lay the wrong side of the fabric against the

continued

Our Wedding

COLOR KEY
- ■ Burgundy
- ⊠ Rose
- ⊙ Brown
- ⊡ Yellow
- ⧄ Light Green
- ● Dark Green

Center

1 Square = 1 Cross-stitch

side of the mat board. Tuck the seam allowance around the oval under the board and secure it with filament tape.

To trim the frame: Sew a pearl to the center of each medallion on the Venetian lace. Next, using silicone glue, secure the lace ½ inch from the edge of the oval.

Glue or tape the outer edges of the fabric to the back of the board. Then glue piping around the oval and rectangular edges of the frame.

Next, make a fabric ruffle: Turn under ½ inch on short ends of the 5x75-inch length of fabric. Baste. Fold the strip in half lengthwise, *wrong sides together*. Baste together raw edges, then gather the strip until it fits around the frame with a 2-inch overlap at the ends. Next, sew pregathered lace to the ruffle (¼-inch seam), matching raw edges. Using white glue, secure the right side of the ruffle to the back of the fabric-covered board. Let dry.

Along one long side of the board, stretch filament tape so it is even with the seam line on the ruffle. The tape will allow you to easily slide the picture in and out of this side of the frame.

Tape the remaining two pieces of batting to the two pieces of mat board. Then, on each board, stretch fabric over the batting side and tape the edges to the back of the board.

From the 1x36-inch strip of fabric, make piping. Glue it around the edge of one of the covered mat boards; let dry.

To make the back of the frame: Glue the two boards together back to back and lay them atop a thick folded towel. Weight with books until the glue is dry.

To finish: Glue the frame back to the front on three sides, not including the side with the filament tape. Again, lay the frame on a thick towel and weight with books until dry. Finally, arrange flowers and ribbon on the front of the frame. Secure with silicone glue.

Tatted Flowers

shown on page 172

Materials

No. 8 white pearl cotton thread; white flower stamen with a pearl bead tip and a stem; white 1-inch-diameter silk flower petals; 18-inch lengths of No. 21- or 22-gauge wire; florist's tape; tatting shuttle; white glue.

Tatting abbreviations

CR: Close ring. Pull on the shuttle thread until the just-completed work forms a ring.

Join: Technique of attaching into the previously completed work.

Number: Tat the specified number of double stitches.

P: Picot.

R: Make a ring of . . . .

RW: Reverse work. Turn work upside down; begin new chain or ring according to directions.

Instructions

For each flower, wind 9 yards of pearl cotton onto the shuttle. Start in center of each petal. Leave a ¼-inch length of thread between each ring.

First arm: *Step 1:* R of 2, P, 1, P, 1, P, 2, CR. Leave a ¼-inch length of thread. *Step 2:* R of 2, join to last picot of previous ring, 1, P, 1, P, 2, CR. Leave a ¼-inch length of thread.

Step 3: Repeat step 2 twice more.

Step 4: R of 3, join to last picot of previous ring, 2, P, 3, P, 5, CR. Leave a ¼-inch length of thread.

Step 5: R of 5, join to last picot of previous ring, 5, P, 5, P, 5, CR. Leave a ¼-inch length of thread. *Step 6:* R of 5, join to last picot of previous ring, 14 picots separated by one double stitch, 5, CR. Leave a ¼-inch length of thread.

Step 7: Repeat step 5. *Step 8:* R of 5, join to last picot of previous ring, 3, P, 2, P, 3, CR. Leave ¼-inch of thread.

Step 9: Repeat step 2 twice more.

Step 10: R of 2, join to last picot of previous ring, 1, P, 1, join to *1st* picot of *1st* ring of this arm, 2, CR. Tie a small piece of contrasting-color thread to this ring to mark it as the last ring of this arm. Tie and cut threads. Whipstitch through knot to secure it, using matching sewing thread.

Second arm: *Step 1:* R of 2, P, 1, P, 1, P, 2, CR. Leave a ¼-inch length of thread. *Step 2:* R of 2, join to last picot of previous ring, 1, join to center picot of last ring of previous arm, 1, P, 2, CR. Leave a ¼-inch length of thread.

Step 3: R of 2, join to last picot of previous ring, 1, join to center picot of next to last ring of previous arm, 1, P, 2, CR. Leave ¼-inch length of thread.

Step 4: Repeat step 2 of first arm.

Step 5: Repeat steps 4-10 of first arm.

Third, fourth, and fifth arms: Add in the same manner as the second arm. Be sure to join the center picot of 11th and

12th picots of 5th arm to the center picots of 2nd and 3rd rings of first arm.

To stiffen the flowers: Wet the lace and place each flower over a cap from a shampoo or dishwashing detergent bottle. Dab the flowers with a solution of ⅓ water and ⅔ glue and finger them into the desired shape. Allow them to dry for 12 to 24 hours.

To assemble flowers: Glue a single round silk flower petal in the center of each flower. Make a slit in the center of the silk petal and insert the pearl tip on the stamen through the bottom of the flower to the top. Place an 18-inch length of wire next to the stamen stem so one end touches the center bottom of the flower. Wrap the stamen stem around the wire, then wrap the stem with florist's tape, starting at the base of the head of the flower.

Three-Button Lace Gloves

shown on page 172

Materials

Two balls white size 30 American Thread Gem crochet cotton (or suitable substitute); size 12 steel crochet hook, or size to obtain gauge given below.

Gauge: 2 shells (4 tr, ch 1, and sc) = 1 inch; 6 rows = 1 inch.

Abbreviations: See pages 218-219.

Instructions

Directions are for size 6; changes for size 7 follow in parentheses.

Fifth finger: *Rnd 1*—Ch 4, 7 dc in 4th ch from hook; join to top of ch.

Rnd 2: Ch 1, sc in same st as join; (ch 3, sc in next dc) 7 times; ch 3, sl st in first sc—8 ch-3 lps. Sl st into next 2 ch and in same ch-3 lp.

Rnd 3: Ch 4, * dc in next lp, ch 1, dc in same lp, ch 1, dc in next lp, ch 1. Rep from * twice more; dc in next lp, ch 1, dc in same lp, ch 1, sc in ch-4 sp.

Rnd 4: Ch 1, skip ch-loop where join was just completed. * 4 tr in next ch-1 sp, ch 1, sk next ch-1 sp, sc in next dc, ch 1, sk next ch-1 sp. Rep from * around, ending with ch 1, join to 1st sc.

Rnd 5: Ch 5, * dc bet 1st and 2nd tr, ch 1, dc bet 2nd and 3rd tr, ch 1, dc bet 3rd and 4th tr, ch 1, tr in next sc, ch 1. Rep from * around, ending with ch 1 before tr in sc, sl st in ch-5 sp to join.

178

Rnd 6: Ch 4, sk ch-loop where join was just completed. * dc in next ch-1 sp, ch 1. Rep from * around, ending with ch 1, sc in ch-4 sp to join.

Rnd 7: Ch 1, skip ch-lp where join was just completed. * 4 tr in next ch-1 sp, ch 1, sk next ch-1 sp, sc in next ch 1 sp, ch 1, sk next ch-1 sp. Rep from * around, ending with 4 tr in next ch-1 sp, ch 1, sl st in 1st sc to join.

Rep Rnds 5-7 for pat until total length measures around 2 (2½) inches, ending with Rnd 5. Fasten off.

Fourth finger: Work as for fifth finger until length measures about 2½ (3) inches, ending with Rnd 5. Fasten off.

Middle finger: Work as for fifth finger until length measures about 3 (3½) inches, ending with Rnd 5. Fasten off.

Index finger: Work as for fifth finger until length measures about 2½ (3) inches, ending with Rnd 5. Fasten off.

Now join fingers as follows: Sew 2 ch-1 sps directly above a 4-tr grp on last rnd of fifth finger to 2 ch-1 sps directly above a 4-tr grp on last rnd of fourth finger; sew middle finger to opposite edge of fourth finger and index finger to middle finger in the same way.

Palm: *Rnd 1:* Join thread in a ch-1 sp at side of index finger , ch 4, * dc in next ch-1 sp, ch 1. Rep from * around working in each finger, ending with ch 1, sc in ch-4 sp at beg—52 ch-1 sps. Continue in pat until length past Rnd 1 of palm measures 2 inches, ending with Rnd 5. Fasten off.

Thumb: Work as for fifth finger until length is about 2 (2½) inches; end with Rnd 5. Fasten off. Sew 2 ch-1 sps above sc bet two 4-tr grps of last rnd to 2 ch-2 sps at side of last rnd of Palm. Sk 22 ch-1 sps to the left of where thumb joins palm, join thread in next ch-1 sp, ch 4, * dc in next ch-1 sp, ch 1. Rep from * around palm and thumb, ending with ch 1 sc in ch-4 sp—67 ch-1 sps. Continue pat for 7 rnds.

Shape base of thumb as follows: *Dec Rnd 1:* Work in pat until 27 ch-1 sps are made, ending with a tr in next sc, ch 1, dc bet 2nd and 3rd dc of next 4-tr grp, ch 1, dc bet 3rd and 4th ch of same grp, ch 1, tr in next sc, continue in pat over next two 4-tr grps, ch 1, dc bet first and 2nd dc of next tr grp, ch 1, dc bet 2nd and 3rd dc of same grp, ch 1, tr in next sc; complete rnd in pat.

Dec Rnd 2: Work in pat until 26 ch-1 sps have been made, ch 1, dc in next sp, dc in following sp—dec made; (ch 1, dc in next sp) 12 times; ch 1, dc in next sp, dc in following sp—dec made; complete rnd in pat.

Dec Rnd 3: Work in pat until 7 tr grps have been made, ending with sk next ch-1 sp, sc in next ch-1 sp, ch 1, dc in next ch-1 sp, ch 1, dc in next ch-1 sp, ch 1, sk 1 sp, 4 tr in next sp, ch 1, sk 1 sp, sc in next sp, ch 1, sk 1 sp, 4 tr in next sp, ch 1, sk 1 sp, dc in next sp, ch 1, dc in next sp, ch 1, sc in next sp, ch 1, sk 1 sp; in next ch-1 sp complete row in pat as established; ch 5, turn.

Work button opening and rem of thumb shaping as follows: *Dec Row 4:* Dc bet first 2 tr, ch 1 and continue in pat until 24 sps have been made including ch-5 sp, sk 1 sp, dc in next sp, ch 1, sk 1 sp, dc bet next 2 tr, ch 1, dc bet 2nd and 3rd tr, ch 1, dc bet 3rd and 4th tr, ch 1, tr in sc, ch 1, dc bet next 2 tr, ch 1, dc bet 2nd and 3rd tr, ch 1, dc bet 3rd and 4th tr, ch 1, sk 1 sp, dc in next sp, ch 1, tr in sc, ch 1; complete row in pat, ending with tr in sc; ch 4; turn.

Dec Row 5: Dc and ch 1 in each sp across, ending with ch 1, dc in ch-5 sp; ch 1, turn.

Dec Row 6: Sc in turning dc, sk 1st sp, work in pat until 6 tr grps have been made, ch 1, dc in next 2 sps, ch 1, sk 1 sp, 4 tr in next sp, ch 1, sk 1 sp, dc in next 2 sps, ch 1, sc in next sp; complete row in pat, ending with sc in turning ch sp; ch 5, turn.

Next row: Work in pat across; work st only in scs and between trs. Do not work in or between the 2 dc groups. End row with ch 1, tr in sc; ch 4, turn.

Following row: Skip first ch-1 sp. Dc in next sp, ch 1, complete row in pat, ending with dc in ch-5 sp; ch 1, turn.

Next row: Sc in turning dc, ch 1, sk first sp; work in pat until 9 tr grps have been made, ch 1, sc in next ch-1 sp; ch 1, sk sp, work in pat ending with sc in ch-4 sp, ch 5, turn. Work next 6 rows in pat as established. Beg and end rows as directed in last 3 rows.

Next row: Work in pat to 1st sc, * 3 tr in sc, ch 1, work in pat to next sc. Rep from * across, ending ch 1, tr in last sc; ch 5, turn. *Following row:* Dc in next sp, * ch 2, dc in next sp. Rep from * across, ending with dc in turning ch sp, join with sc to 3rd ch of beg ch-5.

Cuff: *Rnd 1*—Ch 1, sk 1st ch-2 sp, * tr in next sp, (ch 1, tr in same sp) 3 times, ch 1, sk 1 sp, sc in next sp, ch 1, sk 1 sp. Rep from * around, ending ch 1, 4 tr in first sc—cluster made; mark for end of rnd.

Rnd 2: * Ch 2, dc bet 1st 2 tr, ch 2, dc bet 2nd and 3rd tr, ch 2, dc bet 3rd and 4th tr, ch 2, 4 tr in next sc—cluster made. Rep from * around, ending with ch 2, dc in last ch-1 sp.

Rnd 3: * Ch 2, dc in next ch-2 sp. Rep from * around, ending with ch 2, sc in ch-2 sp over 1st 4-tr cluster. Rep last 3 rnds for pat 3 times more, ending last rep with ch 2, sc in next sp.

Edging rnd: * Ch 1, sk 1 sp, tr in next sp, ch 3, sc around top of tr just made for a picot (pt), (ch 1, tr in same sp, ch 3, pt) 4 times; ch 1, sk 1 sp, sc in next sp. Rep from * around, join to 1st sc. Fasten off.

Button openings: With right side facing, join thread and sc evenly around, working 3 button lps evenly spaced across one side of opening as follows: Sc to position, ch 12, turn, sl st in last sc made, ch 1, turn, 18 sc in lp just made to complete; sc to next position; rep; continue around. Fasten off.

Button (make 3): *Rnd 1*—Ch 2, 8 sc in 2nd ch from hook; do not join this or following rnds, place a marker to establish end of rnd. *Rnd 2:* Work 2 sc in each sc—16 sc. Then work even for 1 rnd more; fasten off, leaving a 4-inch length of thread. Stuff; weave end through last rnd of sts and pull to close; secure end. Attach buttons.

Work other glove in same way, reversing position of button opening.

Bridal Sampler

shown on page 173

Materials

18x20 inches of white hardanger cloth; embroidery floss in the following colors: burgundy, rose, pink, light and dark green, blue, yellow, and light brown; embroidery hoop and needle; masking tape; water-soluble marking pen; graph paper; colored pencils.

Instructions

Following the diagrams (pages 180-181), use colored pencils to transfer pattern to graph paper. Next, chart names and dates of your choice onto the sampler pattern.

Bind edges of the hardanger fabric with masking tape to prevent raveling.
continued

(first names)

(last name)

(month, date and year)

COLOR KEY

◪ Light Blue	◪ Rose	◪ Celery Green	⊡ Bright Yellow
⊠ Light Pink	■ Burgundy	◉ Olive Green	⊞ Light Brown

1 Square = 1 Stitch

180

Locate the exact center of the fabric and mark with a water-soluble marking pen. Mount fabric in embroidery hoop.

Locate center of diagram and center of fabric; begin cross-stitching here. Use two strands of floss throughout. Refer to the diagram for colors and placement. Work each cross-stitch over two threads.

When entire piece is stitched, block the fabric by pressing it lightly, using a clean, damp press cloth.

Center the sampler on a piece of mat board, over a layer of batting, if desired. Tape raw edges of fabric to back of board. Frame.

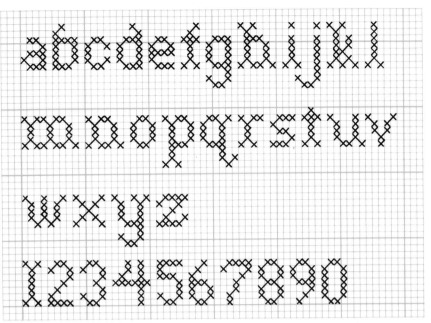

1 Square = 1 Stitch

Floral Appliquéd Vests and Caps

shown on page 174

Materials

For two vests and two caps (sets A and B): 2 yards *each* of ecru crepe and of contrasting fabric for lining; 1¼ yards of patterned ecru satin for borders on vests and caps; ⅛ yard *each* of light and dark green fabrics for leaves; scraps of pink, dark pink, rose, and purple fabrics for flowers and centers; 1 yard *each* of stabilizer (or paper if stabilizer is unavailable) and lightweight iron-on interfacing; 1 yard of thin polyester quilt batting; ¼ yard of polyester fleece; silk thread to blend and contrast with appliqués; pink and bronze metallic threads; 100 tiny glass beads for blossom stamens; dressmaker's carbon.

Instructions

Note: Each finished vest is approximately 14 inches wide and 16 inches long. Also, each vest and cap contains a combination of flat, trapunto, and sculptured appliqués.

Flat appliqués are stitched directly onto the vest or cap (pattern pieces 1, 2, 5, 10-12, 16-18, 22, 23, 25, 32-35, 38, 39, 42, 45, 47-50).

Trapunto appliqués are filled with quilt batting for a textured, puffy effect (pieces 4, 6, 8, 9, 14, 15, 20, 21, 28, 30, 37, 41, 43, 46).

Sculptured appliqués are separate, three-dimensional flowers and leaves that are tacked to the background (pieces 3, 7, 13, 19, 24, 26, 27, 29, 31, 36, 40, 44, and 51-61).

continued

VEST A-Front

_ _ _ _ **Quilting Line** .... **Position Line** 1 Square = 1 Inch

To begin: Enlarge patterns (right and on page 181). Transfer the patterns to brown paper, adding ½-inch seam allowances to all pieces. Using dressmaker's carbon, transfer the patterns for the cap pieces and vest front and back, including numbers, onto *wrong* side of crepe fabric. Also transfer flower and leaf patterns to appliqué fabric, grouping flat, trapunto, and sculptured leaf and flower pieces together. Mark each piece of the pattern on the wrong side with its designated pattern number. *Do not cut out pattern pieces yet.*

Apply iron-on interfacing to green fabric for flat leaves, to pink fabric for blossom centers, and to leaf pattern on the hanging blossom (on Cap B).

To make sculptured blossoms: Pin two or three layers of stabilizer or typing paper underneath each blossom design. Machine satin-stitch along the tapered decorative lines on each blossom. Cut out flower centers and leaf patterns; satin-stitch these to the blossoms with pink metallic thread. Tear away paper or stabilizer.

Baste the blossom top, batting, and fabric for blossom backing together along outlines; cut out each blossom.

Machine satin-stitch around each blossom until raw edges are completely covered. Pull and stretch edges of each blossom for a slightly ruffled effect.

Note: For the hanging blossom on cap B, satin-stitch only along the curved lines. Make a vine streamer from a ½-inch-wide green fabric strip cut to desired length. With right sides together, stitch ¼-inch seam lengthwise; trim and turn to right side. Fold blossom in half, inserting tip of vine streamer; satin-stitch along curved line again to bind streamer in place. Stretch to ruffle curved edge of blossom.

For stamens of blossoms: Hand-sew two crisscrossing loops of beads—four beads on the first loop, five on the second—to center of flowers. With bronze metallic thread, stitch a scattering of French knots around the stamen and onto the petals for pollen.

To make leaves: Cut out flat leaves and set aside. For trapunto leaves, baste batting to wrong side of each leaf; cut out. For sculptured leaves, place batting between leaf top and a piece of fabric for backing; baste, and satin-stitch together along seam lines and center veins. Cut out all shapes.

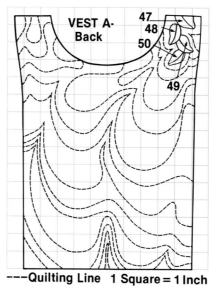

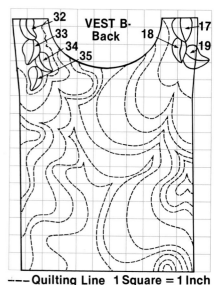

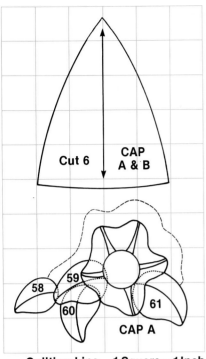

Cut 6 CAP A & B

58 59
60 61
CAP A

---–Quilting Line   1 Square = 1 Inch
·······Position Line

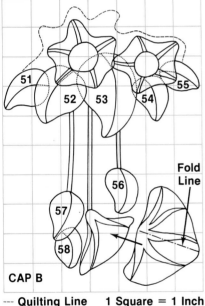

51 55
52 53 54
56
57
58

Fold Line

CAP B

--- Quilting Line   1 Square = 1 Inch
······· Position Line

Note: For the hanging leaves on Cap B, insert end of the streamers when stitching across the base of the leaves.

To assemble vest: Cut out vest front, matching back and lining pieces. Stitch vest front to back at shoulders; repeat for lining pieces. Press.

Baste two layers of stabilizer to wrong side of vest front and back.

Satin-stitch flat and trapunto leaves in place, including vine streamers on

vest B. Remove stabilizer. Steam-press. Next baste batting between vest front and lining; machine- or hand-quilt along all quilting lines, using silk thread. Tack blossoms to vest front as indicated on pattern.

To make borders: From patterned ecru satin, cut four 3-inch-wide strips on the bias. Bind edges of vest, allowing ¼ inch for seam allowances and mitering all corners.

To make neckband: From patterned ecru satin, cut a bias strip 1¼ inches wide to fit around neck. With right sides facing, sew bias strip to neck edge (¼-inch seam). Press under ¼ inch on remaining raw edge of bias strip, then fold strip in half. Slip-stitch to neck. Add ribbons on sides, front and back, for fastening, if desired.

To make caps: (See notes above on preparing flowers and leaves.) Cut 6 triangles *each* from satin, lining fabric, and quilt batting. Add ⅜-inch seam allowances to all pieces.

Stitch satin pieces together along long sides of triangles. Press seams open; repeat for lining pieces. Seam batting triangles together by overlapping the ⅜-inch seam allowances; stitch and trim to eliminate bulkiness.

Sandwich the satin cap, batting, and lining together; baste. Quilt the three layers together in the pattern of your choice. Bind the bottom raw edge with a bias strip, as for neckline.

For cap B, attach streamers to cap; cover streamer ends by tacking blossoms and leaves to side of cap. For cap A, tack leaves and blossoms in place.

Bridesmaid's Puff-Sleeved Pullover

shown on page 175

Materials
Reynolds Velourette yarn (30-gram balls): 10 (11, 12) balls; sizes 3 and 6 needles, or size to obtain gauge.

Gauge: With larger needles over st st, 9 sts = 2 inches; 6 rows = 1 inch
Abbreviations: See pages 218-219.

Instructions
Back: Beg at lower edge with smaller needles, cast on 65 (71, 79) sts. Work in k 1, p 1 ribbing for 8 rows. Change to larger needles and work in st st for 8

rows. Inc 1 st at each edge of next and each following row 5 times in all—75 (81, 89) sts. Work even until total length from beg measures 9 (9½, 10) inches, or desired length to underarm, and ending on wrong side. Mark last row.

Armhole shaping: Cast off 4 (4, 5) sts at beg of next 2 rows. Dec 1 st at each edge every other row twice—63 (69, 75) sts. Work even until length past beg of armholes measures 7 (7½, 8) inches, ending on wrong side.

Shoulder shaping: Cast off 7 (8, 8) sts at beg of next 4 rows; then cast off 6 (6, 8) sts at beg of next 2 rows—23 (25, 27) sts. Sl rem sts to holder for back of neck.

Front: Work same as for back until length past beg of armholes measures 5 (5½, 6) inches, ending on wrong side.

Neck shaping: Work across 25 (27, 29) sts, sl next 13 (15, 17) sts to holder; complete row. Working both sides at once, dec 1 st at each neck edge every other row 5 times—20 (22, 24) sts each side. When length past beg of armholes equals that of back, work shoulder shaping as for back.

Sleeves: With smaller needles, cast on 49 (53, 59) sts. Work in ribbing same as for back. Change to larger needles and work in st st, inc 1 st each edge of every other row 5 times—59 (63, 69) sts. Work even until total length measures 3½ (4, 4) inches, ending on wrong side. Mark last row.

Top shaping: Keeping to st st, cast off 4 (4, 5) sts at beg of next 2 rows. Dec 1 st at each edge every other row 8 (10, 10) times—35 (35, 39) sts. Work even until total length past marked row measures 5¾ (6¼, 6¾) inches. Work 4 sts tog at beg of each of next 6 rows—17 (17, 21) sts. Cut yarn, leaving an 8-in. tail. Sl sts off needle; draw yarn through rem sts.

Finishing: Sew left shoulder, side, and sleeve seams.

Neckband: *Row 1:* From right side with smaller needles, k across the 23 (25, 27) sts of back neck, pick up and k 15 (16, 17) sts along left neck edge, k across the 13 (15, 17) sts of front neck, pick up and k 15 (16, 17) sts along right neck edge—66 (72, 78) sts.

Row 2: Work in k 1, p 1 ribbing. Work 10 more rows ribbing. Sew right shoulder and neckband seam. Sew in sleeves, gathering fullness at top of sleeve as necessary.

Heirloom Treasures

Elegant Gifts to Craft with Love

Certain occasions call for an all-out effort—the creation of an extraordinary (if not extravagant) gift to mark a once-in-a-lifetime event. In this chapter you'll find a selection of gifts that beautifully suit just such an occasion. Each is a joy to make and can be given with real pride, like the romantic, rose-inspired gifts shown here.

Everyone responds to the loveliness of a rose, and these unique needle-art creations capture the essence of that timeless beauty in elegant gifts that will be cherished for years to come.

♦ A formal wreath of full-blown roses graces the perfect frame for a treasured family photograph (far right). Worked in needlepoint on 14-count interlock canvas, the frame is a generous 16 inches square, with a 6x8-inch oval opening for the portrait.

♦ Charming trinket boxes pick up the rose motif in pretty petit point (foreground) or needlepunch embroidery (rear). You might fill one with homemade pot-pourri, or nestle a cherished piece of antique jewelry inside.

♦ For a more fanciful floral gift, stitch an entire "bouquet" of rose bloom pillows. For a cozy little 10-inch cushion like the one shown here, needlepoint the posy pattern on 14-count interlock canvas. To make a set of pillows in graduated sizes, stitch the same pattern on different size canvases.

For more floral gifts, turn the page. And for more on the gold crochet doily, see page 188. Instructions for all the designs in this section begin on page 192.

184

Elegant Gifts
to Craft with Love

Whatever the message, "saying it with flowers" is a time-honored tradition. And what better way to deliver a message of love, thanks, or congratulations than with a flower-bedecked gift that continues to bloom, season after season.

♦ The very first flower that a pioneer bride planted round her doorway was apt to be that queen of the prairie, the wild rose. This hearty, humble flower welcomed visitors to the door, inviting them to share the simple pleasures of hearth and home within.

We've captured the delicate colors and robust spirit of that winsome rose in a handsome crocheted coverlet (left). Worked in afghan stitches and then embroidered in simple cross-stitches, the 58x70-inch coverlet features a lacy filet crochet edging, with satin ribbons in soft shades of pink, green, and lavender woven throughout.

♦ A plump basket of fake blossoms (above) is another way to add a garden touch to any room. This soft, shaped pillow is appliquéd with leaves and petals cut from plush and satiny fabrics, then embellished here and there with a touch of embroidery.

Elegant Gifts
to Craft with Love

Delicate doilies and elaborately edged linens have long been pet projects of those who love to crochet. But for a new twist to an old-fashioned gift idea, work up a batch of these ultra-elegant table settings from the marvelous assortment of new metallic threads available.

♦ Gilded doilies like these (below) add sparkle and spirit to any festive occasion or holiday

table. The two doilies on the right are worked in rounds from the center, while the third (left) features a lovely filet crochet center of diamonds and squares set off by delicate, decorative scallops.

♦ Shimmery metallic edgings also can transform the simplest linens into wonderful party-time place settings, like these elegant place mats and napkins (right).

Although the glitter gives these table accessories a special holiday flavor, you can always work the same patterns in white, ecru, or colored cotton crochet threads for a more subtle and traditional look.

For example, the lacy curtains (above, right) feature the same graceful, bell-shaped edging as the round, gilt-edged doily (far right), but the effect is totally different.

Elegant Gifts
to Craft with Love

G reat things, as everyone knows, often come in small packages. Here are several small but elegant projects that are sure to be a big success with anyone on your gift list.

♦ The two lovely book covers (left) are consummate examples of the needlecrafter's art. Embroider the first (far left) in rich crewel yarns; the second (near left) is appliquéd with a delicate tracery of tatting. Slip an inexpensive address book or a slender volume of poems into either cover for a delightfully personal gift.

♦ Just imagine the uses a sweet young miss might find for the charming ceramic heart box (below). The palm-size shape is ideal for jewelry, or for corralling the heady scent of sachet powder or potpourri.

You'll have to work with a local ceramic studio to make a box like this one (unglazed boxes are usually available in a variety of shapes for a nominal fee). And the sky's the limit when it comes to decorating the top—dab on a few free-hand posies, or just paint the entire box a single glorious color.

♦ The oval boxes, bedecked with violets, (above) are only 2½, 3½, and 4½ inches long. The designs are cross-stitched with floss on perforated paper, then glued to felt-lined boxes made from tag-board. The designs can be adjusted to suit square or rectangular boxes as well.

♦ Make the rose and pansy boxes from 6- and 7-inch wooden containers (available in craft and hobby shops). Paint the designs with acrylics, using just a delicate wash of color to enhance the beauty of the wood.

♦ Nestled among the boxes above is a satin and lace sachet. To make one like it, first stitch up a single, small cathedral pattern quilt block, then back the small square with satin, stuff with sweet smelling sachet, and trim with a lace bow. Any 4- to 6-inch quilt block square can be turned into an attractive sachet in the same way. (For a cathedral window pattern and other quilt block patterns, refer to any good quilt design book.)

Needlepoint Rose Pillow

shown on page 184

Materials

For a 10-inch-diameter pillow as shown: 14x14 inches of 14-mesh interlock canvas; 32-inch strands of 3-ply wool in the following amounts and colors: 10 deep burgundy, 12 wine, 45 dark rose, and 42 medium rose; size 19 tapestry needle; masking tape; permanent needlepoint marker; polyester fiberfill; velour backing fabric.

Note: For a larger or smaller pillow, change the scale when enlarging the pattern. Adjust size of canvas and amount and ply of wool accordingly.

Instructions

Enlarge the pattern (above, right) and transfer onto canvas, using the permanent marker. Bind the edges of the canvas with masking tape to prevent raveling, and mount the canvas in a needlepoint frame, if desired, to minimize distortion.

Work the rose pillow using two strands of yarn. Work a single area of color at a time in either continental or basket-weave stitch, referring to the pattern for color placement.

Block finished canvas and cut out rose shape, leaving ½ inch of unworked canvas around the edges. Cut velour backing fabric same size as pillow front and, with right sides facing, stitch the two pieces together, leaving an opening for turning. Turn right side out, stuff with polyester fiberfill, and slip-stitch the opening closed.

Trinket Boxes

shown on page 185

Materials

Leftover wool yarn and/or embroidery floss in shades of green, rose, blue, lavender, and brown; wooden dresser boxes with recessed tops (available in craft and hobby shops); 22-count petit point canvas *or* finely woven lightweight blue fabric; tapestry needle *or* needlepunch embroidery tool; quilt batting; white glue.

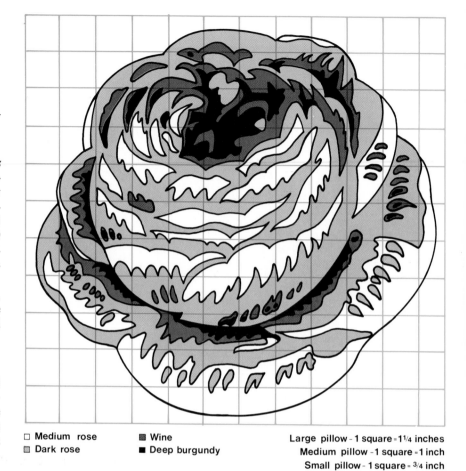

☐ Medium rose	■ Wine
☐ Dark rose	■ Deep burgundy

Large pillow - 1 square = 1¼ inches
Medium pillow - 1 square = 1 inch
Small pillow - 1 square = ¾ inch

Instructions

Choose a small design element from any of the overall floral patterns given here (or elsewhere in the book) and transfer it to tracing paper. (For example, choose a single rose from the crocheted afghan shown on page 186, or select a posy from the basket-of-blossoms pillow on page 187.)

Enlarge the pattern to the desired size and transfer it with indelible marker to 22-count canvas for petit point or with water-erasable pen to blue fabric for needlepunch.

Stitch the design, using one strand of wool yarn for petit point and one strand of embroidery floss for needlepunch. Block the finished design and mount it on a piece of cardboard cut to fit the recessed box top.

Add a layer of quilt batting between the fabric and the cardboard; turn under raw edges and glue fabric to back of cardboard.

Finish box with varnish or paint, as desired. Glue the petit point or needlepunch design in place on box top and let dry.

Flower Garland Picture Frame

shown on page 185

Materials

One-half yard of 14-mesh interlock canvas; 32-inch strands of Paternayan (or a suitable substitute) 3-ply wool yarn in the following amounts and colors: 110 white, 60 tan, 8 deep burgundy, 12 wine, 32 dark rose, 20 medium rose, 30 light rose, 5 light pink, 8 blue, 12 light blue, 5 yellow, 18 dark leaf green, 30 medium leaf green, 20 light leaf green.

In addition, you will need five 32-inch strands of 3-ply wool yarn in blue-green, 6 strands of medium blue-green, and 10 strands of light blue-green for the bow.

Also: No. 19 tapestry needle; masking tape; quilt batting; 16-inch square of ⅛-inch plywood and matching square of white felt for backing; 2 yards of white braid or decorative cording; craft glue; graph paper; colored pencils or felt pens.

Instructions

Use the chart on pages 194-195 to work the design. If desired, transfer the pattern to graph paper before you begin, using colored pencils or felt-tipped marking pens to represent symbols in the chart. Note that the chart represents half of the total design. Reverse the pattern to complete the design.

Before you begin, bind the edges of the canvas with masking tape to prevent raveling. Remember that the oval space (for the photograph) will be cut out; it should not be filled in with stitches. Do *not* cut out the oval until the stitching is completed.

To minimize distortion from the pull on the stitches, mount the painted canvas in a needlepoint frame. Then, using 2-ply strands of yarn, begin stitching the design. Use continental stitches for outlining and basket-weave stitches for filling large areas of color and for the background. Work one area of color at a time.

To prevent unsightly knots, begin each strand of yarn with a waste knot. Weave ends of strands through stitches on the back of the work to secure them.

After completing the design, work the background in vertical stripes, alternating two rows of white stitches with one row of tan stitches.

Block the finished canvas and let it dry overnight.

Next, carefully cut away the center oval, leaving a ½-inch margin of unworked canvas. Using small, sharp scissors, clip curves. Turn raw edges under and steam-press lightly, using a pressing cloth between the needlepoint stitches and the iron. Then trim the outside edges of the canvas, leaving a 1-inch margin. Turn under raw edges and steam-press lightly.

Cut a 16-inch-square piece of ⅛-inch plywood and sand the edges. Cover the plywood with a layer of quilt batting cut to size; glue in place.

Mount the photograph on the underside of the needlepointed frame, centering the picture inside the oval cutout. Secure the photograph with masking tape.

Next, lay the canvas atop the batting-covered board. Carefully pull the raw edges of the canvas to the back of the board, making sure that the rows of needlepoint stitches are parallel to the edges of the board. Staple the canvas to the plywood.

Cover the back of the plywood with white felt. Trim the outside edges of the frame and inside the curve of the oval with white braid or decorative trim; glue in place. Add an easel stand or brass loop for hanging.

Wild Rose Afghan

shown on page 186

Finished size, including border, is 58x70 inches.

Materials

Four-ply knitting worsted (4-ounce skeins) in the following amounts and colors: 12 skeins off-white; 4 skeins each of dark, medium, and light rose; 3 skeins each of dark and light green; 2 skeins each of violet, lavender, and medium blue; size G aluminum afghan crochet hook, or size to obtain gauge below; size H aluminum crochet hook; 8 yards each of 5 colors of ⅜-inch-wide satin ribbon (to match cross-stitch designs); yarn needle.

Gauge: 5 afghan stitches = 1 inch.
Abbreviations: See pages 218-219.

Instructions

Panel: With off-white yarn and afghan hook, ch 61.

Row 1: Working from right to left, sk 1st ch, insert hook into 2nd ch from hook, yo and draw through a lp, * insert hook into next ch, yo and draw through a lp. Rep from * across, keeping all lps on hook.

Row 2: Working from left to right, yo and draw through 1st 2 lps on hook, * yo and draw through next 2 lps on hook. Rep from * across to end until 1 lp rem on hook.

Row 3: Working from right to left, sk 1st vertical bar on the front of the fabric, * insert hook from right to left into next vertical bar, yo and draw through a lp. Rep from * to end, keeping all lps on hook.

Row 4: Rep Row 2.

Rep Rows 3 and 4 until total length measures approximately 60 inches, having an even multiple of 30 rows.

Make 3 more panels similarly.

To assemble: Arrange panels with wrong sides on top; carefully align rows. Whipstitch panels together.

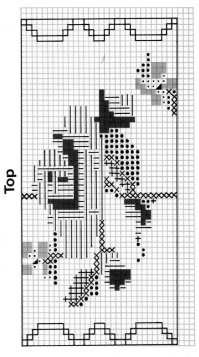

Top

1 square = 1 stitch

⊠ Dark green	⊟ Light pink
⊙ Medium green	⊡ Violet
⊞ Light green	▨ Lavender
■ Dark pink	◣ Gold
⊞ Medium pink	□ Blue

For the cross-stitch embroidery: Refer to the chart (above). Work the rose motif over each 60-stitch-wide panel, using the yarn needle and the colors indicated in the color key.

Begin at the lower edge of the left panel, and cross-stitch motifs up to the upper edge of the left panel. Then work the motifs on the 2nd panel, beginning the motif at the bottom of the panel at Row 16 of the chart.

Work the remainder of the 2nd panel with complete motifs (see photograph on page 188). Finish the last motif where the 1st one started. Work the 3rd panel in the same manner as the 1st one and the 4th panel in the same manner as the 2nd panel.

Border: *Rnd 1:* With crochet hook, 1 strand of off-white, and right side facing, sc in each st around. (To keep work flat, you may have to work 1 sc in every other st on short sides, and work 3 sc in each corner.) End with sl st in 1st sc; ch 1.

continued

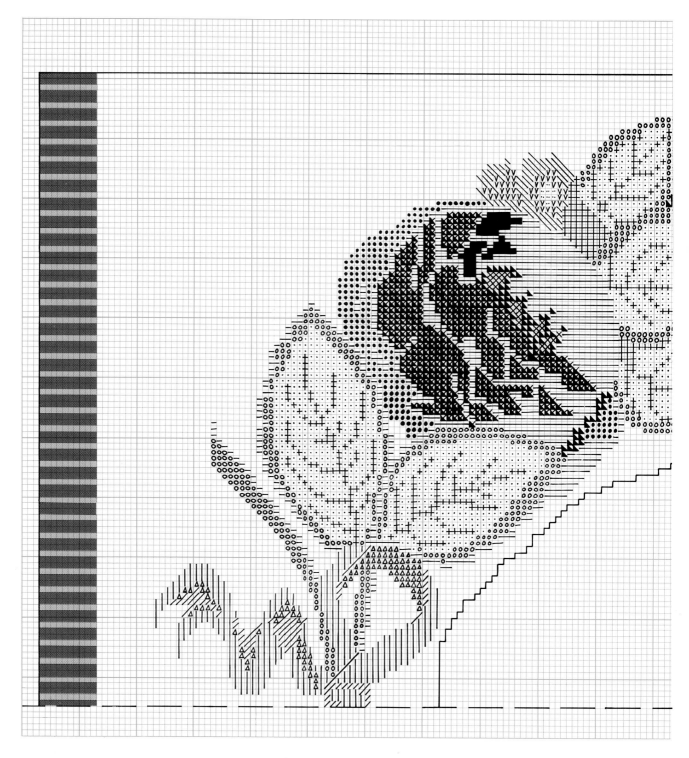

Rnd 2: Work 2 sc in each sc around, working 3 sc in each corner st. End with sl st in 1st sc.

Rnd 3: Work sc in each sc around, working 3 sc in corner.

Rnd 4: Ch 5, dc in 3rd sc from hook, * ch 2, sk 2 sc, dc in next sc. Rep from * around, ending with ch 2, sl st to 3rd ch of ch-5 at beg of rnd.

Rnd 5: Ch 5, * dc in top of dc of pre-

vious rnd, ch 2. Rep from * to corner sp, dc in corner sp, ch 2. Rep from * around, ending with sl st in 3rd ch of ch-5 at beg of rnd.

Rnds 6-8: Rep Rnd 5.

Rnd 9: Ch 4, dc in 1st sp, *ch 3, sl st in 3rd ch from hook*—picot made; dc in same sp, ch 1, dc in same sp, ch 1, * sl st in next sp, ch 1, in next sp work (dc, ch 1, dc, ch 3, sl st in 3rd ch from hook—

picot made; dc, ch 1, dc, ch 1). Rep from * around, ending with sl st in last sp, ch 1, sl st in 3rd ch of beg ch-4. Fasten off.

Using 1 color of ribbon for each of the 5 dc rnds, cut lengths to fit along each side, allowing for bows in each corner. Thread ribbons along sides; tie ribbons into bows.

continued

COLOR KEY

Background

⬜ Tan (#492)
⬛ White (#005)

Roses

◩ Deep burgundy (#236)
◣ Wine (#231)
⊟ Dark rose (#232)
◉ Medium rose (#282)
◪ Light rose (#288)
⬛ Light pink (#865)

Blue Flowers

Ⅴ Blue (#395)
◣ Light blue (#385)
∷ Yellow (#441)

Leaves

⊞ Dark leaf green (#340)
∴ Medium leaf green (#546)
◎ Light leaf green (#556)
⊟ Dark rose (#232)

Bow

◩ Dark blue-green (#367)
◭ Medium blue-green (#342)
⊓ Light blue-green (#535)

1 Square = 1 Stitch

195

Basket of Blossoms Pillow

shown on page 187

Materials

½ yard dark blue velour fabric; ⅛ yard each of 3 shades of pink crepe-backed satin; small pieces of lavender and light blue polyester lining fabric; scraps of light and dark green velour for leaves; 1 yard each of gold and rust 1-inch-wide satin ribbon; lavender, blue, green, and gold embroidery floss; glazed quilt batting; polyester fiberfill; lightweight iron-on interfacing; white tailor's pencil or water-erasable marker; tracing paper.

Instructions

Enlarge the pattern (below) onto tracing paper and cut around outside edges. (This is your master pattern; do not cut it apart.)

Cut blue velour fabric in half widthwise (for front and back of pillow). Lay the tracing paper pattern on front of one piece of fabric, pin in place, and trace around the outside edges of the pattern using a white tailor's pencil.

Cut ribbon into lengths slightly longer than the basket slats shown on the pattern. Weave the ribbons together to form the basket; stitch in place on the pillow front, turning raw edges under. Before sewing the ribbon along the bottom edge of the basket, insert a narrow strip of batting to give the base of the basket dimension.

Cut separate paper pattern pieces for each flower part and leaf, including overlapping areas of each piece. (Do not add seam allowances at this point.) On each pattern piece, note the color the leaf or flower segment should be, using the photograph for reference. Then trace around pattern pieces onto the appropriate fabrics. Iron interfacing to the back of each piece of sheer fabric and machine-stay-stitch around the traced outlines. Cut out each piece ¼ inch beyond stitched line.

Place the master pattern on top of the pillow front again, to aid in positioning the appliqués. Working from the outside toward the center, slip individual fabric shapes between the pattern and fabric. Pin each of the fabrics in place and turn raw edges under along stitched lines. Pad some of the flowers with small amounts of stuffing for added dimension.

To make three-dimensional rosebuds, first roll and stitch a narrow tube of green velour for stems. For sepals, cut a small rectangle of green velour and, with right sides facing, stitch short ends together. Turn right side out, insert stem into bottom of sepal, and stitch, turning raw edges in.

Next, cut a 3½-inch square of pink satin for the rosebud. Fold satin in half diagonally, tucking a small amount of stuffing inside. Fold the top two corners of the triangle down to meet the bottom point; gather the raw edges.

Insert the bud into the top of the sepal and sew in place. Embroider the veins in the leaves using stem stitches. Embroider flowers as shown on pattern, working centers in clusters of French knots.

For a smooth finish, pin and then baste a sheet of quilt batting to the wrong side of the pillow front and back. Machine-stitch around the pillow top ¼ inch outside the appliqué design. Next, with right sides facing, sew together the front and back pillow pieces, using the stitched line as a guide and leaving the bottom edge open. Trim the seams and clip the corners.

Turn pillow right side out, stuff to the desired fullness, and slip-stitch the opening closed.

Round Doily

shown on page 188

Materials

Mangelsen's 3-ply metallic thread in gold or the color of your choice; size 10 crochet hook.

(*Note:* One ball of size 30 crochet cotton may be substituted for metallic thread. Also note that changing the type or size of thread may alter the size of the finished doily.)

Abbreviations: See pages 218–219.

Instructions

Finished size (in recommended thread) is 9 inches in diameter.

Beg at center, ch 10; join with sl st to form ring.

Rnd 1: Ch 3, make 24 dc in ring; join to top of ch-3—25 dc (counting ch-3 as 1 dc).

Rnd 2: Ch 3 (2 dc in next dc, dc in next dc) 12 times—37 dc.

Rnd 3: Ch 3, dc in the joining, (dc in the next 2 dc, 2 dc in the next dc) 12 times—50 dc.

■ = Blue Background   ▨ = Roses   1 Square = 2 Inches

Rnd 4: Ch 11, (sk next 4 dc, dc in next dc, ch 8) 9 times; join to 3rd ch of ch-11.

Rnd 5: Ch 5, dc in joining, (8 dc in next lp; in next dc make dc, ch 2, and dc) 9 times; 8 dc in last lp; join to 3rd ch of ch-5.

Rnd 6: Ch 6, dc in next dc, (ch 10, sk next 8 dc, dc in next dc, ch 3, dc in next dc) 9 times; ch 10; join to 3rd ch of ch-6.

Rnd 7: Ch 6, dc in next dc, (10 dc in next lp, dc in next dc, ch 3, dc in next dc) 9 times; 10 dc in last lp; join to 3rd ch of ch-6.

Rnd 8: Ch 6, * dc in next 5 dc, 2 dc in each of next 2 dc, dc in next 5 dc, ch 3. Rep from * around, ending with dc in last 4 dc; join as before.

Rnd 9: Ch 6, * dc in next 6 dc, 2 dc in each of next 2 dc, dc in next 6 dc, ch 3. Rep from * around, ending with dc in last 5 dc; join as before.

Rnd 10: Ch 6, * dc in next 7 dc, 2 dc in each of next 2 dc, dc in next 7 dc, ch 3. Rep from * around, ending with dc in last 6 dc; join as before.

Rnd 11: Ch 6, * dc in next 8 dc, 2 dc in each of next 2 dc, dc in next 8 dc, ch 3. Rep from * around, ending with dc in last 7 dc; join as before.

Rnd 12: Ch 5, * dc in next 9 dc, 2 dc in each of next 2 dc, dc in next 9 dc, ch 2. Rep from * around, ending with dc in last 8 dc; join to 3rd ch of ch-5.

Rnd 13: Ch 3, * 2 dc in next ch-2 sp, dc in next 11 dc, ch 5, dc in next 11 dc. Rep from * around, ending with dc in last 10 dc; join to top of ch-3.

Rnd 14: Ch 3, dc in next 11 dc, * ch 6, sc in next lp, ch 6, sk next 2 dc, dc in next 20 dc. Rep from * around, ending with dc in last 8 dc; join to top of ch-3.

Rnd 15: Ch 3, dc in next 9 dc, * (ch 6, sc in next lp) twice; ch 6, sk next 2 dc, dc in next 16 dc. Rep from * around, ending with dc in last 6 dc; join to top of ch-3.

Rnd 16: Ch 3, dc in next 7 dc, * ch 6, sc in next lp, ch 7, 9 tr tr in next lp, ch 7, sc in next lp, ch 6, sk next 2 dc, dc in next 12 dc. Rep from * around, ending with dc in last 4 dc; join to top of ch-3.

Rnd 17: Ch 3, dc in next 5 dc, * ch 6, sc in next lp, ch 7, 3 dc in next tr tr, (sk next tr tr, 3 dc in next tr tr) 4 times; ch 7, sk next lp, sc in next lp, ch 6, sk next 2 dc, dc in next 8 dc. Rep from * around, ending with last 2 dc; join to top of ch-3.

Rnd 18: Ch 3, dc in next 4 dc, * ch 6, sc in next lp, ch 7, *holding back on hook last lp of each dc, dc in next 3 dc, thread over and draw through all lps on hook—cluster made: (ch 3, make a cluster over next 3 dc) 4 times; ch 7, sk next lp, sc in next lp, ch 6, sk next dc, dc in next 6 dc. Rep from * around, ending with dc in last dc; join to top of ch-3.

Rnd 19: Ch 5, * sk next 2 dc, dc in next dc, ch 5; *in next sc make tr, ch 1, and tr—V-stitch made;* ch 5, make a V-stitch in next cluster, (ch 3, make a V-stitch in next cluster) 4 times; ch 5, make a V-stitch in next sc, ch 5, sk next dc, dc in next dc, ch 2. Rep from * around, ending with ch 5; join to 3rd ch of ch-5.

Rnd 20: Sl st in ch-2 sp, ch 3, dc in same sp; *ch 5, sc in last dc worked—picot made;* 2 dc in same sp where last dc was made; * (ch 2, *in ch-1 sp of next V-stitch make 2 dc, picot, and 2 dc—picot shell made*) 7 times; ch 2, sk next lp, make a picot shell in next ch-2 sp. Rep from * around, ending with ch-2; join to top of ch-3. Fasten off; block.

Square Doily

shown on page 188

Materials

Mangelsen's 3-ply metallic thread in gold or the color of your choice; size 9 steel crochet hook, or size to obtain gauge given below.

(*Note:* One ball of size 20 crochet cotton may be substituted for metallic thread. Changing the size and type of thread may alter the size of the doily.)

Gauge: 5 sps or bls = 1 inch; 5 rows = 1 inch.

Abbreviations: See pages 218-219.

Instructions

Finished size of the doily is about 8½ inches square.

Center square: Beg at lower edge, ch 56, with 15 ch sts = 1 inch.

Row 1 (right side): *Dc in 8th ch from hook—starting sp made; * ch 2, sk next 2 ch, dc in next ch—sp made. Rep from * across—17 sps; ch 5, turn.

Row 2: Sk 1st 2 ch, dc in next dc—sp over sp made; * ch 2, dc in next dc—sp over sp made. Rep from * to last sp; *ch 2, sk next 2 ch, dc in next ch—end sp over sp made;* ch 5, turn.

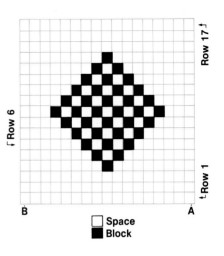

Row 6 / Row 17 / Row 1 / B / A

☐ Space
■ Block

Row 3: Rep Row 2.

Row 4: Make starting sp, 7 sps; *make 2 dc in next sp, dc in next dc—bl over sp made;* make 8 sps; ch 5, turn.

Row 5: Make a starting sp, 6 sps, 1 bl; *ch 2, sk next 2 dc, dc in next dc—sp over bl made;* make 1 bl and 7 sps; ch 5, turn. Beg with Row 6 on chart (above), follow wrong-side row from B to A and every right-side row from A to B until Row 17 is completed. *Do not turn.*

Border: Work in rnds as follows:
Rnd 1: (Note: To make a bl, work 2 dc in the sp and 1 dc in the following st.) *Ch 3, 2 dc in corner sp just made, dc in following st—corner started; * make 15 bls; 6 dc in next corner sp, dc in following st—corner made.* Rep from * around, ending last rep with 3 dc in 1st corner sp used at beg of rnd. Join with sl st to top of ch-3.

Rnd 2: Ch 3, dc in joining, * make 16 sps, ch 2, sk next 2 dc, 2 dc in next dc, ch 5, 2 dc in next dc. Rep from * around, ending with ch 5. Join to top of ch-3.

Rnd 3: Ch 10, * sk next 2 sps, dc in following dc, (make 1 bl, 1 sp) 6 times and 1 bl; ch 6, sk next 2 sps, 16 tr in next ch-6 lp, ch 6. Rep from * around, ending with 15 tr in last ch-5 lp. Join to 4th ch of ch-10.

Rnd 4: Ch 10, * sk next 3 dc, dc in next dc, make 1 bl, (1 sp, 1 bl) 5 times; ch 6, tr in next tr, (ch 1, tr in next tr) 15 times; ch 6. Rep from * around, ending with ch 1; join as before.

Rnd 5: Ch 11, * sk next 3 dc, dc in next dc, make 1 bl, (1 sp, 1 bl) 4 times; ch 7, tr in next tr, (ch 2, tr in next tr) 15 times; ch 7. Rep from * around, ending with ch 2; join to the 4th ch of the initial ch-11.

continued

Rnd 6: Ch 11, * sk next 3 dc, dc in next dc, make 1 bl, (1 sp, 1 bl) 3 times; ch 7, tr in next tr, (ch 3, tr in next tr) 15 times; ch 7. Rep from * around, ending with ch 3; join as before.

Rnd 7: Ch 12, * sk next 3 dc, dc in next dc, make 1 bl, (1 sp, 1 bl) twice; ch 8, tr in next tr, (ch 4, tr in next tr) 15 times; ch 8. Rep from * around, end with ch 4; join to 4th ch of ch-12.

Rnd 8: Ch 12, * sk next 3 dc, dc in next dc, make 1 bl, 1 sp, 1 bl; ch 8, tr in next tr, (ch 5, tr in next tr) 15 times; ch 8. Rep from * around, ending with ch 5; join as before.

Rnd 9: Ch 13, * sk next 3 dc, dc in next dc, make 1 bl, ch 9, tr in next tr, (ch 6, tr in next tr) 15 times; ch 9. Rep from * around, ending with ch 6; join to 4th ch of ch-13.

Rnd 10: Ch 1, * in ch-9 lp make 5 sc; ch 3 and 5 sc; sc in next 2 dc, ch 3, sc in next 2 dc; in next ch-9 lp make 5 sc, ch 3, and 5 sc; (in next ch-6 lp make 4 sc, ch 3 and 4 sc) 15 times. Repeat from * around, joining to the 1st sc. Fasten off and press to block.

Crocheted Bell Edging

shown on page 189

Materials

One 175-yard ball of ecru Coats and Clark Knit-Cro-Sheen and size 7 steel crochet hook, *or* H. Sherley No. 22 Starbright gold metallic thread and size B aluminum crochet hook; 15½x20½ inches of ecru linen for a place mat *or* 12½-inch-diameter circle of linen for a doily.

Gauge: 1 repeat = 1¾ inches.
Abbreviations: See pages 218-219.

Instructions

This edging is worked in gold metallic thread on the round doily and in ecru thread on the panels hanging in the window.

Ch 4. *Row 1:* 2 dc in 4th ch from hook, *ch 3, 3 dc in same ch—shell made;* ch 5, turn.

Row 2: In ch-3 sp of shell work 3 dc, *ch 3, 3 dc—shell over shell made;* ch 3, turn.

Row 3: Shell over shell, *do not turn;* work 8 dc in ch-5 sp of turning lp bet 2 rows below; ch 3, turn.

Row 4: Dc in 1st dc and each dc across—9 dc in row, counting turning ch as dc; ch 3, turn.

Row 5: Dc in 1st dc and each dc across and in top of turning ch—10 dc in row, counting turning ch as dc; ch 2, turn.

Row 6: Sk 1st dc, hdc in next dc, dc in next 2 dc, trc in next dc, *ch 5, sl st in 5th ch from hook—picot made;* trc in next dc, dc in next 2 dc, hdc in next dc and top of turning ch, ch 7, work shell over shell; ch 3, turn.

Row 7: Shell over shell; ch 5, turn.
Row 8: Shell over shell; ch 3, turn.
Rows 9-10: Rep Rows 3-4.

Row 11: Rep Row 5, *do not turn* after ch-2 at end of row; join bell units with a sl st into 3rd ch of ch-7; ch 1, turn; sl st into each of next 2 ch and 1st dc; ch 2, hdc in next dc, dc in next 2 dc, trc in next dc, ch 5, sl st in 5th ch from hook —picot, trc in next st, dc in next 2 dc, hdc in next dc and top of turning ch, ch 7, shell over shell; ch 3, turn.

Rep Rows 7-11 to reach the desired length.

Tack the finished edging to hemmed linen.

To join work into a circle, end with Row 11; ch 4 instead of ch 7, sl st into top of ch-2 of next bell, ch 1, sl st back into next 2 ch, ch 5, 3 dc in ch-3 sp of shell, ch 1, sl st into bottom of next bell, ch 1, 3 dc in same ch-3 sp; ch 3, turn and sl st into top of 1st dc. Fasten off. Tack to hemmed edge of linen.

Gold Crocheted Edging

shown on page 189

Materials

One 20-gram ball of Phildar Sunset Gold metallic thread; 12x12 inches of linen (or fabric sufficient for your project; adjust thread quantities accordingly); size 9 steel crochet hook.

Abbreviations: See pages 218-219.

Instructions

This doily is shown on the far right in the photograph.

Rnd 1: Attach thread to any corner of the linen, 3 sc in same corner, sc closely around, making 3 sc in each corner. Work same number of sts on each side of square. Sl st in 1st sc.

Rnd 2: In same place as sl st make sc and half dc, 3 dc in next sc, make half dc and sc in next sc, sc in next 7 sc, * half dc in next sc, dc in next 3 sc, half dc in next sc (scallop), sc in next 8 sc. Rep from * around, making sc and half dc in the 1st sc on each 3-sc grp at corners, 3 dc in the center sc and half dc and sc in the 3rd sc of each 3-sc grp at corners. Join sl st to 1st sc.

Rnd 3: Sl st in next half dc, ch 8, dc in 5th ch from hook (dc in next dc on scallop, ch 5, dc in last dc) 2 times; dc in next half dc of scallop, * ch 5, sk 4 sc, sc in next sc, ch 5, (dc in next dc on scallop, ch 5, dc in last dc) 3 times; dc in next half dc of scallop. Rep from * around. In corners make (dc in next dc on scallop, ch 5, dc in last dc) 3 times, dc in next half dc, ending with ch 5, sk 4 sc, sc in next sc, ch 5. Join ch-5 with sl st in 1st dc of rnd. Break off.

Ecru and Silver Crocheted Edging

shown on page 189

Materials

One 100-yard ball of Coats and Clark Knit-Cro-Sheen; No. 1S white and silver thread; 16x16 inches of ecru linen (or fabric sufficient for your project); size 8 steel crochet hook.

Abbreviations: See pages 218-219.

Instructions

This doily is shown second from the right in the photograph.

Rnd 1: Attach thread to any corner of linen, sc closely all around, making 3 sc in each corner, sl st in 1st sc.

Rnd 2: Sl st in next 3 sc, sc in same sc, ch 5, sk 2 sc, sc in next sc. * Ch 5, sk 3 sc, dc in next sc, ch 5, dc in last dc (picot), dc in same sc as the dc preceding the picot was made, ch 5, sk 3 sc, sc in next sc, ch 5, sk 2 sc, sc in next sc. Rep from * around, making sc, ch 5, and sc in center sc of each corner and ending with ch 5, sl st in 1st sc.

Rnd 3: Sl st in next 2 ch, sc in same lp, * ch 5, dc in next dc, (ch 5, dc in next dc) 3 times (3 picots made); sk next picot, dc in next dc, ch 5, sk next ch-5, sc in next ch-5 lp. Rep from * around. In corner make dc in next sc, (ch 5, dc in last dc) 4 times, sk next sp, dc in next sc, ch 5. Join ch-5 with sl st in 1st sc of rnd. Break off.

Ecru and Gold Crocheted Edging

shown on page 189

Materials

One 100-yard ball of Coats and Clark Knit-Cro-Sheen; No. 61G white and gold; 16x16 inches of ecru linen (or sufficient fabric for your project; adjust thread quantities accordingly); Size 8 steel crochet hook.

Abbreviations: See pages 218-219.

Instructions

This doily is shown in the center of the photograph.

Rnd 1: Attach thread to one corner of linen, 3 sc in same place, make sc all around outer edges—12 sc to 1 inch; 3 sc in each corner. Sl st in 1st sc.

Rnd 2: Sl st in next sc, ch 8, dc in same place as sl st, * ch 5, sk 3 sc, sc in next sc, ch 3, sk 1 sc, sc in next sc, ch 5, sk 3 sc, in next sc make dc, ch 3 and dc. Rep from * around, making dc, ch 5 and dc in center sc of each corner. Join with sl st to 3rd ch of ch-8.

Rnd 3: Sl st in next sp, ch 9, dc in 6th ch from hook, (dc in same sp, ch 5, dc in top of last dc made) 3 times; dc in same sp, * ch 5, sk next sp, sc in next lp, ch 5, sk next sp, in next sp make (dc, ch 5, dc in top of last dc made) 3 times and dc. Rep from * to corner, in corner sp make (dc, ch 5, dc in top of last dc made) 4 times and dc. Work other 3 sides to correspond. Join and break off.

Silver and Gold Lace Edging

shown on page 189

Materials

One 20-gram ball each of Phildar Sunset Gold and Sunset Silver metallic thread; 12x12 inches of white linen (or fabric sufficient for your project; adjust thread quantities accordingly); Size 9 steel crochet hook.

Abbreviations: See pages 218-219.

Instructions

This doily is shown on the far left in the photograph.

Rnd 1: Attach silver to corner of linen and sc closely around (24 sc to 1 inch), making 3 sc in each corner. Join with sl st to 1st sc. Break off.

Rnd 2: Attach gold to 1st sc, sc in same place, ch 4, sk 1 sc, sc in next sc, * ch 6, sk 4 sc, trc in next sc, ch 5, dc in last trc made, trc in same sc as last trc, ch 6, sk 4 sc. Sc in next sc, ch 4, sk 2 sc, sc in next sc. Rep from * across to within 4 sc of corner 3-sc grp, ending with ch-6. Sk 4 sc, sc in next sc, ch 4, sk 1 sc, sc in next sc. Work other sides and corners the same way. Join with sl st to 1st sc.

Rnd 3: Sl st in next lp, ch 7, in same lp make (double treble, ch 2) 4 times; * sk next sp, in next lp make (dtr, ch 2) 5 times; sk next sp, tr tr (triple treble) in next lp, ch 2. Rep from * across to next corner lp, ending with ch 2, in corner lp make (dtr, ch 2) 5 times. Work other sides and corners in the same way. Join last ch-2 with sl st to 5th ch of ch-7. Break off.

Rnd 4: Attach silver thread to 1st sp, sc in same place, * (ch 3, sc) 3 times; ch 5, sc in next sp, ch 5, sc in next sp, (ch 3, sc) 2 times. Rep from * around. Join and break off.

Protecting your lace

If you decide to put away your lace-edged place mats or doilies between holidays, store them properly so they won't be damaged during the year by dampness, yellowing, or fold marks that may weaken the threads.

First, find a box that is large enough to hold the unfolded place mats flat. Layer pieces in the box with sheets of acid-free tissue paper between. Store the box in a cool, dry, dark place.

Tatted Address Book Cover

shown on page 190

Materials

A 4½x6½-inch address book (for a larger address book, adjust the pattern accordingly; see *Note* at the end of the

tatting instructions); ¼ yard linen or other fabric suitable for covering the book; small piece of quilt batting; 2 tatting shuttles; size 9 steel crochet hook; 1 ball each of DMC No. 8 pearl cotton in the following colors: No. 352 (color A), No. 954 (color B), and No. 353 (color C).

Tatting abbreviations

R: Ring. Make a ring of. . . .

Rnd: Round.

Numbers: Make a ring or a chain of the specified number of double stitches.

P: Picot. A space between two double stitches.

CR: Close ring. Pull on shuttle thread until work just completed forms a ring.

RW: Reverse work. Turn the work just completed upside down and begin a new chain or ring according to the directions.

DNRW: Do not reverse work. Continue with a new ring or chain without changing the position of the work.

Ch: Chain. Make a chain of. . . .

Join: Technique of attaching the thread into previously completed work.

Instructions

Finished size is 4½x6½ inches; tatted rectangle measures 4⅛x6⅛ inches.

Tatted rectangle: For Rnd 1, wind 10½ yards of color A onto shuttle 1; 5½ yards of color B will be used off the ball. For Rnd 2, wind 3½ yards of color C onto shuttle 1 and 6 yards of color B onto shuttle 2.

(If you substitute one color throughout, use masking tape to mark shuttles No. 1 and No. 2.)

Note: Traditionally, tatting rounds are worked from the center. For this piece, however, Rnd 1 forms the outside of the work; Rnd 2 is on the inside.

Rnd 1: Step 1: R of 2, (P, 2) 9 times, CR, RW.

Step 2: Ch 2, P, 2, P, 2, P, 2, P, 2, P, RW.

Step 3: Repeat Steps 1 and 2 alternately until a total of 34 rings and chains have been made. Cut work off. Tie shuttle and chain threads in two knots. Dab knots with glue or whipstitch with sewing thread.

Step 4: Mark 1st, 7th, 18th, and 24th rings by tying a scrap of thread through them in a double overhand knot. These rings are the 4 corners. Chains leading

continued

into and out of marked rings are omitted as joined points when working Rnd 2. When the outside of Rnd 2 is complete, remove markers.

Inside Rnd 2: Step 1: Shuttle 1 R of 2, P, P, 2, CR, RW.

Step 2: Use thread off shuttle No. 2 to chain in same manner as thread off ball. Ch 2, P, 2, P, 2, DNRW.

Step 3: Shuttle 2 R of 4, join in center P of ch to right of 1st marker of Rnd 1, 4, CR, DNRW.

Step 4: Repeat Steps 2, 1, and 2 again.

Step 5: Shuttle 2 R of 4, join in center P of next ch to the right in Rnd 1, 4, CR, DNRW.

Step 6: Repeat Steps 2, 1, 2, and 5 twice more.

Step 7: Repeat Steps 2, 1, and 2 again.

Step 8: Shuttle 2 R of 4, join in center P of 2nd ch to the right of marker 2 of Rnd 1, 4, CR, DNRW.

Step 9: Repeat Steps 2, 1, 2, and 5 in order 8 times more. Half of Rnd 2 is completed. Continue 2nd half of Rnd 2 as for 1st half. Omit joinings in chs leading into and out of markers 3 and 4. Cut, tie, and glue or whipstitch tails as for Rnd 1.

Block the tatted lace by pinning the completed work into a rectangle atop an ironing board or cloth-covered porous board (such as a piece of heavy cardboard). Use rustproof pins. Spray lightly with starch and let dry. Remove from the board and stitch to the cloth book cover. (Directions for the book cover follow.)

Note: To make a rectangle for a larger book, increase the number of rings and chains between the marker rings of Rnd 1 and add rings and chains of Rnd 2 accordingly.

Address book cover: Using a ruler and brown paper, draw a rectangle the length of the cover and the width of the circumference (from flap to flap). Add ½ inch all around for seam allowances.

Next, draw onto brown paper another rectangle equal to the length and width of the *front* cover, adding ½ inch all around for seam allowances.

Using your brown paper patterns, cut two shapes for each rectangle from linen. Cut one long rectangle from quilt batting. Hem one long side on each of the smaller rectangles.

To create pocket flaps, place one hemmed rectangle along the end of one large rectangle, with right sides facing and raw edges matching. Repeat, placing remaining hemmed rectangle along remaining end of large rectangle. Baste.

To assemble the book cover, stack pieces in the following order: batting first, then the large rectangle of linen with the two hemmed rectangles at either side (faceup), and, finally, the large rectangle on top (wrong side up). Stitch all layers together, leaving one short side open. Clip corners, turn to right side, and press carefully. Slip-stitch the opening closed.

Center the tatted piece atop the front cover, and whipstitch it in place. Insert book into pockets.

Embroidered Photograph Album

shown on page 190

Materials

Photograph album or other booklet that is approximately 7 inches square (or, use an album in a different size and adjust materials and pattern); ½ yard of ecru wool; 3-ply yarn in the following colors: purple, pink, rust, peach, and light, medium, and dark green; 1½ yards of ecru rayon rattail cording; ¼ yard of quilt batting; embroidery hoop; crewel needle; dressmaker's carbon paper; masking tape.

Instructions

To begin, draw a 7x15-inch rectangle on brown paper, adding ½-inch seam allowances all around. On the right-hand side of the pattern, center and trace the full-size pattern (right).

Next, transfer the pattern onto the fabric using light-colored dressmaker's carbon. Do not cut out the fabric rectangle until all of the embroidery is complete.

Before beginning to stitch, mount the fabric in an embroidery hoop. Use one strand of yarn for stitching.

Using outline stitches, work stems in dark green yarn, and outline the center of the flower in the upper right-hand corner of the design in rust.

Stitch French knots as follows: in peach on the leaf center, in light green to trim leaf, and in pink for the sepals of the left-hand flower (see photograph).

Satin-stitch remaining areas as follows: For leaves, use dark green on dotted areas, medium green on solid areas, and light green on plain areas.

For flowers, use pink yarn on areas marked with crosses, purple yarn on striped areas, rust yarn on gridded areas, and peach on plain areas. Work decorative straight stitches in purple over peach on the center of the flower in the upper right-hand corner. Press and cut out.

Cut a second rectangle from ecru fabric (for backing) and a matching piece from batting, adding seam allowances. Cut two 7-inch squares (plus seam allowances) for pocket flaps, then assemble book cover as described for the Address Book Cover, left.

Ceramic Heart Box

shown on page 190

Materials

Note: Materials and individual instructions are available through local ceramic studios and workshops. If you wish the professional assistance of a ceramics instructor, check the Yellow Pages of your telephone directory under "Ceramics—Equipment and Supplies" to find a studio in your area. The materials listed below are from Duncan Enterprises.

Bisque heart-shape box; bisque stain in the following colors: dark yellow, light pink, lime, purple, grape, black, olive moss, white mist, gold mist, watermelon, and purple iris; clear matte fixative; assorted paintbrushes; glazed tile or dish to use as a palette.

Instructions

Using a soft, ¾-inch-wide paintbrush, apply a generous coat of pink stain to the interior and exterior of the box. Clean the brush thoroughly with water to prevent its hardening.

Place a small amount of purple iris and grape stain on separate areas of the glazed tile or dish. Load a small, round-tip brush with purple iris and cover the tip with the grape stain.

Using the photograph on page 190 as a guide for color placement, create three violets on the box lid, in a roughly triangular composition, in the following manner: Lay the paint-laden brush gently down on the surface of the lid.

Then pull and twist it slightly to form a commalike shape, lifting the brush as you pull it toward the flower center. (For best results, practice on scrap paper before working on the box.)

Make five comma-shape petals for each violet. Clean the brush with water after each stroke, and reload as before.

Next, place small amounts of watermelon and white mist stains on separate areas of the dish. Load the same round-tip brush that you used for the violets with watermelon and tip with white mist. Paint small, five-petal flowers around the violets on the lid. Clean the brush as before.

Place small amounts of olive moss and lime stain on the dish. Load a fine-point brush with olive moss and tip with lime. Paint three leaves on the lid with small, closely placed comma-shape strokes. Create flower stems, tendrils, and some small leaves along the stems of the pink flowers with the same small brush. Clean as before.

Again using the fine brush, make small dark yellow dots as centers for the violets and the small pink flowers. Create a row of dots on each side of the tendrils for blossom sprays.

With the fine brush, use gold mist stain to create latticework on the tip of the lid. Then outline the top of the lat-

ticework with curved, scroll-like lines and add a teardrop shape above. Use the photograph as a guide for placement. Also paint shallow, ½-inch-wide scallops below the rim on the base of the box, and fill each scallop with more latticework pattern.

Use the very tip of the fine brush dipped in black to partially outline the centers of the violets and small pink flowers on the lid, and to carefully outline the gold latticework.

Use the ¾-inch-wide brush to apply two smooth coats of protective matte fixative to the inside and outside of the box. Let dry between coats.

continued

201

Painted Wooden Boxes

shown on page 191

Materials

6-inch-diameter wooden box for pansy design or 7-inch-diameter box for rose design; acrylic paints in jars or tubes in the following colors: dark red, maroon, dark green, antique gold, purple, and black for rose box; bright yellow, pale blue, lavender, purple, olive green, black, and white for pansy box; No. 8 or No. 10 flat watercolor brush; No. 1 or No. 2 fine liner brush; sandpaper; varnish; graphite or carbon paper.

Instructions

Sand the boxes lightly, then paint the bases dark green. Carefully transfer the rose or pansy design (right and opposite) to the center of the box lid, using graphite or carbon paper.

To paint the designs, thin each of the colors of paint with water to a wash consistency. Using the photograph as a guide for shading, paint the flowers and leaves in the colors noted on the patterns. Then, using a fine brush, add stems, shadows, and other details. Use green acrylic to paint the lattice designs along the lip of the lid.

Finish each box with two coats of clear varnish to protect the designs, allowing each coat to dry thoroughly before applying the second coat.

Embroidered Boxes

shown on page 191

Materials

For three boxes: Sheet of perforated paper (11x14 inches); embroidery floss in yellow and three shades each of purple and green; No. 26 tapestry needle; tagboard; felt for lining; craft glue; clear acrylic finish.

Instructions

Work the cross-stitch design on perforated paper following the pattern (opposite). The pattern given is for the large box; work variations or small portions of the design for the two smaller boxes. Stitch through one hole at a time (to prevent tearing the paper), using two strands of embroidery floss.

To assemble the boxes, follow the instructions for the large box; adjust accordingly for the smaller sizes.

For the large box, cut a 3¾-inch-wide by 4½-inch-long oval lid from tagboard. Measure the perimeter of the oval and cut a ⅝-inch-wide tagboard strip that length (plus a small excess for overlap) for the lip of the box top. Glue the lip to the edge of the oval, using a ⅞-inch-wide strip of tagboard folded in half and glued to the inside of the lid to secure the piece. Clip halfway through the strip, as needed, to allow for a smooth curve when attaching the strip to the box top.

From tagboard, cut an oval base slightly smaller than the inside of the lid; then cut a 1¼-inch-long tagboard strip for the sides. Secure the side strip to the base (see instructions for the lip of the top, above).

Cut another strip of tagboard slightly longer than the first and glue it to the inside of the box for added strength. Finally, cut an oval of tagboard slightly smaller than the base oval and glue it to the inside bottom of the box. Cut felt lining pieces in desired color and glue them to the inside of the box.

Cut a ⅝-inch-wide strip of perforated paper long enough to go around the perimeter of the box top. Cross-stitch with a random floral pattern, using the photograph on page 191 as a guide.

Glue each of the cross-stitch designs in place on the box tops and sides, using glue sparingly. Trim the edges carefully. Apply several coats of clear acrylic spray to protect the boxes from soiling.

Instead of using perforated paper, you may wish to make these boxes with cross-stitches or tent stitches on regular needlepoint canvas.

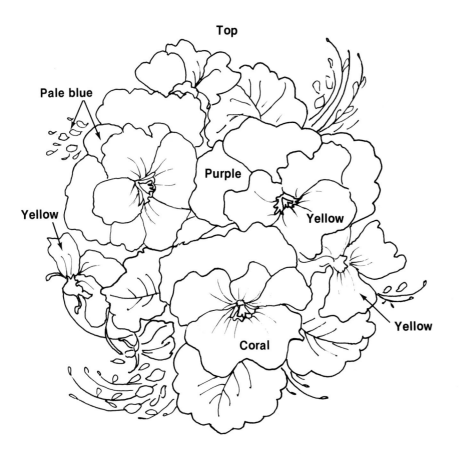

Top

Pale blue

Purple

Yellow

Yellow

Yellow

Coral

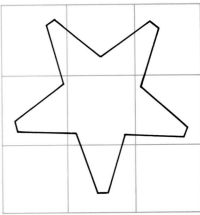

1 Square = 1 Inch

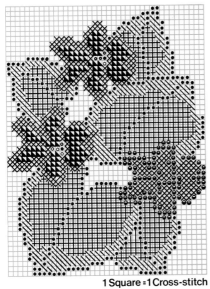

1 Square = 1 Cross-stitch

COLOR KEY

◣ Lavender   ⊡ Yellow

⊠ Purple   ⊞ Light Green

◉ Dark Purple   ⬓ Green

                 ◙ Forest Green

American Flag

shown on page 9

Materials

⅝ yard of blue calico; 2 yards each of red and white calico; ⅛ yard of muslin; white and gold thread; stiff cardboard; two gold eyelets.

Instructions

The finished size of the flag measures 34x60 inches. It is constructed in three segments: the field of stars, the upper section of short stripes, and the lower section of long stripes.

First, enlarge the star pattern (above, right) and make a template of the pattern from a piece of stiff cardboard or a coffee can lid. Use the template to trace 50 stars on the white calico. Cut out.

Cut a 20x28-inch rectangle from the blue calico. Leaving 2½-inch margins around the edge of the background, pin the stars on the blue calico so that five rows of six stars each alternate with four rows of five stars each. Each star should point up. When the stars are arranged as desired, appliqué them to the blue background by machine-zig-zag-stitching around all raw edges with gold thread.

To make the short stripes on the flag, cut four red strips and three white ones, each measuring 3¾x36½ inches. With *wrong* sides facing and using ½-inch seam allowances, sew the strips together along the long edges, alternating red and white, and beginning and ending with red strips. All the raw edges will be on the *right* side of the flag.

Finish all the seam-line edges with flat fell seams as follows: Press all seams toward the bottom of the flag. Trim one raw edge of each seam to ⅛ inch and fold the other raw edge under ¼ inch. Lay the folded side over the trimmed side of the seam and topstitch along the fold.

With *wrong* sides facing and matching short ends, sew the blue calico field to the section of short stripes. Finish with a flat fell seam.

To make the section of long stripes, cut three 3¾x63½-inch strips each of red and white calico. With *wrong* sides facing, stitch the long strips together as for the short strips, beginning with a white strip and ending with a red one. Along the white strip, stitch the lower section of stripes to the upper portion of the flag (*wrong* sides facing). Finish with a flat fell seam.

Cut a 4x37-inch strip of muslin. Fold it in half lengthwise, then turn the raw edges to the inside and sew the strip on the left-hand end of the flag. Hem the remaining raw edges of the flag and set eyelets in the corners of the muslin strip for hanging.

Fanciful Dolls and Playthings

Most of us cherish the memory of at least one special toy from our childhood. And although the fads and fashions in children's playthings come and go, certain toys are often inexplicably special—possessed of the power to charm the child in each of us, forever and always.

You'll find the dolls and toys on these pages reminiscent of those youthful favorites. Here are soft and simple shapes that are meant to be cuddled and clung to and carted along whenever and wherever children wander.

And these pretty playthings are made with posterity in mind: Each has the sort of contemporary folk-art styling that's sure to make it an almost instant family heirloom to treasure.

♦ The adorable needlepoint pillow dolls shown here are a case in point. Adapted from the design for a nineteenth-century cookie jar, these charmingly chubby ladies are bound to delight doll lovers of all ages.

Why not stitch up a whole family of pillow dolls in graduated sizes, if you like, simply by changing the size of the needlepoint canvas that you use. The 12-inch-high doll on the far left is worked with three-ply Persian yarn on 10-mesh-to-the-inch canvas, and the 5½-inch-high lady (near left) is stitched with a single ply of Persian yarn on petit point canvas with 24 meshes to the inch.

So, whether you're a beginning stitcher eager to start your first project or a seasoned expert accustomed to the intricacies of petit point, you'll be able to craft one of these sweet, old-fashioned dolls for yourself or for someone you love.

Instructions for all the projects in this section begin on page 212.

Fanciful Dolls
and Playthings

Pretty is as pretty does, and these lovely, lace-trimmed treasures do very prettily indeed. Our sophisticated kitty and frankly old-fashioned "rag" dolls are sure to delight every young lady from eight to eighty.

♦ The plump pussycat (left) graces grandma's front parlor or a little girl's bedroom with equal aplomb. Smart, striped fabric, simple lines, and an elegant smattering of appliqués turn this simple design into a softly sculpted work of art.

♦ And mass-produced dolls just can't compare with these special lace-bedecked lasses (above). Sweet and simple and just made to be loved, these dainty dolls are sure to be shared from mother to daughter for generations.

To fashion their "antique" outfits, collect mismatched scraps of trim and fabric from flea markets, thrift shops, and attic trunks. Then dip fabrics and trim into the same dye bath to create subtly coordinated materials for one-of-a-kind costumes.

Fanciful Dolls
and Playthings

If fine handiwork is not your forte, count on splashy, eye-catching fabrics and fanciful machine stitchery to give your creations the appearance of timeless, keepsake quality.

♦ For example, our updated rag doll (left) has all the cuddly appeal of her hand-embroidered sisters on the preceding page, but she's ever-so-much quicker to stitch. With her plush velveteen hair, winsome smile, and gloriously beribboned and laced outfit, she's the perfect playmate for a special little girl.

♦ For a truly regal gift, present your own sweet prince (or princess) with this noble steed and dashing hat with colorful plumes (right).

Stitched of satin and corduroy and trimmed in felt and silver lamé, this handsome hobbyhorse makes a wonderfully imaginative toy for the youngsters, or a show-stopping piece of soft sculpture for the young at heart.

And the gallant swashbuckler's hat is just the right touch for a child's travels in the land of Make-Believe.

Fanciful Dolls
and Playthings

Though they look like costly antiques, the elegant bisque beauties (above) and the porcelain peddler doll (right) all began as purchased kits. Fortunately for the growing number of doll makers and collectors across the country, high quality china doll kits are now widely available through local craft and hobby shops and from specialty mail order sources.

Such kits usually contain a bisque or porcelain head, hands, and feet, plus patterns and instructions for making a muslin body and assembling the doll. Once the basic doll is stitched and put together, the fun has just begun.

Raid your cache of fancy fabrics and elegant trims to create stunning "sampler" dresses like those shown above. Or fashion a traditional costume of a nineteenth-century English peddler woman (right). Regardless of whether you dress your doll as a bride or a ballerina, a flapper or a cancan girl, her costume is yours to create.

Needlepoint
China Dolls

shown on pages 204-205

Materials

Note: The finished size of the doll depends on the size of the needlepoint canvas used. For a 12-inch-high doll, you'll need 14x16 inches of 10-count canvas; for an 8½-inch doll, 11x13 inches of 14-count canvas; and for a 5½-inch doll, 9x10 inches of 24-count needlepoint canvas.

You will also need 3-ply Persian wool yarn in sufficient quantities for the size doll you want to make and in the following colors: off-white, black, pink, rose, red, dark and light blue; a tapestry needle in a size appropriate for your canvas; backing fabric to match canvas size; polyester fiberfill for stuffing; graph paper; colored pencils; masking tape.

Instructions

Transfer the pattern (right) to graph paper, using colored pencils. To complete the chart, flop the pattern along the center. When working the design, eliminate the pocket and handkerchief on the right-hand side of the doll.

Bind the edges of the canvas with masking tape to prevent raveling. Mount the canvas on a needlepoint frame to minimize distortion.

Follow the chart and color key to work the design. On 10-count canvas, use all three plies of yarn to cover the canvas; on 14-count canvas, use two plies; and on 24-count canvas, use only one ply of yarn.

Block the finished needlepoint by tacking it facedown on a blocking board; stretch as needed to restore the original shape of the canvas. Dampen with water. When the needlepoint is dry, remove it from board.

Trim canvas to within ½ inch of stitches. Cut backing fabric to match, then stitch back to front, leaving open along lower edge. Clip curves to make smooth, flat seams, and trim excess canvas to within ¼ inch of seams. Turn, press, and stuff with fiberfill. Whipstitch the opening closed.

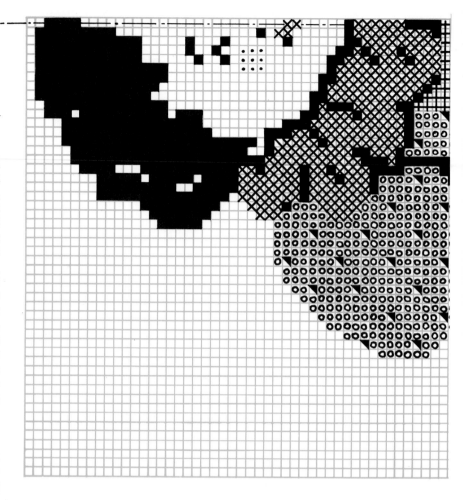

Lace-Trimmed Cat

shown on page 206

Materials

⅝ yard of 45-inch-wide white-and-blue-striped fabric; ¼ yard each of 45-inch-wide blue narrow-stripe, solid blue, and blue calico fabrics; scraps of medium blue felt; embroidery floss to match felt; 10-inch-square white handkerchief with blue embroidery in the corner; 3⅔ yards of ⅛-inch-wide blue satin ribbon; polyester fiberfill; three blue rosebud appliqués; two 6½-inch-diameter doilies; 28 inches of ¾-inch-wide white crocheted lace; 9 inches of ½-inch-wide white pregathered lace; graph paper; dressmaker's carbon.

Instructions

Enlarge the patterns (page 214) onto graph paper, including all lines designating the areas to be appliquéd.

With pattern arrows on the straight grain of the fabric, and following cutting directions on patterns, cut the body, underbody, and tail from blue-and-white-striped fabric. Cut one face peak from blue fabric. (These pattern pieces include ¼-inch seam margins.)

Using dressmaker's carbon, transfer design lines to body front. These lines are appliqué guidelines.

Shaded areas on the cat body are appliqué patterns. Trace these, add ¼-inch seam allowances, and cut appliqués as follows: 2 inner ears from narrow-striped fabric; 2 cheeks from solid blue; a collar from the handkerchief; and upper and lower fan center pieces from solid blue. For fans, cut 6 pieces from solid blue, 5 from calico, and 4 from the narrow-stripe.

From felt, cut 2 eyes and a nose without adding seam allowances.

On the ears and cheeks, staystitch ¼ inch from the outer edges. Clip curves. Turn under raw edges on the stitching line; baste. Pin and slip-stitch the pieces to the front body along the lines indicated on the pattern.

Along the two straight sides of the face peak, staystitch ¼ inch from the

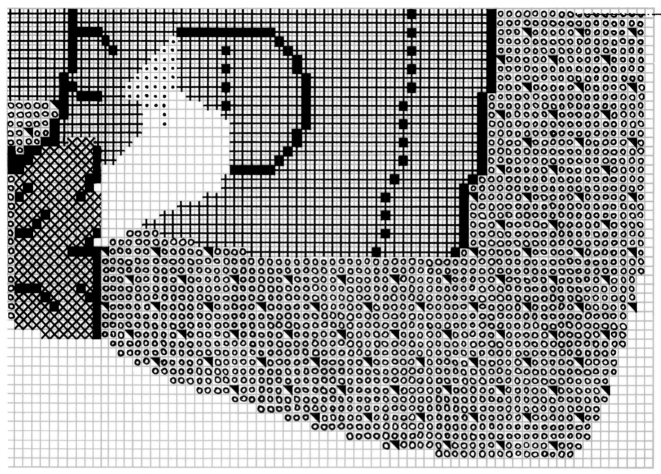

COLOR KEY

□ **Off-White**	⊡ **Pink**	⊠ **Red**	⊞ **Light Blue**
■ **Black**	◎ **Rose**	◩ **Dark Blue**	

edge. Appliqué the peak to the front body, turning under raw edges. Pin and slip-stitch the felt eyes and nose in position on the face of the cat.

With one strand of embroidery floss, straight-stitch the whiskers, make small freckles using French knots, and outline-stitch the eyebrows. (Refer to the photograph for placement.) Use two strands of embroidery floss to outline-stitch the mouth.

For the cat's collar, stitch ¼ inch from the cut edge of the handkerchief and press under along the seam line.

Stitch white gathered lace to the neckline along the line indicated on the pattern. Pin and topstitch the pressed edge of the handkerchief over the lower edge of the lace, leaving the bottom end of the handkerchief free.

To assemble fan decorations, refer to photograph for fabric selection. For upper fan, stitch together the long edges of 8 of the fan pieces, right sides facing. Repeat for lower fan, using 7 pieces. Press the seams open.

With right sides together, pin crocheted lace to the fans ¼ inch from the curved edges. Stitch; press under at the stitching line. Topstitch the fans to the body through the lace and along the edge of the fans. Weave blue ribbon through the lace; turn under the ends and tack them to the pieced sections.

Staystitch ¼ inch from the curved edges of the center fan pieces; clip the curves. Press under the seam allowance along the stitching line. Topstitch centers to fans along curved edges.

Trim straight edges of fans even with front body. Stitch fans to body along the seam lines.

With right sides facing, sew body front to back. Stitch bottom in place, leaving an opening as shown on the pattern. Clip the curves to ensure smooth seams before turning.

With right sides together, pin the underbody to the body. Stitch together, leaving an opening as indicated. Clip curves. Turn, stuff, and whipstitch the opening closed.

Weave ribbon through the doilies and tie the ends into bows, referring to the photograph as a guide. Then pin the doilies over the fans so they extend to the back and bottom of the cat; tack in place. Sew rosebud appliqués to the centers of the doilies.

Tie 11 inches of blue ribbon into a bow; sew to the base of one ear and tack a rosebud to the center. Pin the other ear forward and secure with a tuck slip-stitched along the base.

With right sides together, pin and stitch the tail, leaving it open as shown on the pattern. Clip the curves.

continued

213

Turn the tail right side out; stuff. Blindstitch the opening closed. Stitch the broad end of the tail to the side of the cat; tack to body.

Old-Fashioned Dolls

shown on page 207

Materials

⅓ yard of muslin for body of each doll; water-erasable marking pen; assorted fabrics and laces in soft, old-fashioned colors for clothing; No. 5 pearl cotton in peach or old rose, beige, and light and dark brown for features; sport-weight wool yarn for hair; polyester fiberfill; embroidery needle.

Instructions

For doll bodies: Enlarge patterns (opposite, left) to size and transfer them to muslin, using a water-erasable pen.

Embroider features for each doll *before* cutting out the heads. Work the mouth in peach or old rose satin stitches, the nostrils in dark brown French knots, the pupils in dark brown satin stitches, and the irises in light brown satin stitches. The eyebrows and lines beneath eyes should be worked in beige chain stitches, and the eyelid (lash) line in dark brown chain stitches.

Cut out the pattern pieces. With right sides facing and using ⅜-inch seam allowances, stitch together the head, arms, legs, and body. Clip curves, press, turn, and stuff. Whipstitch the head to the body at the neck, and the arms and legs to the body as shown on the pattern.

For doll's hair: First, wind about ¾ of a skein of yarn lengthwise around a 3x12-inch strip of cardboard. Carefully remove the yarn (without clipping) and machine-stitch through center of bundle to make a part in the hair. (Bundle should measure about 2½ x 12 inches.) Set wig aside. Now fold eight 6-inch-long pieces in half and tack to forehead of doll, along seam line, to make bangs. Trim bangs even at eyebrow level.

For chestnut-haired doll (in front): Using a matching yarn to stitch with, tack wig along center of head, concealing machine stitches with yarn. Spread loops of yarn down to base of head along sides and back; tack carefully and evenly to head, taking backstitches with matching yarn.

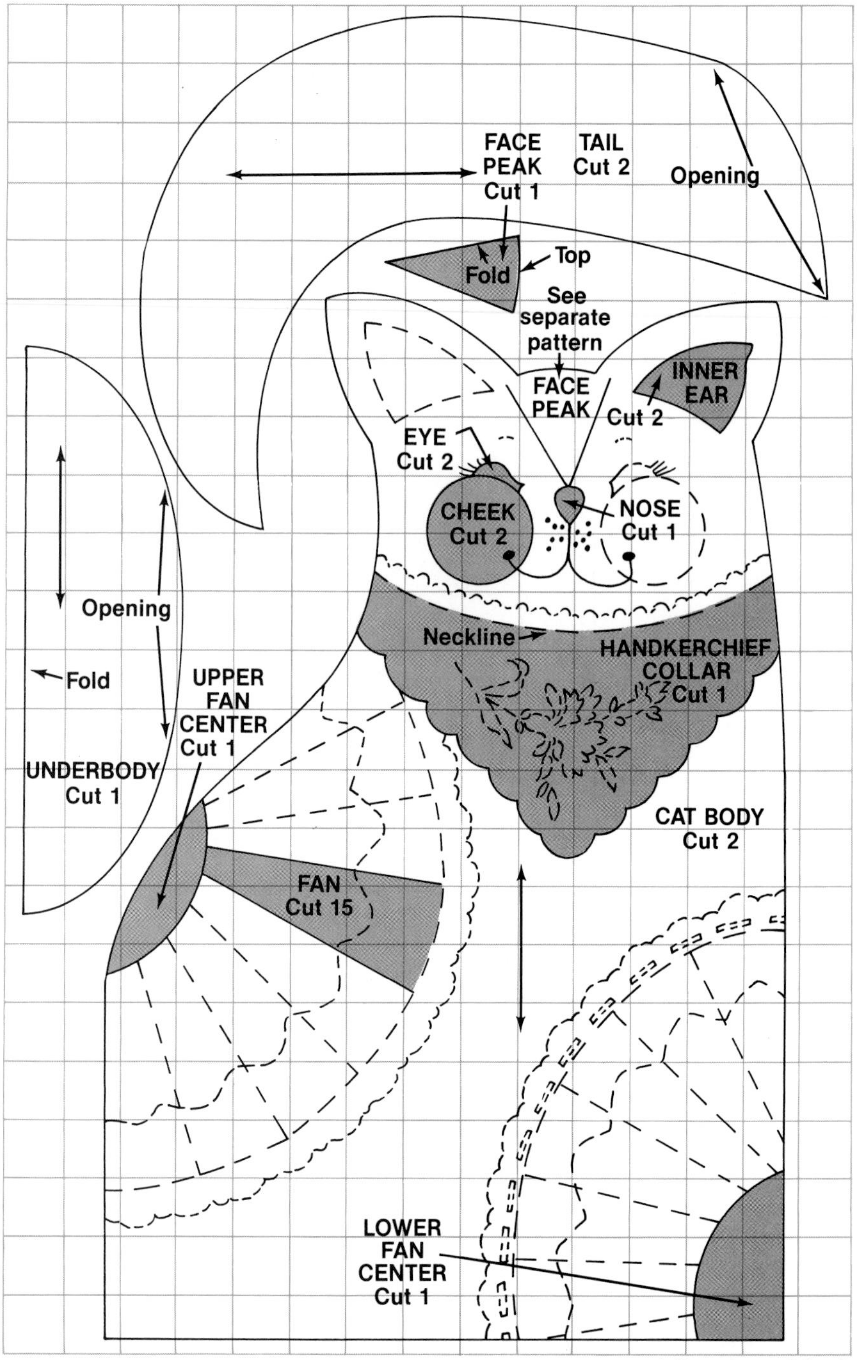

To make "sausage curls," cut 30 strands of yarn, each 36 inches long. With strands together, knot each end of this bundle, then tightly twist together until it begins to curl. Shape the twisted bundle into four or five loops, and tack these loops to one side of the doll's wig at cheek level, concealing any raw ends under the strands of the wig. Repeat the curls on the other side of head.

For flaxen-haired doll (rear): Tack wig in place, as described above. Then cut 39 strands of yarn, each 12 inches long. Divide the yarn into three bunches and braid them tightly together; tie ends with matching yarn. Fold braid in half and tuck folded end under wig at ear level; tack in place. Draw the raw ends of the braid up to the side of the doll's head, tuck raw edges beneath the strands of the wig at eyebrow level, and tack in place. Repeat for other side of head. Trim with bows, as shown.

1 Square = 1 Inch

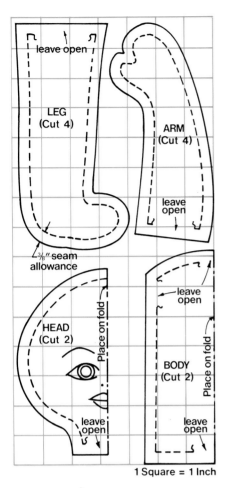

1 Square = 1 Inch

To dress dolls: Make simple clothing from squares, rectangles, and strips of fabric and lace. Use the pattern for doll's body as a guide in determining size and proportions of clothing; refer to the photography on page 207 for design ideas. Sew clothing directly onto doll, or use tiny snaps and hooks and eyes to make clothing removable.

For example, for the flaxen-haired doll, whipstitch beige print fabric to front and back of body to form dress bodice. For sleeves, cut a 3½x7-inch rectangle of beige voile; seam together short ends. Turn under raw edges. Slip sleeve over arm; gather and tack one edge at shoulder. Gather and tack the other edge at elbow; border with a band of dyed-to-match lace.

For pinafore top, tack a 1½-inch-wide band of dyed lace across bodice. Gather two 2¼x9-inch strips of lace; tack over shoulders for ruffled sleeves.

Make a slip from a 7x14-inch rectangle of fabric; trim the bottom with lace. For a skirt, sew a hem and gather an 8½x21-inch piece of fabric; for an overskirt, gather a 5x21-inch piece of

lace. Stitch both the skirt and the overskirt to a ribbon waistband.

Finally, add ribbons and lace to neckline and waist to conceal all seams and raw edges. Trim with buttons, beads, or a few fake flowers, if desired.

Machine-Embroidered Doll

shown on page 208

Materials

½ yard of 45-inch-wide muslin; ¾ yard of white printed satin; ¼ yard *each* of purple velveteen and ecru satin; scraps of white satin, purple corduroy, and pink cotton; ½ yard of 1-inch-wide white lace; 2½ yards of 2-inch-wide pregathered white lace; 2¾ yards of ½-inch-wide ecru lace; ½ yard of 2-inch-wide ecru lace; 2 white ⅝-inch-diameter buttons; navy embroidery floss; polyester fiberfill; ¼-inch-wide elastic; graph paper.

Also, satin ribbon in the following amounts and colors: 1¾ yards (⅜ inch wide) of violet, pink, and mauve; 1⅜ yards (1 inch wide) of dark pink, ecru, light blue, and pale pink; 1½ yards (1 inch wide) of ecru; 1½ yards (1½ inch wide) of mauve; ¾ yard (¼ inch wide) of purple.

Instructions

Enlarge the patterns (right) onto graph paper. Following the cutting instructions on the pattern pieces, cut the legs, arms, body, and head front from muslin. Then transfer all the design lines to the fabric. Cut the head back from velveteen.

Following the guidelines on the leg and head front patterns, cut the following appliqués *without adding seam allowances* (because appliqués will be machine-stitched in place): 2 shoes from purple corduroy, 2 stockings from white satin, trim for the stockings from 1-inch-wide lace, 2 cheeks from pink fabric, and the hair for the head front from purple velveteen.

Machine zigzag-stitch the stockings, shoes, and lace trim to the muslin legs, and the hair and cheeks to the head front. Embroider the eyes, nose, and mouth with navy floss.

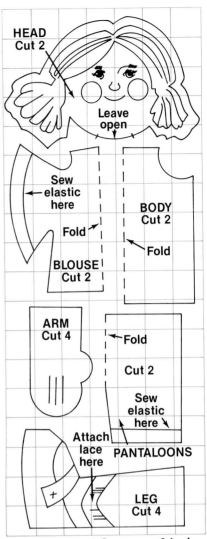

Pattern includes ½-inch seam allowance.

1 Square = 2 Inches

With right sides facing, using ½-inch seam allowances and leaving an opening for turning, sew together each of the body parts—the two arms and legs, the body, and the head. Turn right side out; stuff and stitch closed. Sew the arms and legs to the body.

From white printed satin, cut out two blouse pieces. Using a ½-inch seam allowance, sew the shoulder and underarm seams. Trim sleeve and neck edges. Gather sleeves at cuff by sewing elastic on the inside.

Slit the blouse about halfway down the center back and slip it onto the body. Tuck under the raw edges along the slit; stitch closed. Tack the blouse along sleeve and neck edges. Then sew the head to the body.

continued

215

To make the skirt, refer to the photograph for colors and widths of ribbon. Lay the 1¾-yard lengths of ribbon out flat, faceup, side by side. Overlap them slightly and zigzag-stitch the ribbons together lengthwise until you have a piece approximately 5 inches wide.

Stitch ½-inch-wide lace over the seams where desired. Stitch 2-inch-wide gathered lace to one long side for the hem. Sew the short ends of the piece together, right sides facing, to make the back seam of the skirt.

Gather the skirt along the top to fit the doll's waist. Sew the skirt to the doll at the waist (atop blouse seam), then tie a mauve ribbon around the waist to hide the raw edges of the skirt top.

Cut pantaloons from ecru satin; trim hems with 2-inch-wide gathered lace. Sew the inseam and gather the waist to fit the doll. On the wrong side, sew elastic to the pantaloon above lace.

Turn the pantaloons right side out and slip onto the doll. Over the elastic, tie bows from 13-inch lengths of ¼-inch-wide purple ribbon.

To finish, sew buttons to the shoe fronts; tie bows from the 1-inch-wide ecru satin ribbon and tack to the hair.

Elegant Hobbyhorse

shown on page 209

Materials

½ yard of blue velveteen; ¼ yard of white satin; ¼ yard of black felt; white, pink, and gold felt scraps; fusible webbing; polyester fiberfill; 36-inch length of ¾-inch-diameter dowel; feathers for plume; 4½ feet of black seam binding.

Instructions

Enlarge pattern (above, right) and transfer to brown paper. (*Note:* Pattern is for right side of horse; reverse pattern when cutting pieces for left side.)

Cut two heads from blue velveteen. Cut two satin ears and two velveteen ears. Then cut two pattern pieces for each satin and felt appliqué and for each black and silver rein.

To embellish the head: Secure mane, halter, eyes, mouth, and teeth to each side of head with fusible webbing; machine zigzag-stitch each piece in place.

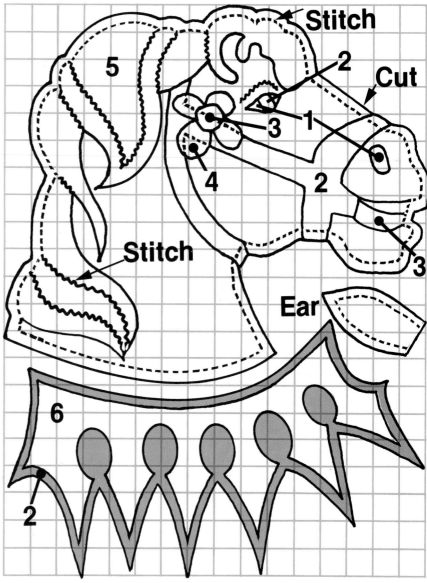

1 = White felt
2 = Black felt
3 = Pink felt
4 = Gold felt
5 = White flannel-backed satin
6 = Metallic fabric

For ears: stitch satin back to velveteen front, right sides together; leave bottom open for turning. Turn, press, and slip-stitch the opening closed. Stitch the ears to the head at dots (beneath flower). Fuse the pink center to the gold petals of the flower and stitch the flower center to the base of the ear; do not stitch down the petals.

For fancy black and silver reins: Fuse the silver metallic fabric to the black felt backing; satin-stitch around the edges of the silver appliqué. Lay the reins end to end. Center seam binding along the top edge of the reins; stitch, binding the edge of the felt.

To assemble the horse: With right sides facing, sew the head back to the front, leaving the bottom open. Clip curves, turn, and press gently. Stuff the head firmly with polyester fiberfill. As you stuff the neck, insert a wooden dowel 6 inches into the head. Whip-stitch the opening closed, applying glue to the dowel at the base of the neck before the stitching is completed.

Attach the reins at the base of the halter and slip-stitch in place. Trim the hobbyhorse with a colorful feather plume, stitched along top seam line.

Swashbuckler's Hat

shown on page 209

Materials

A 21-inch circle of corduroy or velvet; matching strip of 6-inch-wide fabric long enough to fit around child's head, plus 1 inch (for seams); feathers.

Instructions

Stitch the short ends of the hatband together (½-inch seam). Gather the circle to fit the hatband; with right sides together, stitch the crown of the hat to the band. Fold the hatband in half, turn under the raw edge and slip-stitch the band to the inside of hat. Trim with feathers.

Sampler Dolls

shown on page 210

Materials

Ceramic or porcelain doll kit (which includes head, hands, and feet)—or any 15-inch-high doll of your choice; muslin and polyester fiberfill for body; scraps of fabric and lace, ribbon, appliqués, buttons, beads, and other trims for clothing; pearl cotton embroidery floss in assorted colors.

Instructions

Construct the body of the doll according to the directions contained in the kit.

Fashion the doll's clothing following the kit patterns, or create your own clothing designs by using the body of the doll as a guide for the size of the pattern pieces.

For example, the doll pattern will help determine the sleeve length based on the length of the arm, and the shape of the bodice can be derived from the width and length of the doll's torso.

Hints on making doll clothes: Use as many different fabrics for the doll's clothes as possible, and make her clothing as simple or elaborate as whimsy and available materials suggest.

Make a petticoat from scraps of an old silk scarf or pretty handkerchief.

For the blouse, cut the sleeves, bodice, and collar from a variety of lightweight, silky fabrics and trim with scraps of lace and tiny antique buttons.

For the skirt, stitch a crazy-quilt-patterned rectangle, using scraps of wool and/or silk overlaid with bits of ribbon, lace, purchased appliqués, and the like. Finish the seams of the crazy-quilt patching with rows of featherstitching, if desired, using No. 8 pearl cotton floss in complementary colors. Gather the skirt to fit doll's waist and stitch into a narrow waistband. Hem the bottom.

For doll jewelry, collect odds and ends of junk jewelry and old buttons, as well as strings of tiny beads. Single earrings or fancy antique buttons make wonderful brooches, and single pearl beads or knots of smaller glass beads make elegant buttons.

Peddler Doll

shown on page 211

Materials

Ceramic or porcelain doll kit (which includes head, hands, and feet)—or any 15-inch-high doll of your choice; ½ yard of striped cotton fabric for dress; ½ yard of contrasting striped fabric plus strip of binding for overskirt; ⅔ yard of lightweight wool or flannel for cape, plus one package of contrasting seam binding for trim; scraps of velveteen, satin, and lace for mob cap; cardboard box top for peddler's tray (approximately 4x5½x½ inches), plus scraps of fabric to cover it; white glue; assorted small notions with which to stock the peddler's tray (see ideas and suggestions at end of instructions).

Instructions

Construct the doll according to the kit directions. Stitch the doll's pantaloons and dress from squares and rectangles of fabric, pin-fitting pieces and adjusting clothing to fit the doll's body.

For striped overskirt: Gather a 9x30-inch rectangle of fabric into a narrow waistband (make the waistband long enough to tie in a bow at the waist back). Border the overskirt with a strip of contrasting fabric and hem.

For the peddler's cape: Cut a 20-inch-diameter circle of lightweight wool. Snip a 2-inch circle from the center of the wool circle, then cut from the edge of the circle to the center to make the front opening of the cape. Next, cut a 6-inch-diameter circle of wool for the cape's collar. Cut a 2-inch-circle from the center and snip from the perimeter in toward the center hole to match the front opening on the cape.

With the right side of the collar facing the wrong side of the cape, stitch the collar to the cape around the neckline, using a ¼-inch seam allowance. Clip the seam allowance and press the collar toward the right side of the cape. Bind the edges of the cape and collar with a contrasting seam binding.

Run a gathering thread along the seam line and gather the neckline of the cape slightly; adjust to fit the doll's shoulders and tie off the gathering thread. Tack one yard of narrow satin ribbon over the seam, under the collar, matching the center of the ribbon to the center back of neckline. Leave the ends of the ribbon free as ties for the cape.

For the mobcap: Cut a 6½-inch-diameter circle of velveteen and a matching circle of satin for lining. With right sides together, stitch the two circles together, with a ¼-inch seam allowance; leave an opening for turning. Clip the seam allowance around the entire circle; turn, press, and slip-stitch the opening closed.

Using pearl cotton, sew a running stitch 1½ inches in from the edge of the circle; gather the cap to fit the doll's head and tie off. Sew a ruffle of 1-inch-wide lace just inside the cap's brim.

To make the peddler's tray: Cover the box top inside and out with striped fabric; secure with white glue. Cut a strip of fabric or ribbon to fit around the doll's neck. The strip should be long enough to hold the tray at waist height. Attach the ends of the strap to tray with buttons, sewing through button, strap, and cardboard.

To stock peddler's tray: For best results, try to give the tray a full-to-overflowing look. Fill the tray with assorted "notions"—any small things you can turn up in miniature shops, junk stores, garage sales, or around the house. For example, wrap small rectangles of colored cardboard with scraps of fabric to simulate fabric bolts. Fill tiny baskets with buttons, beads, or small balls of yarn or embroidery floss. Dangle miniature kitchen items (pots and pans, for example) from lengths of chain (clipped from old junk jewelry) tacked along the front and sides of the tray, using a few whipstitches to hold the chains in place.

Basic Knitting Stitches

Knitting and Crocheting Abbreviations

beg . . . . begin(ning)	lp(s) . . . . loop(s)	sc . . . . single crochet
ch . . . . chain	MC . . . . main color	sk . . . . skip
dc . . . . double crochet	p . . . . purl	sl st . . . . slip stitch
dec . . . . decrease	pat . . . . pattern	sp . . . . space
dp . . . . double pointed	psso . . . . pass slip st over	st(s) . . . . stitch(es)
dtr . . . . double treble	rem . . . . remaining	st st . . . . stockinette stitch
hdc . . . . half-double crochet	rep . . . . repeat	tog . . . . together
inc . . . . increase	rnd . . . . round	yo . . . . yarn over
k . . . . knit		* . . . . . repeat from * as indicated

Casting on

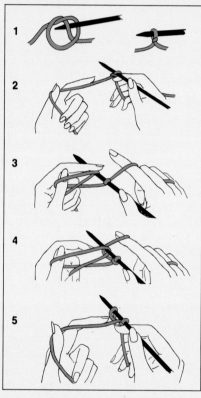

Make a slipknot around the needle at a distance from the yarn end that equals 1 inch for each stitch to be cast on (1, above). Hold the needle with the slip-knot in your right hand; make a loop of the short length of yarn around your left thumb (2). Insert the point of the needle in your right hand under the loop on your left thumb (3). Loop yarn from the ball over the fingers of your right hand (4). Wind yarn from ball under and over the needle; draw it through the loop, leaving the stitch on the needle (5). Tighten stitches on the needle; bring the yarn end around your thumb. Repeat steps (2) through (5) for the desired number of stitches. Switch hands so stitches are on your left.

Knitting

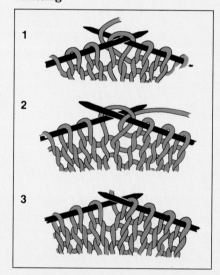

Hold the needle with the stitches on it in your left hand and the other needle in your right hand. Insert the right needle through the stitch on the left needle from the front to the back. Pass the yarn around the point of the right needle to form a loop (1, above).

Pull this loop through the center of the stitch on the left needle; draw the loop onto the right needle (2, above).

Now, slip the stitch completely off the left needle (3).

Repeat these three steps until you have transferred all the stitches from the left needle to the right needle. This completes one row. When working the next row, move the needle holding the stitches to the left hand, and the other needle to the right hand.

Purling

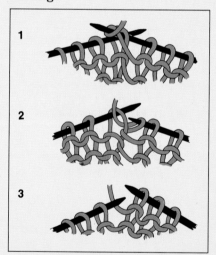

Hold the needle with the stitches in your left hand and the other needle in your right hand. Insert the right needle through the stitch on the left needle from the back to the front. Wind the yarn around the point of the right needle to form a loop (1, above). Draw a loop through the stitch on the needle in your left hand and transfer it to the needle in your right hand (2). Slip the stitch completely off the left needle (3). Repeat these steps until all loops are transferred to right needle.

Basic Crocheting Stitches

Chain stitch

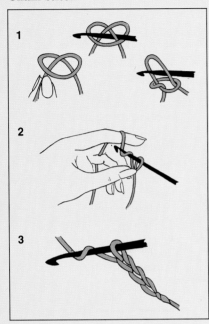

Make a slipknot on the crochet hook about 6 inches from end of yarn (1, above). Pull one end to tighten knot. Hold hook between right index finger and thumb, as you would a pencil. Wrap yarn over ring finger, under middle finger, and over index finger; hold short end between thumb and index finger. For more tension, wrap yarn around little finger. Insert hook under and over strand of yarn (2).

To make a foundation chain, catch the strand of yarn with the hook; draw through the loop (3). Make chain the length pattern calls for.

Single crochet

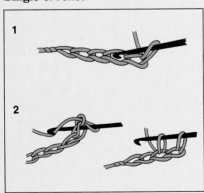

Single crochet (continued)

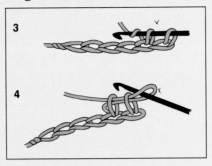

Insert hook into second chain from hook under two upper strands of yarn (1, bottom left). Draw up a loop (2). Draw yarn over hook (3, above). Pull yarn through two loops, making a single crochet stitch (4). Insert hook into next stitch; repeat steps.

Half-double crochet

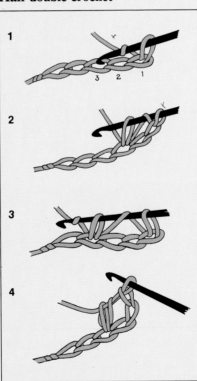

With yarn over hook, insert the hook into the third chain, under the two upper strands of yarn (1, above). Draw up a loop (2). Draw yarn over hook (3). Pull through three loops, completing half-double crochet (4).

Double crochet

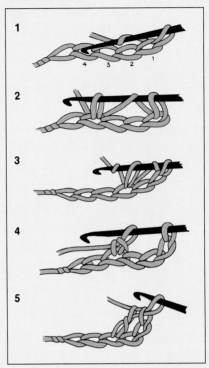

Holding yarn over hook, insert hook into fourth chain under two upper strands of yarn (1, above). Draw up a loop (2). Wrap yarn over hook (3). Draw yarn through two loops as shown (4). Yarn over again and draw through the last two loops on the hook (5) to complete the stitch.

Slip stitch

After you have made the foundation chain, insert crochet hook under top strand of second chain from hook; yarn over. With a single motion, pull yarn through stitch and loop on hook. Insert hook under top strand of next chain, then yarn over and draw yarn through stitch and loop on the hook. Repeat this procedure to end of chain. Use this stitch for decreasing.

Basic Embroidery Stitches

Backstitch

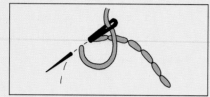

Buttonhole Stitch

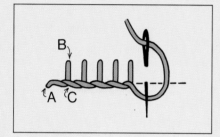

Chain Stitch

Couching Stitch

Laid Work

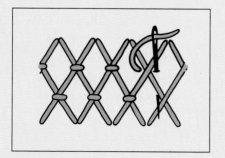

Featherstitch

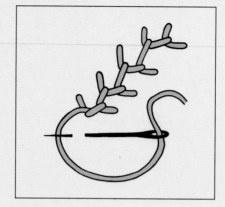

French Knot

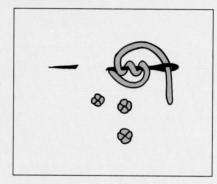

Outline (or Stem) Stitch

Long-and-Short Stitch

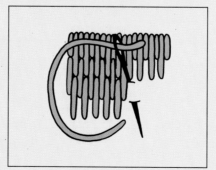

Running Stitch

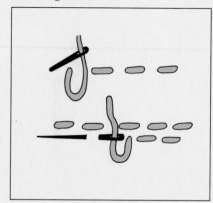

Satin Stitch

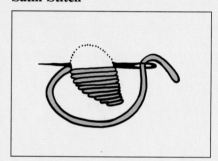

Seed Stitch

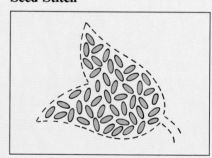

Straight Stitch

Basic Needlepoint Stitches

Bargello Stitch

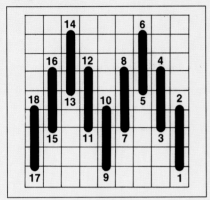

Basket-Weave Stitch

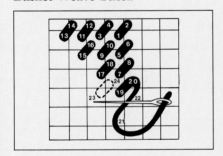

Continental Stitch

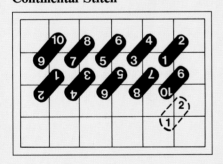

Cross-Stitch

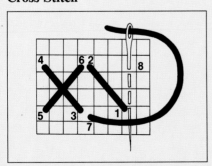

Diamond Eyelet Stitch

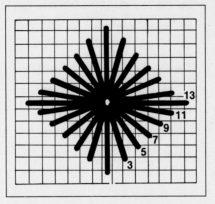

Mosaic Stitch

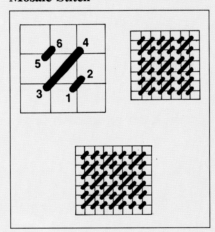

Smyrna Stitch

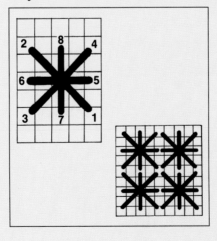

Slanting Gobelin Stitch

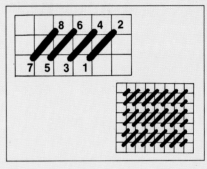

Straight Gobelin Stitch

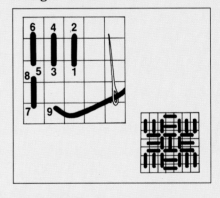

Upright Cross-Stitch

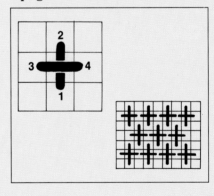

Waste Knot

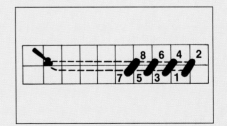

Index

Numbers listed by entries refer to how-to instructions. See the reference with the instructions for the page number of the color photograph.

Design and Photography Credits

Designers

We extend our sincere thanks to all who contributed designs and projects to this book.

American Thread—doily (left), 126; gloves, 172
David Ashe—horse, wagon, 148
Pauline Asmus—boxes, 191
Susie and Joe Barber—wreaths, baskets, 13, 161-162
Ginger Bassett—doily, 129; pillows, 132
Carl Bern—candle holders, 18
Kathy Best—ruffled shirt, 43
Margot Blair—flag, 9
Curt Boehringer—wall hanging, pillows, 79
Taresia Boernke—geese, 55; goose, 146; cat, 206
Gary Boling—hat and collar, 41; afghans, 109, 112, 130
B. J. Casselman—baby blocks, 100
Coats and Clark, Inc.—vest, 40; afghan, 133
Joan Cravens—jar lids, 14
Jackie Curry—crocheted boxes, 14
Patricia Deery—painted hat, 43
Joy Dial—clown mobile, 101
Hugie Dufresne—doilies, 188
Deborah Dugan—jabot, 36
Duncan Enterprises—heart box, 190
Phyllis Dunstan—dolls, 8, 30; animals, 26-27; beads, 38-39; dolls, furniture, 63; gift wraps, 86-87; cat, 147
Dorothy Egan—pitchers, 78
Linda Emmerson—stenciled boxes, 14-15; castle, 65; racquet covers, 80; gift wraps, 91
Dixie Falls—gowns, 106-107
Bobbi Jo Free—dog, 50
Mary Hardy—bears, 52
Ron Hawbaker, Don Wipperman—doll furniture, 144-145
Beverly Hettick—ABC book, 100
Shirley Hewlett—handprint projects, 19
Laura Holtorf—portfolio, 20; cross-stitch boxes, 21; birth announcement, 99; guest book, album, 170-171; sampler, 173; embroidered book cover, 190

Rebecca Jerdee—beaded sweater, 43; autograph projects, 74-75; basket, 76; cover, pincushion, 77; picnic cloth, 81; wraps, 88-89; quilt, toy, 96-97; ponies, 147; dolls, 149, 208; hat, horse, 209
Gail Kinkead—white afghan, 133
Mary Sue Kuhn—tatted flowers, 170-172; tatted book cover, 190
Pamela Kvitne—glass jars, 14-15
Danielle Labourne—bear, 29
Charles Lane—pewter, 10-11
Barbara Lee—vests, 174
Ann Levine—beaded sweater, 42; sampler, 161
Jan Lewis—corn husk doll, 162
Melissa Weston Luppi—bunting, 7
Janet McCaffery—purse, 37; rose projects, 184-187
Mimi McLellan—lampshades, 163
Jill Mead—pillows, 17; snake, 28; dollhouse, 62; playhouse, 64
Nancy Merrell and Karen Strauss—pillow, 17
Thelma Mortley, for King Features—tablecloth, 128-129
Mitch Noah and Don Wipperman—kiddy car, 67
Dawn Paradis—ABC quilt, 100
Pingouin Corp.—shorts, shirt, 108; overalls, 110; rompers, cloud outfit, 111; bow-tie outfit, 113
Katie Ragsdale—house number, 18; painted boxes, 191
Yvonne Resche—frame, 171
Reynolds Yarn—sweaters, 175
Terry Ryder—sheep, 54
Bonnie Schermerhorn—child's vest, 41
Mimi Shimmin—apron, mats, 78
Marilyn Snyder—cow rocker, 66
Karen Strauss and Nancy Merrell—pillow, 17
Laurie Swanson—cat cushion, 51
Gerry Tandy—bib, 109
Shelly Thornton—dolls, 145, 204-205
Sara Jane Treinen—pillow, 106; doily (right), 127; edgings, 189
Ciba Vaughan—pincushion, 16; pins, 39; cloth, pillow, guest

book, 158-159; dolls, 207, 210-211
Elizabeth Vernier—cats, 53
Jim Williams—coasters, 18; wall hanging, 20; blocks, 28; cradle, 31; gift wraps, 90; sheep, 97; tote, 98
Tom Williams—decoys, 160
Judy Williamson—giraffe, 29
Don Wipperman and Mitch Noah—kiddy car, 67
Don Wipperman, Ron Hawbaker—doll furniture, 144-145
Wolf Creek Toys—airplane, 67

Photographers

Our thanks as well to the photographers who contributed to this book.

Ernest Braun—8
Mike Dieter—29, 51, 62, 63, 66, 67, 78, 79, 81, 86, 88-89, 99, 100, 101, 106-108, 110, 129, 190, 207
Hedrich-Blessing—10-13, 39, 42, 43, 74-75, 126-127, 173, 175, 184-187
Thomas Hooper—6-7, 9, 39, 40, 77, 109, 111, 113, 128-129, 174, 204-205
William N. Hopkins—Cover, 16, 18, 19, 26-28, 29, 53, 64-65, 67, 78, 90-91, 98, 100, 109, 112, 130, 131, 144-149, 158-161, 163, 170-172, 188, 189, 190, 191, 206, 208, 209, 211
Scott Little—18, 20-21, 30-31, 50, 52, 54-55, 80, 87, 162
Maris-Semel—132
Bradley Olman—17, 36, 37, 41, 43
Perry Struse—14-15, 76, 96-97, 133